ARCHITECTS OF FATE, OR, STEPS TO SUCCESS AND POWER
BY

Orison Swett Marden

FOREWORD

Orison Swett Marden (1848-1924) was an inspirational American author who wrote on achieving successin life. Marden created SUCCESS magazine in 1897 and his ideas are still sound in modern times.

Architects of Fate; Or, Steps to Success and Power

PREFACE.

The demand for more than a dozen editions of "Pushing to the Front" during its first year and its universally favorable reception, both at home and abroad, have encouraged the author to publish this companion volume of somewhat similar scope and purpose. The two books were prepared simultaneously, and the story of the first, given in its preface, applies equally well to this.

Inspiration to character-building and worthy achievement is the keynote of the present volume, its object, to arouse to honorable exertion youth who are drifting without aim, to awaken dormant ambitions in those who have grown discouraged in the struggle for success, to encourage and stimulate to higher resolve those who are setting out to make their own way, with perhaps neither friendship nor capital other than a determination to get on in the world.

Nothing is so fascinating to a youth with high purpose, life, and energy throbbing in his young blood as stories of men and women who have brought great things to pass. Though these themes are as old as the human race, yet they are ever new, and more interesting to the young than any fiction. The cry of youth is for life! more life! No didactic or dogmatic teaching, however brilliant, will capture a twentieth-century boy, keyed up to the highest pitch by the pressure of an intense civilization. The romance of achievement under difficulties, of obscure beginnings and triumphant ends; the story of how great men started, their struggles, their long waitings, amid want and woe, the obstacles overcome, the final triumphs; examples, which explode excuses, of men who have seized common situations and made them great, of those of average capacity who have succeeded by the use of ordinary means, by dint of indomitable will and inflexible purpose: these will most inspire the ambitious youth. The author teaches that there are bread and success for every youth under the American flag who has the grit to seize his chance and work his way to his own loaf; that the barriers are not yet erected which declare to aspiring talent, "Thus far and no farther"; that the most forbidding circumstances cannot repress a longing for knowledge, a yearning for growth; that poverty, humble birth, loss of limbs or even eyesight, have not been able to bar the progress of men with grit; that poverty has rocked the cradle of the giants who have wrung civilization from barbarism, and have led the world up from savagery to the Gladstones, the Lincolns, and the Grants.

The book shows that it is the man with one unwavering aim who cuts his way through opposition and forges to the front; that in this electric age, where everything is pusher or pushed, he who would succeed must hold his ground and push hard; that what are stumbling-blocks and defeats to the weak and vacillating, are but stepping-stones and victories to the strong and determined. The author teaches that every germ of goodness will at last struggle into bloom and fruitage, and that true success follows every right step. He has tried to touch the higher springs of the youth's aspiration; to lead him to high ideals; to teach him that there is something nobler in an occupation than merely living-getting or money-getting; that a man may make millions and be a failure still; to caution youth not to allow the maxims of a low prudence, dinned daily into his ears in this money-getting age, to repress the longings for a higher life; that the hand can never safely reach higher than does the heart.

The author's aim has been largely through concrete illustrations which have pith, point, and purpose, to be more suggestive than dogmatic, in a style more practical than elegant, more helpful than ornate, more pertinent than novel.

The author wishes to acknowledge valuable assistance from Mr. Arthur W. Brown, of W. Kingston, R. I.

O. S. M.
43 BOWDOIN ST., BOSTON, MASS.
December 2, 1896.

CHAPTER I. WANTED—A MAN.

"Wanted; men:
Not systems fit and wise,
Not faiths with rigid eyes,
Not wealth in mountain piles,
Not power with gracious smiles,
Not even the potent pen:
Wanted; men."
Run ye to and fro through the streets of Jerusalem, and see now, and know, and seek in the broad places thereof, if ye can find a man.—JEREMIAH.

All the world cries, Where is the man who will save us? We want a man! Don't look so far for this man. You have him at hand. This man,—it is you, it is I, it is each one of us!… How to constitute one's self a man? Nothing harder, if one knows not how to will it; nothing easier, if one wills it.—ALEXANDRE DUMAS.

"'Tis life, not death for which we pant!
'Tis life, whereof our nerves are scant:
More life and fuller, that we want."
I do not wish in attempting to paint a man to describe an air-fed, unimpassioned, impossible ghost. My eyes and ears are revolted by any neglect of the physical facts, the limitations of man.—EMERSON.

But nature, with a matchless hand, sends forth her nobly born,
And laughs the paltry attributes of wealth and rank to scorn;
She moulds with care a spirit rare, half human, half divine,
And cries exulting, "Who can make a gentleman like mine?"
ELIZA COOK.

"In a thousand cups of life," says Emerson, "only one is the right mixture. The fine adjustment of the existing elements, where the well-mixed man is born with eyes not too dull, nor too good, with fire enough and earth enough, capable of receiving impressions from all things, and not too susceptible, then no gift need be bestowed on him. He brings his fortune with him."

Diogenes sought with a lantern at noontide in ancient Athens for a perfectly honest man, and sought in vain. In the market place he once cried aloud, "Hear me, O men;" and, when a crowd collected around him, he said scornfully: "I called for men, not pygmies."

The world has a standing advertisement over the door of every profession, every occupation, every calling; "Wanted—A Man."

Wanted, a man who will not lose his individuality in a crowd, a man who has the courage of his convictions, who is not afraid to say "No," though all the world say "Yes."

Wanted, a man who, though he is dominated by a mighty purpose, will not permit one great faculty to dwarf, cripple, warp, or mutilate his manhood; who will not allow the over-development of one facility to stunt or paralyze his other faculties.

Wanted, a man who is larger than his calling, who considers it a low estimate of his occupation to value it merely as a means of getting a living. Wanted, a man who sees self-development, education and culture, discipline and drill, character and manhood, in his occupation.

A thousand pulpits vacant in a single religious denomination, a thousand preachers standing idle in the market place, while a thousand church committees scour the land for men to fill those same vacant pulpits, and scour in vain, is a sufficient indication, in one direction at least, of the largeness of the opportunities of the age, and also of the crying need of good men.

Wanted, a man who is well balanced, who is not cursed with some little defect or weakness which cripples his usefulness and neutralizes his powers. Wanted, a man of courage, who is not a coward in any part of his nature.

Wanted, a man who is symmetrical, and not one-sided in his development, who has not sent all the energies of his being into one narrow specialty, and allowed all the other branches of his life to wither and die. Wanted, a man who is broad, who does not take half views of things. Wanted, a man who mixes common sense with his theories, who does not let a college education spoil him for practical, every-day life; a man who prefers substance to show, who regards his good name as a priceless treasure.

Wanted, a man "who, no stunted ascetic, is full of life and fire, but whose passions are trained to heed a strong will, the servant of a tender conscience; who has learned to love all beauty, whether of nature or of art, to hate all vileness, and to respect others as himself."

God calls a man to be upright and pure and generous, but he also calls him to be intelligent and skillful and strong and brave.

The world wants a man who is educated all over; whose nerves are brought to their acutest sensibility, whose brain is cultured, keen, incisive, penetrating, broad, liberal, deep; whose hands are deft; whose eyes are alert, sensitive, microscopic, whose heart is tender, broad, magnanimous, true.

The whole world is looking for such a man. Although there are millions out of employment, yet it is almost impossible to find just the right man in almost any department of life. Every profession and every occupation has a standing advertisement all over the world: "Wanted—A Man."

Rousseau, in his celebrated essay on education, says: "According to the order of nature, men being equal, their common vocation is the profession of humanity; and whoever is well educated to discharge the duty of a man cannot be badly prepared to fill any of those offices that have a relation to him. It matters little to me whether my pupil be designed for the army, the pulpit, or the bar. Nature has destined us to the offices of human life antecedent to our destination concerning society. To live is the profession I would teach him. When I have done with him, it is true he will be neither a soldier, a lawyer, nor a divine. Let him first be a man; Fortune may remove him from one rank to another as she pleases, he will be always found in his place."

A little, short doctor of divinity in a large Baptist convention stood on a step and said he thanked God he was a Baptist. The audience could not hear and called "Louder." "Get up higher," some one said. "I can't," he replied. "To be a Baptist is as high as one can get." But there is something higher than being a Baptist, and that is being a man.

As Emerson says, Talleyrand's question is ever the main one; not, is he rich? is he committed? is he well-meaning? has he this or that faculty? is he of the movement? is he of the establishment? but is he anybody? does he stand for something? He must be good of his kind. That is all that Talleyrand, all that State Street, all that the common sense of mankind asks.

When Garfield was asked as a young boy, "what he meant to be," he answered: "First of all, I must make myself a man, if I do not succeed in that, I can succeed in nothing."

Montaigne says our work is not to train a soul by itself alone, nor a body by itself alone, but to train a man.

One great need of the world to-day is for men and women who are good animals. To endure the strain of our concentrated civilization, the coming man and woman must have an excess of animal spirits. They must have a robustness of health. Mere absence of disease is not health. It is the overflowing fountain, not the one half full, that gives life and beauty to the valley below. Only he is healthy who exults in mere animal existence; whose very life is a luxury; who feels a bounding pulse throughout his body, who feels life in every limb, as dogs do when scouring over the field, or as boys do when gliding over fields of ice.

Pope, the poet, was with Sir Godfrey Kneller, the artist, one day, when the latter's nephew, a Guinea slave-trader, came into the room. "Nephew," said Sir Godfrey, "you have the honor of seeing the two greatest men in the world." "I don't know how great men you may be," said the Guinea man, "but I don't like your looks. I have often bought a much better man than either of you, all muscles and bones, for ten guineas."

Sydney Smith said, "I am convinced that digestion is the great secret of life, and that character, virtue and talents, and qualities are powerfully affected by beef, mutton, pie crust, and rich soups. I have often thought I could feed or starve men into virtues or vices, and affect them more powerfully with my instruments of torture than Timotheus could do formerly with his lyre."

What more glorious than a magnificent manhood, animated with the bounding spirits of overflowing health?

It is a sad sight to see thousands of students graduated every year from our grand institutions, whose object is to make stalwart, independent, self-supporting men, turned out into the world saplings instead of stalwart oaks, "memory-glands" instead of brainy men, helpless instead of self-supporting, sickly instead of robust, weak instead of strong, leaning instead of erect. "So many promising youths, and never a finished man!"

The character sympathizes with and unconsciously takes on the nature of the body. A peevish, snarling, ailing man cannot develop the vigor and strength of character which is possible to a healthy, robust, jolly man. There is an inherent love in the human mind for wholeness, a demand that man shall come up to the highest standard; and there is an inherent protest or contempt for preventable deficiency. Nature too demands that man be ever at the top of his condition. The giant's strength with the imbecile's brain will not be characteristic of the coming man.

Man has been a dwarf of himself, but a higher type of manhood stands at the door of this age knocking for admission.

As we stand upon the seashore while the tide is coming in, one wave reaches up the beach far higher than any previous one, then recedes, and for some time none that follows comes up to its mark, but after a while the whole sea is there and beyond it, so now and then there comes a man head and shoulders above his fellow-men, showing that Nature has not lost her ideal, and after a while even the average man will overtop the highest wave of manhood yet given to the world.

Apelles hunted over Greece for many years, studying the fairest points of beautiful women, getting here an eye, there a forehead and there a nose, here a grace and there a turn of beauty, for his famous portrait of a perfect woman which enchanted the world. So the coming man will be a composite, many in one. He will absorb into himself not the weakness, not the follies, but the strength and the virtues of other types of men. He will be a man raised to the highest power. He will be self-centred, equipoised, and ever master of himself. His sensibility will not be deadened or blunted by violation of nature's laws. His whole character will be impressible, and will respond to the most delicate touches of nature.

What a piece of work—this coming man! "How noble in reason. How infinite in faculties. In form and motion how express and admirable, in action how like an angel, in apprehension how like a god. The beauty of the world. The paragon of animals."

The first requisite of all education and discipline should be man-timber. Tough timber must come from well grown, sturdy trees. Such wood can be turned into a mast, can be fashioned into a piano or an exquisite carving. But it must become timber first. Time and patience develop the sapling into the tree. So through discipline, education, experience, the sapling child is developed into hardy mental, moral, physical timber.

What an aid to character building would be the determination of the young man in starting out in life to consider himself his own bank; that his notes will be accepted as good or bad, and will pass current everywhere or be worthless, according to his individual reputation for honor and veracity; that if he lets a note go to protest, his bank of character will be suspected; if he lets two or three go to protest, public confidence will be seriously shaken; that if they continue to go to protest, his reputation will be lost and confidence in him ruined.

If the youth should start out with the fixed determination that every statement he makes shall be the exact truth; that every promise he makes shall be redeemed to the letter; that every appointment shall be kept with the strictest faithfulness and with full regard for other men's time, if he should hold his reputation as a priceless treasure, feel that the eyes of the world are upon him, that he must not deviate a hair's breadth from the truth and right; if he should take such a stand at the outset, he would, like George Peabody, come to have almost unlimited credit and the confidence of all, and would have developed into noble man-timber.

What are palaces and equipages; what though a man could cover a continent with his title-deeds, or an ocean with his commerce, compared with conscious rectitude, with a face that never turns pale at the accuser's voice, with a bosom that never throbs with the fear of exposure, with a heart that might be turned inside out and disclose no stain of dishonor? To have done no man a wrong; to have put your signature to no paper to which the purest angel in heaven might not have been an attesting witness; to walk and live, unseduced, within arm's length of what is not your own, with nothing between your desire and its gratification but the invisible law of rectitude;—this is to be a man.

"He that of such a height hath built his mind,
And reared the dwelling of his thought so strong
As neither fear nor hope can shake the frame
Of his resolved powers; nor all the wind
Of vanity or malice pierce to wrong
His settled peace, or to disturb the same;
What a fair seat hath he; from whence he may
The boundless wastes and wilds of man survey."
[Lines found in one of the books of Beecher's Library.]
A man is never so happy as when he is totus in se; as when he suffices to himself, and can walk without crutches or a guide. Said Jean Paul Richter: "I have made as much out of myself as could be made of the stuff, and no man should require more."

Man is the only great thing in the universe. All the ages have been trying to produce a perfect model. Only one complete man has yet been evolved. The best of us are but prophecies of what is to come.

What constitutes a state?
Not high-raised battlement or labored mound,
Thick wall or moated gate;
Not cities proud with spires and turrets crowned;
Not bays and broad-armed ports,
Where, laughing at the storm, rich navies ride;
Not starred and spangled courts,
Where low-browed baseness wafts perfume to pride.
No: men, high-minded men,
With powers as far above dull brutes endued
In forest, brake, or den,
As beasts excel cold rocks and brambles rude,—

Men who their duties know,
But know their rights, and knowing, dare maintain,
Prevent the long-aimed blow,
And crush the tyrant while they rend the chain.
WILLIAM JONES.
God give us men. A time like this demands
Strong minds, great hearts, true faith and ready hands:
Men whom the lust of office does not kill;
Men whom the spoils of office cannot buy;
Men who possess opinions and a will;
Men who have honor—men who will not lie;
Men who can stand before a demagogue
And scorn his treacherous flatteries without winking;
Tall men sun-crowned, who live above the fog
In public duty, and in private thinking.
ANON.
Open thy bosom, set thy wishes wide,
And let in manhood—let in happiness;
Admit the boundless theatre of thought
From nothing up to God… which makes a man!
YOUNG.
"The wisest man could ask no more of fate
Than to be simple, modest, manly, true."
In speech right gentle, yet so wise; princely of mien,
Yet softly mannered; modest, deferent,
And tender-hearted, though of fearless blood.
EDWIN ARNOLD.

CHAPTER II. DARE.

The Spartans did not inquire how many the enemy are, but where they are.—AGIS II.

What's brave, what's noble, let's do it after the high Roman fashion, and make death proud to take us.—SHAKESPEARE.

Better, like Hector, in the field to die,
Than, like a perfumed Paris, turn and fly.
LONGFELLOW.
Let me die facing the enemy.—BAYARD.

Who conquers me, shall find a stubborn foe.—BYRON.

Courage in danger is half the battle.—PLAUTUS.

No great deed is done
By falterers who ask for certainty.
GEORGE ELIOT.
Fortune befriends the bold.—DRYDEN.

Tender handed stroke a nettle,
And it stings you for your pains;
Grasp it like a man of mettle,
And it soft as silk remains.
AARON HILL.
We make way for the man who boldly pushes past us.—BOVÉE.

Man should dare all things that he knows is right,
And fear to do nothing save what is wrong.
PHEBE CARY.
Soft-heartedness, in times like these,
Shows softness in the upper story.
LOWELL.
O friend, never strike sail to fear. Come into port grandly, or sail with God the seas.—
EMERSON.

To stand with a smile upon your face against a stake from which you cannot get away—that, no doubt, is heroic. But the true glory is resignation to the inevitable. To stand unchained, with perfect liberty to go away, held only by the higher claims of duty, and let the fire creep up to the heart,—this is heroism.—F. W. ROBERTSON.

"Steady, men! Every man must die where he stands!" said Colin Campbell to the Ninety-third Highlanders at Balaklava, as an overwhelming force of Russian cavalry came sweeping down. "Ay, ay, Sir Colin! we'll do that!" was the cordial response from men many of whom had to keep their word by thus obeying.

"Bring back the colors," shouted a captain at the battle of the Alma, when an ensign maintained his ground in front, although the men were retreating. "No," cried the ensign, "bring up the men to the colors." "To dare, and again to dare, and without end to dare," was Danton's noble defiance to the enemies of France.

"The Commons of France have resolved to deliberate," said Mirabeau to De Breze, who brought an order from the king for them to disperse, June 23, 1789. "We have heard the intentions that have been attributed to the king; and you, sir, who cannot be recognized as his organ in the National Assembly,—you, who have neither place, voice, nor right to speak,—you are not the person to bring to us a message of his. Go, say to those who sent you that we are here by the power of the people, and that we will not be driven hence, save by the power of the bayonet."

When the assembled senate of Rome begged Regulus not to return to Carthage to fulfill an illegal promise, he calmly replied: "Have you resolved to dishonor me? Torture and death are awaiting me, but what are these to the shame of an infamous act, or the wounds of a guilty mind? Slave as I am to Carthage, I still have the spirit of a Roman. I have sworn to return. It is my duty. Let the gods take care of the rest."

The courage which Cranmer had shown since the accession of Mary gave way the moment his final doom was announced. The moral cowardice which had displayed itself in his miserable compliance with the lust and despotism of Henry displayed itself again in six successive recantations by which he hoped to purchase pardon. But pardon was impossible; and Cranmer's strangely mingled nature found a power in its very weakness when he was brought into the church of St. Mary at Oxford on the 21st of March, to repeat his recantation on the way to the stake. "Now," ended his address to the hushed congregation before him,—"now I come to the great thing that troubleth my conscience more than any other thing that ever I said or did in my life, and that is the setting abroad of writings contrary to the truth; which here I now renounce and refuse as things written by a hand contrary to the truth which I thought in my heart, and written for fear of death to save my life, if it might be. And, forasmuch as my hand offended in writing contrary to my heart, my hand therefore shall be the first punished; for if I come to the fire it shall be the first burned." "This was the hand that wrote it," he again exclaimed at the stake, "therefore it shall suffer first punishment;" and holding it steadily in the flame, "he never stirred nor cried till life was gone."

"Oh, if I were only a man!" exclaimed Rebecca Bates, a girl of fourteen, as she looked from the window of a lighthouse at Scituate, Mass., during the War of 1812, and saw a British warship anchor in the harbor. "What could you do?" asked Sarah Winsor, a young visitor. "See what a lot of them the boats contain, and look at their guns!" and she pointed to five large boats, filled with soldiers in scarlet uniforms, who were coming to burn the vessels in the harbor and destroy the town. "I don't care, I'd fight," said Rebecca. "I'd use father's old shotgun—anything. Think of uncle's new boat and the sloop! And how hard it is to sit here and see it all, and not lift a finger to help. Father and uncle are in the village and will do all they can. How still it is in the town! There is not a man to be seen." "Oh, they are hiding till the soldiers get nearer," said Sarah, "then we'll hear the shots and the drum." "The drum!" exclaimed Rebecca, "how can they use it? It is here. Father brought it home last night to mend. See! the first boat has reached the sloop. Oh! they are going to burn her. Where is that drum? I've a great mind to go down and beat it. We could hide behind the sandhills and bushes." As flames began to rise from the sloop the ardor of the girls increased. They found the drum and an old fife, and, slipping out of doors unnoticed by Mrs. Bates, soon stood behind a row of sandhills. "Rub-a-dub-dub, rub-a-dub-dub," went the drum, and "squeak, squeak, squeak," went the fife. The Americans in the town thought that help had come from Boston, and rushed into boats to attack the redcoats. The British paused in their work of destruction; and, when the fife began to play "Yankee Doodle," they scrambled into their boats and rowed in haste to the warship, which weighed anchor and sailed away as fast as the wind would carry her.

A woman's piercing shriek suddenly startled a party of surveyors at dinner in a forest of northern Virginia on a calm, sunny day in 1750. The cries were repeated in quick succession, and the men sprang through the undergrowth to learn their cause. "Oh, sir," exclaimed the woman as she caught sight of a youth of eighteen, but a man in stature and bearing; "you will surely do something for me! Make these friends release me. My boy,—my poor boy is drowning, and they will not let me go!" "It would be madness; she will jump into the river," said one of the men who was holding her; "and the rapids would dash her to pieces in a moment!" Throwing on his coat, the youth sprang to the edge of the bank, scanned for a moment the rocks and whirling currents, and then, at sight of part of the boy's dress, plunged into the roaring rapids. "Thank God, he will save my child!" cried the mother, and all rushed to the brink of the precipice; "there he is! Oh, my boy, my darling boy! How could I leave you?"

But all eyes were bent upon the youth struggling with strong heart and hope amid the dizzy sweep of the whirling currents far below. Now it seemed as if he would be dashed against a projecting rock, over which the water flew in foam, and anon a whirlpool would drag him in, from whose grasp escape would seem impossible. Twice the boy went out of sight, but he had reappeared the second time, although frightfully near the most dangerous part of the river. The rush of waters here was tremendous, and no one had ever dared to approach it, even in a canoe, lest he should be dashed to pieces. The youth redoubled his exertions. Three times he was about to grasp the child, when some stronger eddy would toss it from him. One final effort he makes; the child is held aloft by his strong right arm, but a cry of horror bursts from the lips of every spectator as boy and man shoot over the falls and vanish in the seething waters below.

"There they are!" shouted the mother a moment later, in a delirium of joy. "See! they are safe! Great God, I thank Thee!" And sure enough they emerged unharmed from the boiling vortex, and in a few minutes reached a low place in the bank and were drawn up by their friends, the boy senseless, but still alive, and the youth almost exhausted. "God will give you a reward," solemnly spoke the grateful woman. "He will do great things for you in return for this day's work, and the blessings of thousands besides mine will attend you."

The youth was George Washington.

"Your Grace has not the organ of animal courage largely developed," said a phrenologist, who was examining Wellington's head. "You are right," replied the Iron Duke, "and but for my sense of duty I should have retreated in my first fight." That first fight, on an Indian field, was one of the most terrible on record.

In the reverses which followed Napoleon, he met the allies at Arcis. A live shell having fallen in front of one of his young battalions, which recoiled and wavered in expectation of an explosion, Napoleon, to reassure them, spurred his charger toward the instrument of destruction, made him smell the burning match, waited unshaken for the explosion, and was blown up. Rolling in the dust with his mutilated steed, and rising without a wound amid the plaudits of his soldiers, he calmly called for another horse, and continued to brave the grape-shot, and to fly into the thickest of the battle.

When General Jackson was a judge and was holding court in a small settlement, a border ruffian, a murderer and desperado, came into the court-room with brutal violence and interrupted the court. The judge ordered him to be arrested. The officer did not dare to approach him. "Call a posse," said the judge, "and arrest him." But they also shrank in fear from the ruffian. "Call me, then," said Jackson; "this court is adjourned for five minutes." He left the bench, walked straight up to the man, and with his eagle eye actually cowed the ruffian, who dropped his weapons, afterwards saying, "There was something in his eye I could not resist."

One of the last official acts of the late President Carnot, of France, was the sending of a medal of the French Legion of Honor to a little American girl, who lives in Indiana. While a train on the Pan Handle Railroad, having on board several distinguished Frenchmen, was bound to Chicago and the World's Fair, Jennie Carey, who was then ten years old, discovered that a trestle was on fire, and that if the train, which was nearly due, entered it a dreadful wreck would take place. Thereupon she ran out upon the track to a place where she could be seen from some little distance. Then she took off her red flannel skirt and, when the train came in view, waved it back and forth across the track. It was seen, and the train stopped. On board of it were seven hundred people, many of whom must have suffered death but for Jennie's courage and presence of mind. When they returned to France, the Frenchmen brought the occurrence to the notice of President Carnot, and the result was the sending of the medal of this famous French society, the purpose of which is the honoring of bravery and merit, wherever they may be found.

After the battle of Fort Donelson, the wounded were hauled down the hill in rough board wagons, and most of them died before they reached St. Louis. One blue-eyed boy of nineteen, with both arms and both legs shattered, had lain a long time and was neglected. He said, "Why, you see they couldn't stop to bother with us because they had to take the fort. When they took it we all forgot our sufferings and shouted for joy, even to the dying."

Louis IX. of France was captured by the Turks at the battle of Mansoora, during the Seventh Crusade, and his wife Marguerite, with a babe at the breast, was in Damietta, many miles away. The Infidels surrounded the city, and pressed the garrison so hard that it was decided to capitulate. The queen summoned the knights, and told them that she at least would die in armor upon the ramparts before the enemy should become masters of Damietta.

"Before her words they thrilled like leaves
When winds are in the wood;
And a deepening murmur told of men
Roused to a loftier mood."

Grasping lance and shield, they vowed to defend their queen and the cross to the last. Damietta was saved.

Pyrrhus marched to Sparta to reinstate the deposed Cleonymus, and quietly pitched his tents before Laconia, not anticipating resistance. In consternation, the Spartans in council decided to send their women to Crete for safety. But the women met and asked Queen Archidamia to remonstrate. She went to the council, sword in hand, and told the men that their wives did not care to live after Sparta was destroyed.

"We are brave men's mothers, and brave men's wives;
We are ready to do and dare;
We are ready to man your walls with our lives,
And string your bows with our hair."

They hurried to the walls and worked all night, aiding the men in digging trenches. When Pyrrhus attacked the city next day, his repulse was so emphatic that he withdrew from Laconia.

Charles V. of Spain passed through Thuringia in 1547, on his return to Swabia after the battle of Muehlburg. He wrote to Catherine, Countess Dowager of Schwartzburg, promising that her subjects should not be molested in their persons or property if they would supply the Spanish soldiers with provisions at a reasonable price. On approaching Eudolstadt, General Alva and Prince Henry of Brunswick, with his sons, invited themselves, by a messenger sent forward, to breakfast with the Countess, who had no choice but to ratify so delicate a request from the commander of an army. Just as the guests were seated at a generous repast, the Countess was called from the hall and told that the Spaniards were using violence and driving away the cattle of the peasants.

Quietly arming all her retinue, she bolted and barred all the gates and doors of the castle, and returned to the banquet to complain of the breach of faith. General Alva told her that such was the custom of war, adding that such trifling disorders were not to be heeded. "That we shall presently see," said Catharine; "my poor subjects must have their own again, or, as God lives, prince's blood for oxen's blood!" The doors were opened, and armed men took the places of the waiters behind the chairs of the guests. Henry changed color; then, as the best way out of a bad scrape, laughed loudly, and ended by praising the splendid acting of his hostess, and promising that Alva should order the cattle restored at once. Not until a courier returned, saying that the order had been obeyed, and all damages settled satisfactorily, did the armed waiters leave. The Countess then thanked her guests for the honor they had done her castle, and they retired with protestations of their distinguished consideration.

It was the heroic devotion of an Indian girl that saved the life of Captain John Smith, when the powerful King Powhatan had decreed his death. Ill could the struggling colony spare him at that time.

When the consul shouted that the bridge was tottering, Lartius and Herminius sought safety in flight. But Horatius strode still nearer the foe, the single champion of his country and liberty, and dared the ninety thousand to come on. Dead stillness fell upon the Tuscans, so astonished were they at the audacity of the Roman. He first broke the awful silence, so deep that his clear, strong voice could be heard by thousands in both armies, between which rolled the Tiber, as he denounced the baseness and perfidy of the invaders. Not until his words were drowned by the loud crash of fiercely disrupturing timbers, and the sullen splash of the dark river, did his enemies hurl their showers of arrows and javelins. Then, dexterously warding off the missiles with his shield, he plunged into the Tiber. Although stabbed in the hip by a Tuscan spear which lamed him for life, he swam in safety to Rome.

"It is a bad omen," said Eric the Red, when his horse slipped and fell on the way to his ship, moored on the coast of Greenland, in readiness for a voyage of discovery. "Ill-fortune would be mine should I dare venture now upon the sea." So he returned to his house, but his young son Leif decided to go, and, with a crew of thirty-five men, sailed southward in search of the unknown shore upon which Captain Biarni had been driven by a storm, while sailing in another Viking ship two or three years before. The first land that they saw was probably Labrador, a barren, rugged plain. Leif called this country Heluland, or the land of flat stones. Sailing onward many days, he came to a low, level coast thickly covered with woods, on account of which he called the country Markland, probably the modern Nova Scotia. Sailing onward, they came to an island which they named Vinland on account of the abundance of delicious wild grapes in the woods. This was in the year 1000. Here where the city of Newport, R. I., stands, they spent many months, and then returned to Greenland with their vessel loaded with grapes and strange kinds of wood. The voyage was successful, and no doubt Eric was sorry he had been frightened by the bad omen.

May 10, 1796, Napoleon carried the bridge at Lodi, in the face of the Austrian batteries. Fourteen cannon—some accounts say thirty—were trained upon the French end of the structure. Behind them were six thousand troops. Napoleon massed four thousand grenadiers at the head of the bridge, with a battalion of three hundred carbineers in front. At the tap of the drum the foremost assailants wheeled from the cover of the street wall under a terrible hail of grape and canister, and attempted to pass the gateway to the bridge. The front ranks went down like stalks of grain before a reaper; the column staggered and reeled backward, and the valiant grenadiers were appalled by the task before them. Without a word or a look of reproach, Napoleon placed himself at their head, and his aids and generals rushed to his side. Forward again, this time over heaps of dead that choked the passage, and a quick run, counted by seconds only, carried the column across two hundred yards of clear space, scarcely a shot from the Austrians taking effect beyond the point where the platoons wheeled for the first leap. So sudden and so miraculous was it all that the Austrian artillerists abandoned their guns instantly, and their supports fled in a panic instead of rushing to the front and meeting the French onslaught. This Napoleon had counted on in making the bold attack. The contrast between Napoleon's slight figure and the massive grenadiers suggested the nickname "Little Corporal."

The great secret of the success of Joan of Arc was the boldness of her attacks.

When Stephen of Colonna fell into the hands of base assailants, and they asked him in derision, "Where is now your fortress?" "Here," was his bold reply, placing his hand upon his heart.

It was after the Mexican War when General McClellan was employed as a topographical engineer in surveying the Pacific coast. From his headquarters at Vancouver he had gone south to the Columbia River with two companions, a soldier and a servant. One evening he received word that the chiefs of the Columbia River tribes desired to confer with him. From the messenger's manner he suspected that the Indians meant mischief. He warned his companions that they must be ready to leave camp at a moment's notice. Mounting his horse, he rode boldly into the Indian village. About thirty chiefs were holding council. McClellan was led into the circle, and placed at the right hand of Saltese. He was familiar with the Chinook jargon, and could understand every word spoken in the council. Saltese made known the grievance of the tribes. Two Indians had been captured by a party of white pioneers and hanged for theft. Retaliation for this outrage seemed indispensable. The chiefs pondered long, but had little to say. McClellan had been on friendly terms with them, and was not responsible for the forest executions. Still, he was a white man, and the chiefs had vowed vengeance against the race. The council was prolonged for hours before sentence was passed, and then Saltese, in the name of the head men of the tribes, decreed that McClellan should immediately be put to death in retaliation for the hanging of the two Indian thieves.

McClellan had said nothing. He had known that argument and pleas for justice or mercy would be of no avail. He had sat motionless, apparently indifferent to his fate. By his listlessness he had thrown his captors off their guard. When the sentence was passed he acted like a flash. Flinging his left arm around the neck of Saltese, he whipped out his revolver and held it close to the chief's temple. "Revoke that sentence, or I shall kill you this instant!" he cried, with his fingers clicking the trigger. "I revoke it!" exclaimed Saltese, fairly livid from fear. "I must have your word that I can leave this council in safety." "You have the word of Saltese," was the quick response. McClellan knew how sacred was the pledge which he had received. The revolver was lowered. Saltese was released from the embrace of the strong arm. McClellan strode out of the tent with his revolver in his hand. Not a hand was raised against him. He mounted his horse and rode to his camp, where his two followers were ready to spring into the saddle and to escape from the villages. He owed his life to his quickness of perception, and to his accurate knowledge of Indian character.

In 1866, Rufus Choate spoke to an audience of nearly five thousand in Lowell in favor of the candidacy of James Buchanan for the presidency. The floor of the great hall began to sink, settling more and more as he proceeded with his address, until a sound of cracking timber below would have precipitated a stampede with fatal results but for the coolness of B. F. Butler, who presided. Telling the people to remain quiet, he said that he would see if there were any cause for alarm. He found the supports of the floor in so bad a condition that the slightest applause would be likely to bury the audience in the ruins of the building. Returning rather leisurely to the platform, he whispered to Choate as he passed, "We shall all be in —— in five minutes," then he told the crowd that there was no immediate danger if they would slowly disperse, although he thought it prudent to adjourn to a place where there would be no risk whatever. The post of danger, he added, was on the platform, which was most weakly supported, therefore he and those with him would be the last to leave. No doubt many lives were saved by his coolness.

Many distinguished foreign and American statesmen were present at a fashionable dinner party where wine was freely poured, but Schuyler Colfax, then vice-president of the United States, declined to drink from a proffered cup. "Colfax dares not drink," sneered a Senator who had already taken too much. "You are right," said the Vice-President, "I dare not."

When Grant was in Houston several years ago, he was given a rousing reception. Naturally hospitable, and naturally inclined to like a man of Grant's make-up, the Houstonites determined to go beyond any other Southern city in the way of a banquet and other manifestations of their good-will and hospitality. They made great preparations for the dinner, the committee taking great pains to have the finest wines that could be procured for the table that night. When the time came to serve the wine, the head-waiter went first to Grant. Without a word the general quietly turned down all the glasses at his plate. This movement was a great surprise to the Texans, but they were equal to the occasion. Without a single word being spoken, every man along the line of the long tables turned his glasses down, and there was not a drop of wine taken that night.

A deep sewer at Noyon, France, had been opened for repairs, and carelessly left at night without covering or lights to warn people of danger. Late at night four men stumbled in, and lay some time before their situation was known in the town. No one dared go to the aid of the men, then unconscious from breathing noxious gases, except Catherine Vassen, a servant girl of eighteen. She insisted on being lowered at once. Fastening a rope around two of the men, she aided in raising them and restoring them to consciousness. Descending again, she had just tied a rope around a third man, when she felt her breath failing. Tying another rope to her long, curly hair, she swooned, but was drawn up with the man, to be quickly revived by fresh air and stimulants. The fourth man was dead when his body was pulled up, on account of the delay from the fainting of Catherine.

Two French officers at Waterloo were advancing to charge a greatly superior force. One, observing that the other showed signs of fear, said, "Sir, I believe you are frightened." "Yes, I am," was the reply, "and if you were half as much frightened, you would run away."

"That's a brave man," said Wellington, when he saw a soldier turn pale as he marched against a battery; "he knows his danger, and faces it."

"There are many cardinals and bishops at Worms," said a friend to Luther, "and they will burn your body to ashes as they did that of John Huss." Luther replied: "Although they should make a fire that should reach from Worms to Wittenberg, and that should flame up to heaven, in the Lord's name I would pass through it and appear before them." He said to another: "I would enter Worms though there were as many devils there as there are tiles upon the roofs of the houses." Another said: "Duke George will surely arrest you." He replied: "It is my duty to go, and I will go, though it rain Duke Georges for nine days together."

"Here I stand, I cannot do otherwise, God help me," exclaimed Luther at the Diet of Worms, facing his foes.

A Western paper recently invited the surviving Union and Confederate officers to give an account of the bravest act observed by each during the Civil War. Colonel Thomas W. Higginson said that at a dinner at Beaufort, S. C., where wine flowed freely and ribald jests were bandied, Dr. Miner, a slight, boyish fellow who did not drink, was told that he could not go until he had drunk a toast, told a story, or sung a song. He replied: "I cannot sing, but I will give a toast, although I must drink it in water. It is 'Our Mothers.'" The men were so affected and ashamed that some took him by the hand and thanked him for displaying courage greater than that required to walk up to the mouth of a cannon.

It took great courage for the commercial Quaker, John Bright, to espouse a cause which called down upon his head the derision and scorn and hatred of the Parliament. For years he rested under a cloud of obloquy, but Bright was made of stern stuff. It was only his strength of character and masterly eloquence, which saved him from political annihilation. To a man who boasted that his ancestors came over with the Conquerors, he replied, "I never heard that they did anything else." A Tory lordling said, when Bright was ill, that Providence had inflicted upon Bright, for the measure of his talents, disease of the brain. When Bright went back into the Commons he replied: "This may be so, but it will be some consolation to the friends and family of the noble lord to know that that disease is one which even Providence cannot inflict upon him."

"When a resolute young fellow steps up to the great bully, the World, and takes him boldly by the beard," says Holmes, "he is often surprised to find it come off in his hand, and that it was only tied on to scare away timid adventurers."

It takes courage for a young man to stand firmly erect while others are bowing and fawning for praise and power. It takes courage to wear threadbare clothes while your comrades dress in broadcloth. It takes courage to remain in honest poverty when others grow rich by fraud. It takes courage to say "No" squarely when those around you say "Yes." It takes courage to do your duty in silence and obscurity while others prosper and grow famous although neglecting sacred obligations. It takes courage to unmask your true self, to show your blemishes to a condemning world, and to pass for what you really are.

It takes courage and pluck to be outvoted, beaten, laughed at, scoffed, ridiculed, derided, misunderstood, misjudged, to stand alone with all the world against you, but

"They are slaves who dare not be
In the right with two or three."

"There is never wanting a dog to bark at you."

"An honest man is not the worse because a dog barks at him."

"Let any man show the world that he feels
Afraid of its bark, and 'twill fly at his heels.
Let him fearlessly face it, 't will leave him alone,
And 't will fawn at his feet if he fling it a bone."

We live ridiculously for fear of being thought ridiculous.

"'Tis he is the coward who proves false to his vows,
To his manhood, his honor, for a laugh or a sneer:
'Tis he is the hero who stands firm, though alone,
For the truth and the right without flinching or fear."

The youth who starts out by being afraid to speak what he thinks will usually end by being afraid to think what he wishes.

How we shrink from an act of our own. We live as others live. Custom or fashion dictates, or your doctor or minister, and they in turn dare not depart from their schools. Dress, living, servants, carriages, everything must conform, or be ostracized. Who dares conduct his household or business affairs in his own way, and snap his fingers at Dame Grundy?

Many a man has marched up to the cannon's mouth in battle who dared not face public opinion or oppose Mrs. Grundy.

It takes courage for a public man not to bend the knee to popular prejudice. It takes courage to refuse to follow custom when it is injurious to his health and morals. To espouse an unpopular cause in Congress requires more courage than to lead a charge in battle. How much easier for a politician to prevaricate and dodge an issue than to stand squarely on his feet like a man.

As a rule, eccentricity is a badge of power, but how many women would not rather strangle their individuality than be tabooed by Mrs. Grundy? Yet fear is really the only thing to fear.

"Whoever you may be," said Sainte-Beuve, "great genius, distinguished talent, artist honorable or amiable, the qualities for which you deserve to be praised will all be turned against you. Were you a Virgil, the pious and sensible singer par excellence, there are people who will call you an effeminate poet. Were you a Horace, there are people who will reproach you with the very purity and delicacy of your taste. If you were a Shakespeare, some one will call you a drunken savage. If you were a Goethe, more than one Pharisee will proclaim you the most selfish of egotists."

As the strongest man has a weakness somewhere, so the greatest hero is a coward somewhere. Peter was courageous enough to draw his sword to defend his master, but he could not stand the ridicule and the finger of scorn of the maidens in the high priest's hall, and he actually denied even the acquaintance of the master he had declared he would die for.

"I will take the responsibility," said Andrew Jackson, on a memorable occasion, and his words have become proverbial. Not even Congress dared to oppose the edicts of John Quincy Adams.

If a man would accomplish anything in this world, he must not be afraid of assuming responsibilities. Of course it takes courage to run the risk of failure, to be subjected to criticism for an unpopular cause, to expose one's self to the shafts of everybody's ridicule, but the man who is not true to himself, who cannot carry out the sealed orders placed in his hands at his birth, regardless of the world's yes or no, of its approval or disapproval, the man who has not the courage to trace the pattern of his own destiny, which no other soul knows but his own, can never rise to the true dignity of manhood. All the world loves courage; youth craves it; they want to hear about it, they want to read about it. The fascination of the "blood and thunder" novels and of the cheap story papers for youth are based upon this idea of courage. If the boys cannot get the real article, they will take a counterfeit.

Don't be like Uriah Heep, begging everybody's pardon for taking the liberty of being in the world. There is nothing attractive in timidity, nothing lovable in fear. Both are deformities and are repulsive. Manly courage is dignified and graceful. The worst manners in the world are those of persons conscious "of being beneath their position, and trying to conceal it or make up for it by style."

Bruno, condemned to be burned alive in Rome, said to his judge: "You are more afraid to pronounce my sentence than I am to receive it." Anne Askew, racked until her bones were dislocated, never flinched, but looked her tormentor calmly in the face and refused to abjure her faith.

"We are afraid of truth, afraid of fortune, afraid of death, and afraid of each other." "Half a man's wisdom goes with his courage," said Emerson. Physicians used to teach that courage depends on the circulation of the blood in the arteries, and that during passion, anger, trials of strength, wrestling or fighting, a large amount of blood is collected in the arteries, and does not pass to the veins. A strong pulse is a fortune in itself.

"Rage," said Shaftesbury, "can make a coward forget himself and fight."

"I should have thought fear would have kept you from going so far," said a relative who found the little boy Nelson wandering a long distance from home. "Fear?" said the future admiral, "I don't know him."

"Doubt indulged becomes doubt realized." To determine to do anything is half the battle. "To think a thing is impossible is to make it so." Courage is victory, timidity is defeat.

That simple shepherd-lad, David, fresh from his flocks, marching unattended and unarmed, save with his shepherd's staff and sling, to confront the colossal Goliath with his massive armor, is the sublimest audacity the world has ever seen.

"Dent, I wish you would get down, and see what is the matter with that leg there," said Grant, when he and Colonel Dent were riding through the thickest of a fire that had become so concentrated and murderous that his troops had all been driven back. "I guess looking after your horse's legs can wait," said Dent; "it is simply murder for us to sit here." "All right," said Grant, "if you don't want to see to it, I will." He dismounted, untwisted a piece of telegraph wire which had begun to cut the horse's leg, examined it deliberately, and climbed into his saddle. "Dent," said he, "when you've got a horse that you think a great deal of, you should never take any chances with him. If that wire had been left there for a little time longer he would have gone dead lame, and would perhaps have been ruined for life."

Wellington said that at Waterloo the hottest of the battle raged round a farmhouse, with an orchard surrounded by a thick hedge, which was so important a point in the British position that orders were given to hold it at any hazard or sacrifice. At last the powder and ball ran short and the hedges took fire, surrounding the orchard with a wall of flame. A messenger had been sent for ammunition, and soon two loaded wagons came galloping toward the farmhouse. "The driver of the first wagon, with the reckless daring of an English boy, spurred his struggling and terrified horses through the burning heap; but the flames rose fiercely round, and caught the powder, which exploded in an instant, sending wagon, horses, and rider in fragments into the air. For an instant the driver of the second wagon paused, appalled by his comrade's fate; the next, observing that the flames, beaten back for the moment by the explosion, afforded him one desperate chance, sent his horses at the smouldering breach and, amid the deafening cheers of the garrison, landed his terrible cargo safely within. Behind him the flames closed up, and raged more fiercely than ever."

At the battle of Friedland a cannon-ball came over the heads of the French soldiers, and a young soldier instinctively dodged. Napoleon looked at him and smilingly said: "My friend, if that ball were destined for you, though you were to burrow a hundred feet under ground it would be sure to find you there."

When the mine in front of Petersburg was finished, the fuse was lighted, and the Union troops were drawn up ready to charge the enemy's works as soon as the explosion should make a breach. But seconds, minutes, and tens of minutes passed, without a sound from the mine, and the suspense became painful. Lieutenant Doughty and Sergeant Kees volunteered to examine the fuse. Through the long subterranean galleries they hurried in silence, not knowing but they were advancing to a horrible death. They found the defect, fired the train anew, and soon a terrible upheaval of earth gave the signal to march to victory.

At the battle of Copenhagen, as Nelson walked the deck slippery with blood and covered with the dead, he said: "This is warm work, and this day may be the last to any of us in a moment. But, mark me, I would not be elsewhere for thousands." At the battle of Trafalgar, when Nelson was shot and was being carried below, he covered his face, that those fighting might not know their chief had fallen.

In a skirmish at Salamanca, while the enemy's guns were pouring shot into his regiment, Sir William Napier's men became disobedient. He at once ordered a halt, and flogged four of the ringleaders under fire. The men yielded at once, and then marched three miles under a heavy cannonade as coolly as if it were a review.

Execute your resolutions immediately. Thoughts are but dreams till their effects be tried. Does competition trouble you? work away; what is your competitor but a man? Conquer your place in the world, for all things serve a brave soul. Combat difficulty manfully; sustain misfortune bravely; endure poverty nobly; encounter disappointment courageously. The influence of the brave man is a magnetism which creates an epidemic of noble zeal in all about him. Every day sends to the grave obscure men, who have only remained in obscurity because their timidity has prevented them from making a first effort; and who, if they could have been induced to begin, would, in all probability, have gone great lengths in the career of usefulness and fame. "No great deed is done," says George Eliot, "by falterers who ask for certainty." The brave, cheerful man will survive his blighted hopes and disappointments, take them for just what they are, lessons and perhaps blessings in disguise, and will march boldly and cheerfully forward in the battle of life. Or, if necessary, he will bear his ills with a patience and calm endurance deeper than ever plummet sounded. He is the true hero.

Then to side with Truth is noble when we share her wretched crust,
Ere her cause bring fame and profit, and 't is prosperous to be just;
Then it is the brave man chooses, while the coward stands aside,
Doubting in his abject spirit, till his Lord is crucified.
LOWELL.
Our doubts are traitors,
And make us lose the good we oft might win,
By fearing to attempt.
SHAKESPEARE.

After the great inward struggle was over, and he had determined to remain loyal to his principles, Thomas More walked cheerfully to the block. His wife called him a fool for staying in a dark, damp, filthy prison when he might have his liberty by merely renouncing his doctrines, as some of the bishops had done. But he preferred death to dishonor. His daughter allowed the power of love to drive away fear. She remained true to her father when all others, even her mother, had forsaken him. After his head had been cut off and exhibited on a pole on London Bridge, the poor girl begged it of the authorities, and requested that it be buried in the coffin with her. Her request was granted, for her death occurred soon.

When Sir Walter Raleigh came to the scaffold he was very faint, and began his speech to the crowd by saying that during the last two days he had been visited by two ague fits. "If, therefore, you perceive any weakness in me, I beseech you ascribe it to my sickness rather than to myself." He took the axe and kissed the blade, and said to the sheriff: "'T is a sharp medicine, but a sound cure for all diseases."

Don't waste time dreaming of obstacles you may never encounter, or in crossing bridges you have not reached. Don't fool with a nettle! Grasp with firmness if you would rob it of its sting. To half will and to hang forever in the balance is to lose your grip on life.

Abraham Lincoln's boyhood was one long struggle with poverty, with little education, and no influential friends. When at last he had begun the practice of law, it required no little daring to cast his fortune with the weaker side in politics, and thus imperil what small reputation he had gained. Only the most sublime moral courage could have sustained him as President to hold his ground against hostile criticism and a long train of disaster; to issue the Emancipation Proclamation; to support Grant and Stanton against the clamor of the politicians and the press; and through it all to do the right as God gave him to see the right.

Lincoln never shrank from espousing an unpopular cause when he believed it to be right. At the time when it almost cost a young lawyer his bread and butter to defend the fugitive slave, and when other lawyers had refused, Lincoln would always plead the cause of the unfortunate whenever an opportunity presented. "Go to Lincoln," people would say, when these hounded fugitives were seeking protection; "he's not afraid of any cause, if it's right."

As Salmon P. Chase left the court room after making an impassioned plea for the runaway slave girl Matilda, a man looked at him in surprise and said: "There goes a fine young fellow who has just ruined himself." But in thus ruining himself Chase had taken the first important step in a career in which he became Governor of Ohio, United States Senator from Ohio, Secretary of the United States Treasury, and Chief Justice of the United States Supreme Court.

At the trial of William Penn for having spoken at a Quaker meeting, the recorder, not satisfied with the first verdict, said to the jury: "We will have a verdict by the help of God, or you shall starve for it." "You are Englishmen," said Penn; "mind your privileges, give not away your right." At last the jury, after two days and two nights without food, returned a verdict of "Not guilty." The recorder fined them forty marks apiece for their independence.

What cared Christ for the jeers of the crowd? The palsied hand moved, the blind saw, the leper was made whole, the dead spake, despite the ridicule and scoffs of the spectators.

What cared Wendell Phillips for rotten eggs, derisive scorn, and hisses? In him "at last the scornful world had met its match." Were Beecher and Gough to be silenced by the rude English mobs that came to extinguish them? No! they held their ground and compelled unwilling thousands to hear and to heed. Did Anna Dickinson leave the platform when the pistol bullets of the Molly Maguires flew about her head? She silenced those pistols by her courage and her arguments.

"What the world wants is a Knox, who dares to preach on with a musket leveled at his head, a Garrison, who is not afraid of a jail, or a mob, or a scaffold erected in front of his door.

"Storms may howl around thee,
Foes may hunt and hound thee:
Shall they overpower thee?
Never, never, never."

When General Butler was sent with nine thousand men to quell the New York riots, he arrived in advance of his troops, and found the streets thronged with an angry mob, which had already hanged more than one man to lamp-posts. Without waiting for his men, Butler went to the place where the crowd was most dense, overturned an ash barrel, stood upon it, and began: "Delegates from Five Points, fiends from hell, you have murdered your superiors," and the blood-stained crowd quailed before the courageous words of a single man in a city which Mayor Fernando Wood could not restrain with the aid of police and militia.

"Our enemies are before us," exclaimed the Spartans at Thermopylae. "And we are before them," was the cool reply of Leonidas. "Deliver your arms," came the message from Xerxes. "Come and take them," was the answer Leonidas sent back. A Persian soldier said: "You will not be able to see the sun for flying javelins and arrows." "Then we will fight in the shade," replied a

Lacedemonian. What wonder that a handful of such men checked the march of the greatest host that ever trod the earth.

"It is impossible," said a staff officer, when Napoleon gave directions for a daring plan. "Impossible!" thundered the great commander, "impossible is the adjective of fools!" Napoleon went to the edge of his possibility.

Grant never knew when he was beaten. When told that he was surrounded by the enemy at Belmont, he quietly replied: "Well, then we must cut our way out."

The courageous man is an example to the intrepid. His influence is magnetic. He creates an epidemic of nobleness. Men follow him, even to the death.

The spirit of courage will transform the whole temper of your life. "The wise and active conquer difficulties by daring to attempt them. Sloth and folly shiver and sicken at the sight of trial and hazard, and make the impossibility they fear."

"The hero," says Emerson, "is the man who is immovably centred."

Emin Pasha, the explorer of Africa, was left behind by his exploring party under circumstances that were thought certainly fatal, and his death was reported with great assurance. Early the next winter, as his troop was on its toilsome but exciting way through Central Africa, it came upon a most wretched sight. A party of natives had been kidnapped by the slave-hunters, and dragged in chains thus far toward the land of bondage. But small-pox had set in, and the miserable company had been abandoned to their fate. Emin sent his men ahead, and stayed behind in this camp of death to act as physician and nurse. How many lives he saved is not known, though it is known that he nearly lost his own. The age of chivalry is not gone by. This is as knightly a deed as poet ever chronicled.

A mouse that dwelt near the abode of a great magician was kept in such constant distress by its fear of a cat, that the magician, taking pity on it, turned it into a cat itself. Immediately it began to suffer from its fear of a dog, so the magician turned it into a dog. Then it began to suffer from fear of a tiger. The magician therefore turned it into a tiger. Then it began to suffer from fear of hunters, and the magician said in disgust: "Be a mouse again. As you have only the heart of a mouse, it is impossible to help you by giving you the body of a nobler animal."

Men who have dared have moved the world, often before reaching the prime of life. It is astonishing what daring to begin and perseverance have enabled even youths to achieve. Alexander, who ascended the throne at twenty, had conquered the known world before dying at thirty-three. Julius Caesar captured eight hundred cities, conquered three hundred nations, and defeated three million men, became a great orator and one of the greatest statesmen known, and still was a young man. Washington was appointed adjutant-general at nineteen, was sent at twenty-one as an ambassador to treat with the French, and won his first battle as a colonel at twenty-two. Lafayette was made general of the whole French army at twenty. Charlemagne was master of France and Germany at thirty. Condé was only twenty-two when he conquered at Rocroi. Galileo was but eighteen when he saw the principle of the pendulum in the swinging lamp in the cathedral at Pisa. Peel was in Parliament at twenty-one. Gladstone was in Parliament before he was twenty-two, and at twenty-four he was Lord of the Treasury. Elizabeth Barrett Browning was proficient in Greek and Latin at twelve; De Quincey at eleven. Robert Browning wrote at eleven poetry of no mean order. Cowley, who sleeps in Westminster Abbey, published a volume of poems at fifteen. N. P. Willis won lasting fame as a poet before leaving college. Macaulay was a celebrated author before he was twenty-three. Luther was but twenty-nine when he nailed his famous thesis to the door of the bishop and defied the pope. Nelson was a lieutenant in the British Navy before he was twenty. He was but forty-seven when he received his death wound at Trafalgar. Charles the Twelfth was only nineteen when he gained the battle of Narva; at thirty-six, Cortez was the conqueror of Mexico; at thirty-two, Clive had established the British power in India. Hannibal, the greatest of military commanders, was only thirty when, at Cannae, he dealt an almost annihilating blow at the republic of Rome; and Napoleon was only twenty-seven when, on the plains of Italy, he outgeneraled and defeated, one after another, the veteran marshals of Austria.

Equal courage and resolution are often shown by men who have passed the allotted limit of life. Victor Hugo and Wellington were both in their prime after they had reached the age of threescore years and ten. George Bancroft wrote some of his best historical work when he was eighty-five. Gladstone ruled England with a strong hand at eighty-four, and was a marvel of literary and scholarly ability.

"Not every vessel that sails from Tarshish will bring back the gold of Ophir. But shall it therefore rot in the harbor? No! Give its sails to the wind!"

Shakespeare says: "He is not worthy of the honeycomb that shuns the hive because the bees have stings."

"The brave man is not he who feels no fear,
For that were stupid and irrational;
But he whose noble soul its fear subdues
And bravely dares the danger nature shrinks from."

The inscription on the gates of Busyrane: "Be bold." On the second gate: "Be bold, be bold, and ever more be bold;" the third gate: "Be not too bold."

Many a bright youth has accomplished nothing of worth simply because he did not dare to commence.

Begin! Begin!! Begin!!!

Whatever people may think of you, do that which you believe to be right. Be alike indifferent to censure or praise.—PYTHAGORAS.

Fear makes man a slave to others. This is the tyrant's chain. Anxiety is a form of cowardice embittering life.—CHANNING.

Courage is generosity of the highest order, for the brave are prodigal of the most precious things. Our blood is nearer and dearer to us than our money, and our life than our estate. Women are more taken with courage than with generosity.—COLTON.

Who chooses me must give and hazard all he hath.
Merchant of Venice, Inscription on Leaden Casket.
I dare to do all that may become a man:
Who dares do more is none.
SHAKESPEAKE.
For man's great actions are performed in minor struggles. There are obstinate and unknown braves who defend themselves inch by inch in the shadows against the fatal invasion of want and turpitude. There are noble and mysterious triumphs which no eye sees, no renown rewards, and no flourish of trumpets salutes. Life, misfortune, isolation, abandonment, and poverty are battlefields which have their heroes.—VICTOR HUGO.

Who waits until the wind shall silent keep,
Who never finds the ready hour to sow,
Who watcheth clouds, will have no time to reap.
HELEN HUNT JACKSON.
Quit yourselves like men.—1 SAMUEL iv. 9.

CHAPTER III. THE WILL AND THE WAY.

"The 'way' will be found by a resolute will."

"I will find a way or make one."

Nothing is impossible to the man who can will.—MIRABEAU.

A politician weakly and amiably in the right is no match for a politician tenaciously and pugnaciously in the wrong.—E. P. WHIPPLE.

The iron will of one stout heart shall make a thousand quail;
A feeble dwarf, dauntlessly resolved, will turn the tide of battle,
And rally to a nobler strife the giants that had fled.
TUPPER.
"Man alone can perform the impossible. They can who think they can. Character is a perfectly educated will."

The education of the will is the object of our existence. For the resolute and determined there is time and opportunity.—EMERSON.

Invincible determination, and a right nature, are the levers that move the world.—PRESIDENT PORTER.

In the lexicon of youth which fate reserves for a bright manhood there is no such word as fail.—BULWER.

Perpetual pushing and assurance put a difficulty out of countenance and make a seeming difficulty give way.—JEREMY COLLIER.

When a firm and decisive spirit is recognized, it is curious to see how the space clears around a man and leaves him room and freedom.—JOHN FOSTER.

The star of the unconquered will,
He rises in my breast,
Serene, and resolute and still,
And calm and self-possessed.
LONGFELLOW.

"As well can the Prince of Orange pluck the stars from the sky, as bring the ocean to the wall of Leyden for your relief," was the derisive shout of the Spanish soldiers when told that the Dutch fleet would raise that terrible four months' siege of 1574. But from the parched lips of William, tossing on his bed of fever at Rotterdam, had issued the command: "Break down the dikes: give Holland back to ocean:" and the people had replied: "Better a drowned land than a lost land." They began to demolish dike after dike of the strong lines, ranged one within another for fifteen miles to their city of the interior. It was an enormous task; the garrison was starving; and the besiegers laughed in scorn at the slow progress of the puny insects who sought to rule the waves of the sea. But ever, as of old, heaven aids those who help themselves. On the first and second of October a violent equinoctial gale rolled the ocean inland, and swept the fleet on the rising waters almost to the camp of the Spaniards. The next morning the garrison sallied out to attack their enemies, but the besiegers had fled in terror under cover of the darkness. The next day the wind changed, and a counter tempest brushed the water, with the fleet upon it, from the surface of Holland. The outer dikes were replaced at once, leaving the North Sea within its old bounds. When the flowers bloomed the following spring, a joyous procession marched through the streets to found the University of Leyden, in commemoration of the wonderful deliverance of the city.

At a dinner party given in 1837, at the residence of Chancellor Kent, in New York city, some of the most distinguished men in the country were invited, and among them was a young and rather melancholy and reticent Frenchman. Professor Morse was one of the guests, and during the evening he drew the attention of Mr. Gallatin, then a prominent statesman, to the stranger, observing that his forehead indicated great intellect. "Yes," replied Mr. Gallatin, touching his own forehead with his finger, "there is a great deal in that head of his: but he has a strange fancy. Can you believe it? He has the idea that he will one day be the Emperor of France. Can you conceive anything more absurd?"

It did seem absurd, for this reserved Frenchman was then a poor adventurer, an exile from his country, without fortune or powerful connections, and yet, fourteen years later, his idea became a fact,—his dream of becoming Napoleon III. was realized. True, before he accomplished his purpose there were long dreary years of imprisonment, exile, disaster, and patient labor and hope, but he gained his ambition at last. He was not scrupulous as to the means employed to accomplish his ends, yet he is a remarkable example of what pluck and energy can do.

When it was proposed to unite England and America by steam, Dr. Lardner delivered a lecture before the Royal Society "proving" that steamers could never cross the Atlantic, because they could not carry coal enough to produce steam during the whole voyage. The passage of the steamship Sirius, which crossed in nineteen days, was fatal to Lardner's theory. When it was proposed to build a vessel of iron, many persons said: "Iron sinks—only wood can float:" but experiments proved that the miracle of the prophet in making iron "swim" could be repeated, and now not only ships of war, but merchant vessels, are built of iron or steel. A will found a way to make iron float.

Mr. Ingram, publisher of the "London Illustrated News," who lost his life on Lake Michigan, walked ten miles to deliver a single paper rather than disappoint a customer, when he began life as a newsdealer at Nottingham, England. Does any one wonder that such a youth succeeded? Once he rose at two o'clock in the morning and walked to London to get some papers because there was no post to bring them. He determined that his customers should not be disappointed. This is the kind of will that finds a way.

There is scarcely anything in all biography grander than the saying of young Henry Fawcett, Gladstone's last Postmaster-General, to his grief-stricken father, who had put out both his eyes by bird-shot during a game hunt: "Never mind, father, blindness shall not interfere with my success in life." One of the most pathetic sights in London streets, long afterward, was Henry Fawcett, M. P., led everywhere by a faithful daughter, who acted as amanuensis as well as guide to her plucky father. Think of a young man, scarcely on the threshold of active life, suddenly losing the sight of both eyes and yet, by mere pluck and almost incomprehensible tenacity of purpose, lifting himself into eminence, in any direction, to say nothing of becoming one of the foremost men in a country noted for its great men. Most youth would have succumbed to such a misfortune, and would never have been heard from again. But fortunately for the world, there are yet left many Fawcetts, many Prescotts, Parkmans, Cavanaghs.

The courageous daughter who was eyes to her father was herself a marvelous example of pluck and determination. For the first time in the history of Oxford College, which reaches back centuries, she succeeded in winning the post which had only been gained before by great men, such as Gladstone,—the post of senior wrangler. This achievement had had no parallel in history up to that date, and attracted the attention of the whole civilized world. Not only had no woman ever held this position before, but with few exceptions it had only been held by men who in after life became highly distinguished. Who can deny that where there is a will, as a rule, there's a way?

When Grant was a boy he could not find "can't" in the dictionary. It is the men who have no "can't" in their dictionaries that make things move.

"Circumstances," says Milton, "have rarely favored famous men. They have fought their way to triumph through all sorts of opposing obstacles."

The true way to conquer circumstances is to be a greater circumstance yourself.

Yet, while desiring to impress in the most forcible manner possible the fact that will-power is necessary to success, and that, other things being equal, the greater the will-power, the grander and more complete the success, we cannot indorse the preposterous theory that there is nothing in circumstances or environments, or that any man, simply because he has an indomitable will, may become a Bonaparte, a Pitt, a Webster, a Beecher, a Lincoln. We must temper determination with discretion, and support it with knowledge and common sense, or it will only lead us to run our heads against posts. We must not expect to overcome a stubborn fact by a stubborn will. We merely have the right to assume that we can do anything within the limit of our utmost faculty, strength, and endurance. Obstacles permanently insurmountable bar our progress in some directions, but in any direction we may reasonably hope and attempt to go, we shall find that the obstacles, as a rule, are either not insurmountable or else not permanent. The strong-willed, intelligent, persistent man will find or make a way where, in the nature of things, a way can be found or made.

Every schoolboy knows that circumstances do give clients to lawyers and patients to physicians; place ordinary clergymen in extraordinary pulpits; place sons of the rich at the head of immense corporations and large houses, when they have very ordinary ability and scarcely any experience, while poor young men with extraordinary abilities, good education, good character, and large experience, often have to fight their way for years to obtain even very ordinary situations. Every one knows that there are thousands of young men, both in the city and in the country, of superior ability, who seem to be compelled by circumstances to remain in very ordinary positions for small pay, when others about them are raised by money or family influence into desirable places. In other words, we all know that the best men do not always get the best places: circumstances do have a great deal to do with our position, our salaries, and our station in life.

Many young men who are nature's noblemen, who are natural leaders, are working under superintendents, foremen, and managers infinitely their inferiors, but whom circumstances have placed above them and will keep there, unless some emergency makes merit indispensable. No, the race is not always to the swift.

Every one knows that there is not always a way where there is a will, that labor does not always conquer all things; that there are things impossible even to him that wills, however strongly; that one cannot always make anything of himself he chooses; that there are limitations in our very natures which no amount of will-power or industry can overcome; that no amount of sun-staring can ever make an eagle out of a crow.

The simple truth is that a will strong enough to keep a man continually striving for things not wholly beyond his powers will carry him in time very far toward his chosen goal.

The greatest thing a man can do in this world is to make the most possible out of the stuff that has been given to him. This is success, and there is no other.

While it is true that our circumstances or environments do affect us, in most things they do not prevent our growth. The corn that is now ripe, whence comes it, and what is it? Is it not large or small, stunted wild maize or well-developed ears, according to the conditions under which it has grown? Yet its environments cannot make wheat of it. Nor can our circumstances alter our nature. It is part of our nature, and wholly within our power, greatly to change and to take advantage of our circumstances, so that, unlike the corn, we can rise much superior to our natural surroundings simply because we can thus vary and improve the surroundings. In other words, man can usually build the very road on which he is to run his race.

It is not a question of what some one else can do or become, which every youth should ask himself, but what can I do? How can I develop myself into the grandest possible manhood?

So far, then, from the power of circumstances being a hindrance to men in trying to build for themselves an imperial highway to fortune, these circumstances constitute the very quarry out of which they are to get paving-stones for the road.

While it is true that the will-power cannot perform miracles, yet that it is almost omnipotent, that it can perform wonders, all history goes to prove. As Shakespeare says:—

"Men at some time are masters of their fates:

The fault, dear Brutus, is not in our stars,
But in ourselves, that we are underlings."

"There is nobody," says a Roman Cardinal, "whom Fortune does not visit once in his life: but when she finds he is not ready to receive her, she goes in at the door, and out through the window." Opportunity is coy. The careless, the slow, the unobservant, the lazy fail to see it, or clutch at it when it has gone. The sharp fellows detect it instantly, and catch it when on the wing.

Show me a man who is, according to popular prejudice, a victim of bad luck, and I will show you one who has some unfortunate crooked twist of temperament that invites disaster. He is ill-tempered, or conceited, or trifling; lacks character, enthusiasm, or some other requisite for success.

Disraeli says that man is not the creature of circumstances, but that circumstances are the creatures of men.

What has chance ever done in the world? Has it built any cities? Has it invented any telephones, any telegraphs? Has it built any steamships, established any universities, any asylums, any hospitals? Was there any chance in Caesar's crossing the Rubicon? What had chance to do with Napoleon's career, with Wellington's, or Grant's, or Von Moltke's? Every battle was won before it was begun. What had luck to do with Thermopylae, Trafalgar, Gettysburg? Our successes we ascribe to ourselves; our failures to destiny.

Man is not a helpless atom in this vast creation, with a fixed position, and naught to do but obey his own polarity.

Believe in the power of will, which annihilates the sickly, sentimental doctrine of fatalism,—you must but can't, you ought but it is impossible.

Give me the man

"Who breaks his birth's invidious bar,
And grasps the skirts of happy chance,
And breasts the blows of circumstance,
And grapples with his evil star."

It is only the ignorant and superficial who believe in fate. "The first step into thought lifts this mountain of necessity." "Fate is unpenetrated causes." "They may well fear fate who have any infirmity of habit or aim: but he who rests on what he is has a destiny beyond destiny, and can make mouths at fortune."

The indomitable will, the inflexible purpose, will find a way or make one. There is always room for a man of force.

"He who has a firm will," says Goethe, "moulds the world to himself." "People do not lack strength," says Victor Hugo, "they lack will."

"He who resolves upon any great end, by that very resolution has scaled the great barriers to it, and he who seizes the grand idea of self-cultivation, and solemnly resolves upon it, will find that idea, that resolution, burning like fire within him, and ever putting him upon his own improvement. He will find it removing difficulties, searching out, or making means; giving courage for despondency, and strength for weakness."

Nearly all great men, those who have towered high above their fellows, have been remarkable above all things else for their energy of will. Of Julius Caesar it was said by a contemporary that it was his activity and giant determination, rather than his military skill, that won his victories. The youth who starts out in life determined to make the most of his eyes and let nothing escape him which he can possibly use for his own advancement; who keeps his ears open for every sound that can help him on his way, who keeps his hands open that he may clutch every opportunity, who is ever on the alert for everything which can help him to get on in the world, who seizes every experience in life and grinds it up into paint for his great life's picture, who keeps his heart open that he may catch every noble impulse, and everything which may inspire him,—that youth will be sure to make his life successful; there are no "ifs" or "ands" about it. If he has his health, nothing can keep him from final success.

No tyranny of circumstances can permanently imprison a determined will.

The world always stands aside for the determined man. Will makes a way, even through seeming impossibilities. "It is the half a neck nearer that shows the blood and wins the race; the one march more that wins the campaign: the five minutes more of unyielding courage that wins the fight." Again and again had the irrepressible Carter Harrison been consigned to oblivion by the educated and moral element of Chicago. Nothing could keep him down. He was invincible. A son of Chicago, he had partaken of that nineteenth century miracle, that phoenix-like nature of the city which, though she was burned, caused her to rise from her ashes and become a greater and a grander Chicago, a wonder of the world. Carter Harrison would not down. He entered the Democratic Convention and, with an audacity rarely equaled, in spite of their protest, boldly declared himself their candidate. Every newspaper in Chicago, save the "Times," his own paper, bitterly opposed his election: but notwithstanding all opposition, he was elected by twenty thousand majority. The aristocrats hated him, the moral element feared him, but the poor people believed in him: he pandered to them, flattered them, till they elected him. While we would not by any means hold Carter Harrison up to youth as a model, yet there is a great lesson in his will-power and wonderful tenacity of purpose.

"The general of a large army may be defeated," said Confucius, "but you cannot defeat the determined mind of a peasant."

The poor, deaf pauper, Kitto, who made shoes in the almshouse, and who became the greatest of Biblical scholars, wrote in his journal, on the threshold of manhood: "I am not myself a believer in impossibilities: I think that all the fine stories about natural ability, etc., are mere rigmarole, and that every man may, according to his opportunities and industry, render himself almost anything he wishes to become."

Years ago, a young mechanic took a bath in the river Clyde. While swimming from shore to shore he discerned a beautiful bank, uncultivated, and he then and there resolved to be the owner of it, and to adorn it, and to build upon it the finest mansion in all the borough, and name it in honor of the maiden to whom he was espoused. "Last summer," says a well-known American, "I had the pleasure of dining in that princely mansion, and receiving this fact from the lips of the great shipbuilder of the Clyde." That one purpose was made the ruling passion of his life, and all the energies of his soul were put in requisition for its accomplishment.

Lincoln is probably the most remarkable example on the pages of history, showing the possibilities of our country. From the poverty in which he was born, through the rowdyism of a frontier town, the rudeness of frontier society, the discouragement of early bankruptcy, and the fluctuations of popular politics, he rose to the championship of union and freedom.

Lincoln's will made his way. When his friends nominated him as a candidate for the legislature, his enemies made fun of him. When making his campaign speeches he wore a mixed jean coat so short that he could not sit down on it, flax and tow-linen trousers, straw hat, and pot-metal boots. He had nothing in the world but character and friends.

When his friends suggested law to him, he laughed at the idea of his being a lawyer. He said he hadn't brains enough. He read law barefoot under the trees, his neighbors said, and he sometimes slept on the counter in the store where he worked. He had to borrow money to buy a suit of clothes to make a respectable appearance in the legislature, and walked to take his seat at Vandalia,—one hundred miles. While he was in the legislature, John F. Stuart, an eminent lawyer of Springfield, told him how Clay had even inferior chances to his, had got all of the education he had in a log schoolhouse without windows or doors; and finally induced Lincoln to study law.

See Thurlow Weed, defying poverty and wading through the snow two miles, with rags for shoes, to borrow a book to read before the sap-bush fire. See Locke, living on bread and water in a Dutch garret. See Heyne, sleeping many a night on a barn floor with only a book for his pillow. See Samuel Drew, tightening his apron strings "in lieu of a dinner." See young Lord Eldon, before daylight copying Coke on Littleton over and over again. History is full of such examples. He who will pay the price for victory needs never fear final defeat. Why were the Roman legionaries victorious?

"For Romans, in Rome's quarrels,
Spared neither land nor gold,
Nor son, nor wife, nor limb nor life,
In the brave days of old."

Fowell Buxton, writing to one of his sons, says: "I am sure that a young man may be very much what he pleases."

Dr. Mathews has well said that "there is hardly a word in the whole human vocabulary which is more cruelly abused than the word 'luck.' To all the faults and failures of men, their positive sins and their less culpable shortcomings, it is made to stand a godfather and sponsor. Go talk with the bankrupt man of business, who has swamped his fortune by wild speculation, extravagance of living, or lack of energy, and you will find that he vindicates his wonderful self-love by confounding the steps which he took indiscreetly with those to which he was forced by 'circumstances,' and complacently regarding himself as the victim of ill-luck. Go visit the incarcerated criminal, who has imbued his hands in the blood of his fellow-man, or who is guilty of less heinous crimes, and you will find that, joining the temptations which were easy to avoid with those which were comparatively irresistible, he has hurriedly patched up a treaty with conscience, and stifles its compunctious visitings by persuading himself that, from first to last, he was the victim of circumstances. Go talk with the mediocre in talents and attainments, the weak-spirited man who, from lack of energy and application, has made but little headway in the world, being outstripped in the race of life by those whom he had despised as his inferiors, and you will find that he, too, acknowledges the all-potent power of luck, and soothes his humbled pride by deeming himself the victim of ill-fortune. In short, from the most venial offense to the most flagrant, there is hardly any wrong act or neglect to which this too fatally convenient word is not applied as a palliation."

Paris was in the hands of a mob, the authorities were panic-stricken, for they did not dare to trust their underlings. In came a man who said, "I know a young officer who has the courage and ability to quell this mob." "Send for him; send for him; send for him," said they. Napoleon was sent for, came, subjugated the mob, subjugated the authorities, ruled France, then conquered Europe.

What a lesson is Napoleon's life for the sickly, wishy-washy, dwarfed, sentimental "dudes," hanging about our cities, country, and universities, complaining of their hard lot, dreaming of success, and wondering why they are left in the rear in the great race of life.

Success in life is dependent largely upon the willpower, and whatever weakens or impairs it diminishes success. The will can be educated. That which most easily becomes a habit in us is the will. Learn, then, to will decisively and strongly; thus fix your floating life, and leave it no longer to be carried hither and thither, like a withered leaf, by every wind that blows. "It is not talent that men lack, it is the will to labor; it is the purpose, not the power to produce."

It was this insatiable thirst for knowledge which held to his task, through poverty and discouragement, John Leyden, a Scotch shepherd's son. Barefoot and alone, he walked six or eight miles daily to learn to read, which was all the schooling he had. His desire for an education defied the extremest poverty, and no obstacle could turn him from his purpose. He was rich when he discovered a little bookstore, and his thirsty soul would drink in the precious treasures from its priceless volumes for hours, perfectly oblivious of the scanty meal of bread and water which awaited him at his lowly lodging. Nothing could discourage him from trying to improve himself by study. It seemed to him that an opportunity to get at books and lectures was all that any man could need. Before he was nineteen, this poor shepherd boy with no chance had astonished the professors of Edinburgh by his knowledge of Greek and Latin.

Hearing that a surgeon's assistant in the Civil Service was wanted, although he knew nothing whatever of medicine, he determined to apply for it. There were only six months before the place was to be filled, but nothing could daunt him, and in six months' time he actually took his degree with honor. Walter Scott, who thought this one of the most remarkable illustrations of perseverance, helped to fit him out, and he sailed for India.

Webster was very poor even after he entered Dartmouth College. A friend sent him a recipe for greasing his boots. Webster wrote and thanked him, and added: "But my boots need other doctoring, for they not only admit water, but even peas and gravel-stones." Yet he became one of the greatest men in the world. Sydney Smith said: "Webster was a living lie, because no man on earth could be as great as he looked." Carlyle said of him: "One would incline at sight to back him against the world."

What seemed to be luck followed Stephen Girard all his life. No matter what he did, it always seemed to others to turn to his account. His coming to Philadelphia seemed a lucky accident. A sloop was seen one morning off the mouth of Delaware Bay floating the flag of France and a signal of distress. Young Girard was captain of this sloop, and was on his way to a Canadian port with freight from New Orleans. An American skipper, seeing his distress, went to his aid, but told him the American war had broken out, and that the British cruisers were all along the American coast, and would seize his vessel. He told him his only chance was to make a push for Philadelphia. Girard did not know the way, and had no money. The skipper loaned him five dollars to get the service of a pilot who demanded his money in advance.

His sloop passed into the Delaware just in time to avoid capture by a British war vessel. He sold the sloop and cargo in Philadelphia, and began business on the capital. Being a foreigner, unable to speak English, short, stout, and with a repulsive face, blind in one eye, it was hard for him to get a start. But he was not the man to give up. He had begun as a cabin boy at thirteen, and for nine years sailed between Bordeaux and the French West Indies. He improved every leisure minute at sea, mastering the art of navigation.

At the age of eight he first discovered that he was blind in one eye. His father, evidently thinking that he would never amount to anything, would not help him to an education beyond that of mere reading and writing, but sent his younger brothers to college. The discovery of his blindness, the neglect of his father, and the chagrin of his brothers' advancement, soured his whole life.

When he began business for himself in Philadelphia, there seemed to be nothing he would not do for money. He bought and sold anything, from groceries to old junk. He bottled wine and cider, from which he made a good profit. Everything he touched prospered. In 1780, he resumed the New Orleans and St. Domingo trade, in which he had been engaged at the breaking out of the Revolution. Here great success again attended him. He had two vessels lying in one of the St. Domingo ports when the great insurrection on that island broke out. A number of the rich planters fled to his vessels with their valuables, which they left for safe keeping while they went back to their estates to secure more. They probably fell victims to the cruel negroes, for they never returned, and Girard was the lucky possessor of $50,000 which the goods brought in Philadephia.

Everybody, especially his jealous brother merchants, attributed his great success to his luck. While undoubtedly he was fortunate in happening to be at the right place at the right time, yet he was precision, method, accuracy, energy itself. He left nothing to chance. His plans and schemes were worked out with mathematical care. His letters, written to his captains in foreign ports, laying out their routes and giving detailed instruction from which they were never allowed to deviate under any circumstances, are models of foresight and systematic planning. He never left anything of importance to others. He was rigidly accurate in his instructions, and would not allow the slightest departure from them. He used to say that while his captains might save him money by deviating from instructions once, yet they would cause loss in ninety-nine other cases. Once, when a captain returned and had saved him several thousand dollars by buying his cargo of cheese in another port than that in which he had been instructed to buy, Girard was so enraged, although he was several thousand dollars richer, that he discharged the captain on the spot, notwithstanding the latter had been faithful in his service for many years, and thought he was saving his employer a great deal of money by deviating from his instructions.

Girard lived in a dingy little house, poorer than that occupied by many of his employees. He married a servant girl of great beauty, but she proved totally unfitted for him, and died at last in the insane asylum.

Girard never lost a ship, and many times what brought financial ruin to many others, as the War of 1812, only increased his wealth. What seemed luck with him was only good judgment and promptness in seizing opportunities, and the greatest care and zeal in improving them to their utmost possibilities.

Luck is not God's price for success: that is altogether too cheap, nor does he dicker with men.

The mathematician tells you that if you throw the dice, there are thirty chances to one against your turning up a particular number, and a hundred to one against your repeating the same throw three times in succession: and so on in an augmenting ratio. What is luck? Is it, as has been suggested, a blind man's buff among the laws? a ruse among the elements? a trick of Dame Nature? Has any scholar defined luck? any philosopher explained its nature? any chemist shown its composition? Is luck that strange, nondescript fairy, that does all things among men that they cannot account for? If so, why does not luck make a fool speak words of wisdom; an ignoramus utter lectures on philosophy?

Many a young man who has read the story of John Wanamaker's romantic career has gained very little inspiration or help from it toward his own elevation and advancement, for he looks upon it as the result of good luck, chance, or fate. "What a lucky fellow," he says to himself as he reads; "what a bonanza he fell into." But a careful analysis of Wanamaker's life only enforces the same lesson taught by the analysis of most great lives, namely, that a good mother, a good constitution, the habit of hard work, indomitable energy, a determination which knows no defeat, a decision which never wavers, a concentration which never scatters its forces, courage which never falters, a self-mastery which can say No, and stick to it, an "ignominious love of detail," strict integrity and downright honesty, a cheerful disposition, unbounded enthusiasm in one's calling, and a high aim and noble purpose insure a very large measure of success.

Youth should be taught that there is something in circumstances; that there is such a thing as a poor pedestrian happening to find no obstruction in his way, and reaching the goal when a better walker finds the drawbridge up, the street blockaded, and so fails to win the race; that wealth often does place unworthy sons in high positions, that family influence does gain a lawyer clients, a physician patients, an ordinary scholar a good professorship; but that, on the other hand, position, clients, patients, professorships, manager's and superintendent's positions do not necessarily constitute success. He should be taught that in the long run, as a rule, the best man does win the best place, and that persistent merit does succeed.

There is about as much chance of idleness and incapacity winning real success, or a high position in life, as there would be in producing a Paradise Lost by shaking up promiscuously the separate words of Webster's Dictionary, and letting them fall at random on the floor. Fortune smiles upon those who roll up their sleeves and put their shoulders to the wheel; upon men who are not afraid of dreary, dry, irksome drudgery, men of nerve and grit who do not turn aside for dirt and detail.

The youth should be taught that "he alone is great, who, by a life heroic, conquers fate;" that "diligence is the mother of good luck;" that, nine times out of ten, what we call luck or fate is but a mere bugbear of the indolent, the languid, the purposeless, the careless, the indifferent; that the man who fails, as a rule, does not see or seize his opportunity. Opportunity is coy, is swift, is gone, before the slow, the unobservant, the indolent, or the careless can seize her:—

"In idle wishes fools supinely stay:
Be there a will and wisdom finds a way."

It has been well said that the very reputation of being strong willed, plucky, and indefatigable is of priceless value. It often cows enemies and dispels at the start opposition to one's undertakings which would otherwise be formidable.

"If Eric's in robust health, and has slept well, and is at the top of his condition, and thirty years old at his departure from Greenland," says Emerson, "he will steer west and his ships will reach Newfoundland. But take Eric out and put in a stronger and bolder man, and the ships will sail six hundred, one thousand, fifteen hundred miles further, and reach Labrador and New England. There is no chance in results." Obstacles tower before the living man like mountain chains, stopping his path and hindering his progress. He surmounts them by his energy. He makes a new path over them. He climbs upon them to mountain heights. They cannot stop him. They do not much delay him. He transmutes difficulties into power, and makes temporary failures into stepping-stones to ultimate success.

How many might have been giants who are only dwarfs. How many a one has died "with all his music in him."

It is astonishing what men who have come to their senses late in life have accomplished by a sudden resolution.

Arkwright was fifty years of age when he began to learn English grammar and improve his writing and spelling. Benjamin Franklin was past fifty before he began the study of science and philosophy. Milton, in his blindness, was past the age of fifty when he sat down to complete his world-known epic, and Scott at fifty-five took up his pen to redeem an enormous liability. "Yet I am learning," said Michael Angelo, when threescore years and ten were past, and he had long attained the highest triumphs of his art.

Even brains are second in importance to will. The vacillating man is always pushed aside in the race of life. It is only the weak and vacillating who halt before adverse circumstances and obstacles. A man with an iron will, with a determination that nothing shall check his career, if he has perseverance and grit, is sure to succeed. We may not find time for what we would like, but what we long for and strive for with all our strength, we usually approximate if we do not fully reach. Hunger breaks through stone walls; stern necessity will find a way or make one.

Success is also a great physical as well as mental tonic, and tends to strengthen the will-power. Dr. Johnson says: "Resolutions and success reciprocally produce each other." Strong-willed men, as a rule, are successful men, and great success is almost impossible without it.

A man who can resolve vigorously upon a course of action, and turns neither to the right nor the left, though a paradise tempt him, who keeps his eyes upon the goal, whatever distracts him, is sure of success. We could almost classify successes and failures by their various degrees of will-power. Men like Sir James Mackintosh, Coleridge, La Harpe, and many others who have dazzled the world with their brilliancy, but who never accomplished a tithe of what they attempted, who were always raising our expectations that they were about to perform wonderful deeds, but who accomplished nothing worthy of their abilities, have been deficient in will-power. One talent with a will behind it will accomplish more than ten without it. The great linguist of Bologna mastered a hundred languages by taking them singly, as the lion fought the bulls.

I wish it were possible to show the youth of America the great part that the will might play in their success in life and in their happiness also. The achievements of will-power are simply beyond computation. Scarcely anything in reason seems impossible to the man who can will strong enough and long enough.

How often we see this illustrated in the case of a young woman who suddenly becomes conscious that she is plain and unattractive; who, by prodigious exercise of her will and untiring industry, resolves to redeem herself from obscurity and commonness; and who not only makes up for her deficiencies, but elevates herself into a prominence and importance which mere personal attractions could never have given her. Charlotte Cushman, without a charm of form or face, climbed to the very top of her profession. How many young men, stung by consciousness of physical deformity or mental deficiencies, have, by a strong persistent exercise of will-power, raised themselves from mediocrity and placed themselves high above those who scorned them.

History is full of examples of men and women who have redeemed themselves from disgrace, poverty, and misfortune, by the firm resolution of an iron will. The consciousness of being looked upon as inferior, as incapable of accomplishing what others accomplish; the sensitiveness at being considered a dunce in school, has stung many a youth into a determination which has elevated him far above those who laughed at him, as in the case of Newton, of Adam Clark, of Sheridan, Wellington, Goldsmith, Dr. Chalmers, Curran, Disraeli, and hundreds of others. "Whatever you wish, that you are; for such is the force of the human will, joined to the Divine, that whatever we wish to be seriously, and with a true intention, that we become." While this is not strictly true, yet there is a deal of truth in it.

It is men like Mirabeau, who "trample upon impossibilities;" like Napoleon, who do not wait for opportunities, but make them; like Grant, who has only "unconditional surrender" for the enemy, who change the very front of the world. "We have but what we make, and every good is locked by nature in a granite hand, sheer labor must unclench."

What cares Henry L. Bulwer for the suffocating cough, even though he can scarcely speak above a whisper? In the House of Commons he makes his immortal speech on the Irish Church just the same.

"I can't, it is impossible," said a foiled lieutenant, to Alexander. "Be gone," shouted the conquering Macedonian, "there is nothing impossible to him who will try."

Were I called upon to express in a word the secret of so many failures among those who started out in life with high hopes, I should say unhesitatingly, they lacked will-power. They could not half will. What is a man without a will? He is like an engine without steam, a mere sport of chance, to be tossed about hither and thither, always at the mercy of those who have wills. I should call the strength of will the test of a young man's possibilities. Can he will strong enough, and hold whatever he undertakes with an iron grip? It is the iron grip that takes the strong hold on life. What chance is there in this crowding, pushing, selfish, greedy world, where everything is pusher or pushed, for a young man with no will, no grip on life? "The truest wisdom," said Napoleon, "is a resolute determination." An iron will without principle might produce a Napoleon; but with character it would make a Wellington or a Grant, untarnished by ambition or avarice.

"The undivided will
'T is that compels the elements and wrings
A human music from the indifferent air."

CHAPTER IV. SUCCESS UNDER DIFFICULTIES.

Victories that are easy are cheap. Those only are worth having which come as the result of hard fighting.—BEECHER.

Man owes his growth chiefly to that active striving of the will, that encounter with difficulty, which we call effort; and it is astonishing to find how often results that seemed impracticable are thus made possible.—EPES SARGENT.

I know no such unquestionable badge and ensign of a sovereign mind as that tenacity of purpose which, through all change of companions, or parties, or fortunes, changes never, bates no jot of heart or hope, but wearies out opposition and arrives at its port.—EMERSON.

Yes, to this thought I hold with firm persistence;
The last result of wisdom stamps it true;
He only earns his freedom and existence
Who daily conquers them anew.
GOETHE.
Little minds are tamed and subdued by misfortunes; but great minds rise above them.—WASHINGTON IRVING.

"I have here three teams that I want to get over to Staten Island," said a boy of twelve one day in 1806 to the innkeeper at South Amboy, N. J. "If you will put us across, I'll leave with you one of my horses in pawn, and if I don't send you back six dollars within forty-eight hours you may keep the horse."

The innkeeper asked the reason for this novel proposition, and learned that the lad's father had contracted to get the cargo of a vessel stranded near Sandy Hook, and take it to New York in lighters. The boy had been sent with three wagons, six horses, and three men, to carry the cargo across a sand-spit to the lighters. The work accomplished, he had started with only six dollars to travel a long distance home over the Jersey sands, and reached South Amboy penniless. "I'll do it," said the innkeeper, as he looked into the bright honest eyes of the boy. The horse was soon redeemed.

How can you keep a determined man from success: Place stumbling-blocks in his way, and he uses them for stepping-stones. Imprison him, and he produces the "Pilgrim's Progress." Deprive him of eyesight, and he writes the "Conquest of Mexico."

"My son," said this same boy's mother, on the first of May, 1810, when he asked her to lend him one hundred dollars to buy a boat, having imbibed a strong liking for the sea; "on the twenty-seventh of this month you will be sixteen years old. If, by that time, you will plow, harrow, and plant with corn the eight-acre lot, I will advance you the money." The field was rough and stony, but the work was done in time, and well done. From this small beginning Cornelius Vanderbilt laid the foundation of a colossal fortune. He would often work all night; and, as he was never absent from his post by day, he soon had the best business in New York harbor.

In 1813, when it was expected that New York would be attacked by British ships, all the boatmen except Cornelius put in bids to convey provisions to the military posts around New York, naming extremely low rates, as the contractor would be exempted from military duty. "Why don't you send in a bid?" asked his father. "Of what use?" replied young Vanderbilt; "they are offering to do the work at half price. It can't be done at such rates." "Well," said his father, "it can do no harm to try for it." So, to please his father, but with no hope of success, Cornelius made an offer fair to both sides, but did not go to hear the award. When his companions had all returned with long faces, he went to the commissary's office and asked if the contract had been given. "Oh, yes," was the reply; "that business is settled. Cornelius Vanderbilt is the man. What?" he asked, seeing that the youth was apparently thunderstruck, "is it you?" "My name is Cornelius Vanderbilt," said the boatman. "Well," said the commissary, "don't you know why we have given the contract to you?" "No." "Why, it is because we want this business done, and we know you'll do it." Character gives confidence.

In 1818 he owned two or three of the finest coasting schooners in New York harbor, and had a capital of nine thousand dollars. Seeing that steam-vessels would soon win supremacy over those carrying sails only, he gave up his fine business to become the captain of a steamboat at one thousand dollars a year. For twelve years he ran between New York city and New Brunswick, N. J. In 1829 he began business as a steamboat owner, in the face of opposition so bitter that he lost his last dollar. But the tide turned, and he prospered so rapidly that he at length owned over one hundred steamboats. He early identified himself with the growing railroad interests of the country, and became the richest man of his day in America.

Barnum began the race of business life barefoot, for at the age of fifteen he was obliged to buy on credit the shoes he wore at his father's funeral. He was a remarkable example of success under difficulties. There was no keeping him down; no opposition daunted him, no obstacles were too great for him to overcome. Think of a man being ruined at fifty years of age; yes, worse than ruined, for he was heavily in debt besides. Yet on the very day of his downfall he begins to rise again, wringing victory from defeat by his indomitable persistence.

"Eloquence must have been born with you," said a friend to J. P. Curran. "Indeed, my dear sir, it was not," replied the orator, "it was born some three and twenty years and some months after me." Speaking of his first attempt at a debating club, he said: "I stood up, trembling through every fibre, but remembering that in this I was but imitating Tully, I took courage and had actually proceeded almost as far as 'Mr. Chairman,' when, to my astonishment and terror, I perceived that every eye was turned on me. There were only six or seven present, and the room could not have contained as many more; yet was it, to my panic-stricken imagination, as if I were the central object in nature, and assembled millions were gazing upon me in breathless expectation. I became dismayed and dumb. My friends cried, 'Hear him!' but there was nothing to hear." He was nicknamed "Orator Mum," and well did he deserve the title until he ventured to stare in astonishment at a speaker who was "culminating chronology by the most preposterous anachronisms." "I doubt not," said the annoyed speaker, "that 'Orator Mum' possesses wonderful talents for eloquence, but I would recommend him to show it in future by some more popular method than his silence." Stung by the taunt, Curran rose and gave the man a "piece of his mind," speaking quite fluently in his anger. Encouraged by this success, he took great pains to become a good speaker. He corrected his habit of stuttering by reading favorite passages aloud every day slowly and distinctly, and spoke at every opportunity.

Bunyan wrote his "Pilgrim's Progress" on the untwisted papers used to cork the bottles of milk brought for his meals. Gifford wrote his first copy of a mathematical work, when a cobbler's apprentice, on small scraps of leather; and Rittenhouse, the astronomer, first calculated eclipses on his plow handle.

A poor Irish lad, so pitted by smallpox that boys made sport of him, earned his living by writing little ballads for street musicians. Eight cents a day was often all he could earn. He traveled through France and Italy, begging his way by singing and playing the flute at the cottages of the peasantry. At twenty-eight he was penniless in London, and lived in the beggars' quarters in Axe Lane. In his poverty, he set up as a doctor in the suburbs of London. He wore a second-hand coat of rusty velvet, with a patch on the left breast which he adroitly covered with his three-cornered hat during his visits; and we have an amusing anecdote of his contest of courtesy with a patient who persisted in endeavoring to relieve him of his hat, which only made him press it more devoutly to his heart. He often had to pawn his clothes to keep from starving. He sold his "Life of Voltaire" for twenty dollars. After great hardship he managed to publish his "Polite Learning in Europe," and this brought him to public notice. Next came "The Traveller," and the wretched man in a Fleet Street garret found himself famous. His landlady once arrested him for rent, but Dr. Johnson came to his relief, took from his desk the manuscript of the "Vicar of Wakefield," and sold it for three hundred dollars. He spent two years revising "The Deserted Village" after it was first written. Generous to a fault, vain and improvident, imposed on by others, he was continually in debt; although for his "History of the Earth and Animated Nature" he received four thousand dollars, and some of his works, as, for instance, "She Stoops to Conquer," had a large sale. But in spite of fortune's frown and his own weakness, he won success and fame. The world, which so often comes too late with its assistance and laurels, gave to the weak, gentle, loving author of "The Vicar of Wakefield" a monument in the Poets' Corner of Westminster Abbey.

The poor, scrofulous, and almost blind boy, Samuel Johnson, was taken by his mother to receive the touch of Queen Anne, which was supposed to heal the "King's Evil." He entered Oxford as a servant, copying lectures from a student's notebooks, while the boys made sport of the bare feet showing through great holes in his shoes. Some one left a pair of new shoes at his door, but he was too proud to be helped, and threw them out of the window. He was so poor that he was obliged to leave college, and at twenty-six married a widow of forty-eight. He started a private school with his wife's money; but, getting only three pupils, was obliged to close it. He went to London, where he lived on nine cents a day. In his distress he wrote a poem in which appeared in capital letters the line, "Slow rises worth by poverty depressed," which attracted wide attention. He suffered greatly in London for thirteen years, being arrested once for a debt of thirteen dollars. At forty he published "The Vanity of Human Wishes," in which were these lines:—

"Then mark what ills the scholar's life assail;
Toil, envy, want, the patron and the jail."
When asked how he felt about his failures, he replied:

"Like a monument,"—that is, steadfast, immovable. He was an indefatigable worker. In the evenings of a single week he wrote "Rasselas," a beautiful little story of the search for happiness, to get money to pay the funeral expenses of his mother. With six assistants he worked seven years on his Dictionary, which made his fortune. His name was then in everybody's mouth, and when he no longer needed help, assistance, as usual, came from every quarter. The great universities hastened to bestow their degrees, and King George invited him to the palace.

Lord Mansfield raised himself by indefatigable industry from oatmeal porridge and poverty to affluence and the Lord Chief Justice's Bench.

Of five thousand articles sent every year to "Lippincott's Magazine," only two hundred were accepted. How much do you think Homer got for his Iliad? or Dante for his Paradise? Only bitter bread and salt, and going up and down other people's stairs. In science, the man who discovered the telescope, and first saw heaven, was paid with a dungeon: the man who invented the microscope, and first saw earth, died from starvation, driven from his home. It is very clear indeed that God means all good work and talk to be done for nothing. Shakespeare's "Hamlet" was sold for about twenty-five dollars; but his autograph has sold for five thousand dollars.

During the ten years in which he made his greatest discoveries, Isaac Newton could hardly pay two shillings a week to the Royal Society of which he was a member. Some of his friends wanted to get him excused from this payment, but he would not allow them to act.

There are no more interesting pages in biography than those which record how Emerson, as a child, was unable to read the second volume of a certain book, because his widowed mother could not afford the amount (five cents) necessary to obtain it from the circulating library.

Linnaeus was so poor when getting his education, that he had to mend his shoes with folded paper, and often had to beg his meals of his friends.

Who in the days of the First Empire cared to recall the fact that Napoleon, Emperor and King, was once forced to borrow a louis from Talma, when he lived in a garret on the Quai Conti?

David Livingstone at ten years of age was put into a cotton factory near Glasgow. Out of his first week's wages he bought a Latin Grammar, and studied in the night schools for years. He would sit up and study till midnight unless his mother drove him to bed, notwithstanding he had to be at the factory at six in the morning. He mastered Virgil and Horace in this way, and read extensively, besides studying botany. So eager and thirsty for knowledge was he, that he would place his book before him on the spinning-jenny, and amid the deafening roar of machinery would pore over its pages.

George Eliot said of the years of close work upon her "Romola," "I began it a young woman, I finished it an old woman." One of Emerson's biographers says, referring to his method of rewriting, revising, correcting, and eliminating: "His apples were sorted over and over again, until only the very rarest, the most perfect, were left. It did not matter that those thrown away were very good and helped to make clear the possibilities of the orchard, they were unmercifully cast aside." Carlyle's books were literally wrung out of him. The pains he took to satisfy himself of a relatively insignificant fact were incredible. Before writing his essay on Diderot, he read twenty-five volumes at the rate of one per day. He tells Edward Fitzgerald that for the twentieth time he is going over the confused records of the battle of Naseby, that he may be quite sure of the topography.

"All the performances of human art, at which we look with praise and wonder," says Johnson, "are instances of the resistless force of perseverance: it is by this that the quarry becomes a pyramid, and that distant countries are united with canals. If a man was to compare the effect of a single stroke of the pickaxe, or of one impression of the spade, with the general design and last result, he would be overwhelmed by the sense of their disproportion; yet those petty operations, incessantly continued, in time surmount the greatest difficulties, and mountains are leveled, and oceans bounded, by the slender force of human beings."

The Rev. Eliphalet Nott, a pulpit orator, was especially noted for a sermon on the death of Alexander Hamilton, the great statesman, who was shot in a duel by Aaron Burr. Although Nott had managed in some way to get his degree at Brown University, he was at one time so poor after he entered the ministry that he could not buy an overcoat. His wife sheared their only cosset sheep in January, wrapped it in burlap blankets to keep it from freezing, carded and spun and wove the wool, and made it into an overcoat for him.

Great men never wait for opportunities; they make them. Nor do they wait for facilities or favoring circumstances; they seize upon whatever is at hand, work out their problem, and master the situation. A young man determined and willing will find a way or make one. A Franklin does not require elaborate apparatus; he can bring electricity from the clouds with a common kite. A Watt can make a model of the condensing steam-engine out of an old syringe used to inject the arteries of dead bodies previous to dissection. A Dr. Black can discover latent heat with a pan of water and two thermometers. A Newton can unfold the composition of light and the origin of colors with a prism, a lens, and a piece of pasteboard. A Humphry Davy can experiment with kitchen pots and pans, and a Faraday can experiment on electricity by means of old bottles, in his spare minutes while a book-binder. When science was in its cradle the Marquis of Worcester, an English nobleman, imprisoned in the Tower of London, was certainly not in a very good position to do anything for the world, but would not waste his time. The cover of a vessel of hot water blown on before his eyes led to a series of observations, which he published later in a book called "Century of Inventions." These observations were a sort of text-book on the power of steam, which resulted in Newcomen's steam-engine, which Watt afterward perfected. A Ferguson maps out the heavenly bodies, lying on his back, by means of threads with beads stretched between himself and the stars.

Not in his day of bodily strength and political power, but blind, decrepit, and defeated with his party, Milton composed "Paradise Lost."

Great men have found no royal road to their triumph. It is always the old route, by way of industry and perseverance.

The farmer boy, Elihu B. Washburn, taught school at ten dollars per month, and early learned the lesson that it takes one hundred cents to make a dollar. In after years he fought "steals" in Congress, until he was called the "Watchdog of the Treasury." From his long membership he became known as the "Father of the House." He administered the oath to Schuyler Colfax as Speaker three times. He recommended Grant as colonel of a regiment of volunteers. The latter, when President, appointed him Secretary of State, and, later, Minister to France. During the reign of the Commune, the representatives of nearly all other foreign nations fled in dismay, but Washburn remained at his post. Shells exploded close to his office, and fell all around it, but he did not leave even when Paris was in flames. For a time he was really the minister of all foreign countries, in Paris; and represented Prussia for almost a year. The Emperor William conferred upon him the Order of the Red Eagle, and gave him a jeweled star of great value.

How could the poor boy, Elihu Burritt, working nearly all the daylight in a blacksmith's shop, get an education? He had but one book in his library, and carried that in his hat. But this boy with no chance became one of America's wonders.

When teaching school, Garfield was very poor. He tore his only blue jean trousers, but concealed the rents by pins until night, when he retired early that his boarding mistress might mend his clothes. "When you get to be a United States Senator," said she, "no one will ask what kind of clothes you wore when teaching school."

Although Michael Angelo made himself immortal in three different occupations, his fame might well rest upon his dome of St. Peter as an architect, upon his "Moses" as a sculptor, and upon his "Last Judgment" as a painter; yet we find by his correspondence now in the British Museum, that when he was at work on his colossal bronze statue of Pope Julius II., he was so poor that he could not have his younger brother come to visit him at Bologna, because he had but one bed in which he and three of his assistants slept together.

"I was always at the bottom of my purse," said Zola, in describing the struggles of his early years of authorship. "Very often I had not a sou left, and not knowing, either, where to get one. I rose generally at four in the morning, and began to study after a breakfast consisting of one raw egg. But no matter, those were good times. After taking a walk along the quays, I entered my garret, and joyfully partaking of a dinner of three apples, I sat down to work. I wrote, and I was happy. In winter I would allow myself no fire; wood was too expensive—only on fête days was I able to afford it. But I had several pipes of tobacco and a candle for three sous. A three-sous candle, only think of it! It meant a whole night of literature to me."

James Brooks, once the editor and proprietor of the "New York Daily Express," and later an eminent congressman, began life as a clerk in a store in Maine, and when twenty-one received for his pay a hogshead of New England rum. He was so eager to go to college that he started for Waterville with his trunk on his back, and when he was graduated he was so poor and plucky that he carried his trunk on his back to the station when he went home.

When Elias Howe, harassed by want and woe, was in London completing his first sewing-machine, he had frequently to borrow money to live on. He bought beans and cooked them himself. He also borrowed money to send his wife back to America. He sold his first machine for five pounds, although it was worth fifty, and then he pawned his letters patent to pay his expenses home.

The boy Arkwright begins barbering in a cellar, but dies worth a million and a half. The world treated his novelties just as it treats everybody's novelties—made infinite objection, mustered all the impediments, but he snapped his fingers at their objections, and lived to become honored and wealthy.

There is scarcely a great truth or doctrine but has had to fight its way to public recognition in the face of detraction, calumny, and persecution. "Everywhere," says Heine, "that a great soul gives utterance to its thoughts, there also is a Golgotha."

Nearly every great discovery or invention that has blessed mankind has had to fight its way to recognition, even against the opposition of the most progressive men.

Even Sir Charles Napier fiercely opposed the introduction of steam power into the Royal Navy. In the House of Commons, he exclaimed, "Mr. Speaker, when we enter Her Majesty's naval service and face the chances of war, we go prepared to be hacked in pieces, to be riddled by bullets, or to be blown to bits by shot and shell; but Mr. Speaker, we do not go prepared to be boiled alive." He said this with tremendous emphasis.

"Will any one explain how there can be a light without a wick?" asked a member of Parliament, when William Murdock, toward the close of the eighteenth century, said that coal gas would give a good light, and could be conveyed into buildings in pipes. "Do you intend taking the dome of St. Paul's for a gasometer?" was the sneering question of even the great scientist, Humphry Davy. Walter Scott ridiculed the idea of lighting London by "smoke," but he soon used it at Abbotsford, and Davy achieved one of his greatest triumphs by experimenting with gas until he had invented his safety lamp.

Titian used to crush the flowers to get their color, and painted the white walls of his father's cottage in Tyrol with all sorts of pictures, at which the mountaineers gazed in wonder.

"That boy will beat me one day," said an old painter as he watched a little fellow named Michael Angelo making drawings of pot and brushes, easel and stool, and other articles in the studio. The barefoot boy did persevere until he had overcome every difficulty and become a master of his art.

William H. Prescott was a remarkable example of what a boy with "no chance" can do. While at college, he lost one eye by a hard piece of bread thrown during a "biscuit battle," then so common after meals; and, from sympathy, the other eye became almost useless. But the boy had pluck and determination, and would not lead a useless life. He set his heart upon being a historian, and turned all his energies in that direction. By the aid of others' eyes, he spent ten years studying before he even decided upon a particular theme for his first book. Then he spent ten years more, poring over old archives and manuscripts, before he published his "Ferdinand and Isabella." What a lesson in his life for young men! What a rebuke to those who have thrown away their opportunities and wasted their lives!

"Galileo with an opera-glass," said Emerson, "discovered a more splendid series of celestial phenomena than any one since with the great telescopes. Columbus found the new world in an undecked boat."

Surroundings which men call unfavorable cannot prevent the unfolding of your powers. From the plain fields and lowlands of Avon came the Shakespearean genius which has charmed the world. From among the rock-ribbed hills of New Hampshire sprang the greatest of American orators and statesmen, Daniel Webster. From the crowded ranks of toil, and homes to which luxury is a stranger, have often come the leaders and benefactors of our race. Indeed, when Christ came upon earth, His early abode was a place so poor and so much despised that men thought He could not be the Christ, asking, in utter astonishment, "Can any good thing come out of Nazareth?"

"I once knew a little colored boy," said Frederick Douglass, "whose mother and father died when he was but six years old. He was a slave, and had no one to care for him. He slept on a dirt floor in a hovel, and in cold weather would crawl into a meal-bag head foremost, and leave his feet in the ashes to keep them warm. Often he would roast an ear of corn and eat it to satisfy his hunger, and many times has he crawled under the barn or stable and secured eggs, which he would roast in the fire and eat. That boy did not wear pantaloons, as you do, but a tow-linen shirt. Schools were unknown to him, and he learned to spell from an old Webster's spelling-book, and to read and write from posters on cellar and barn doors, while boys and men would help him. He would then preach and speak, and soon became well known. He became presidential elector, United States marshal, United States recorder, United States diplomat, and accumulated some wealth. He wore broadcloth, and didn't have to divide crumbs with the dogs under the table. That boy was Frederick Douglass. What was possible for me is possible for you. Don't think because you are colored you can't accomplish anything. Strive earnestly to add to your knowledge. So long as you remain in ignorance, so long will you fail to command the respect of your fellow-men."

Where shall we find an illustration more impressive than in Abraham Lincoln, whose life, career, and death might be chanted by a Greek chorus as at once the prelude and the epilogue of the most imperial theme of modern times? Born as lowly as the Son of God, in a hovel; of what real parentage we know not, reared in penury, squalor, with no gleam of light, nor fair surrounding; a young manhood vexed by weird dreams and visions; with scarcely a natural grace; singularly awkward, ungainly even among the uncouth about him: it was reserved for this remarkable character, late in life, to be snatched from obscurity, raised to supreme command at a supreme moment, and intrusted with the destiny of a nation. The great leaders of his party were made to stand aside; the most experienced and accomplished men of the day, men like Seward, and Chase, and Sumner, statesmen famous and trained, were sent to the rear, while this strange figure was brought by unseen hands to the front, and given the reins of power.

The story is told of a man in London deprived of both legs and arms, who managed to write with his mouth and perform other things so remarkable as to enable him to earn a fair living. He would lay certain sheets of paper together, pinning them at the corner to make them hold. Then he would take a pen and write some verses; after which he would proceed to embellish the lines by many skillful flourishes. Dropping the pen from his mouth, he would next take up a needle and thread, also with his mouth, thread the needle, and make several stitches. He also painted with a brush, and was in many other ways a wonderful man. Instead of being a burden to his family he was the most important contributor to their welfare.

Arthur Cavanagh, M. P., was born without arms or legs, yet it is said that he was a good shot, a skillful fisherman and sailor, and one of the best cross country riders in Ireland. He was a good conversationalist, and an able member of Parliament. He ate with his fork attached to his stump of an arm, and wrote holding his pen in his teeth. In riding he held the bridle in his mouth, his body being strapped to the saddle. He once lost his means of support in India, but went to work with his accustomed energy, and obtained employment as a carrier of dispatches.

People thought it strange that Gladstone should appoint blind Henry Fawcett Postmaster-General of Great Britain; but never before did any one fill the office so well.

John B. Herreshoff, of Bristol, R. I., although blind since he was fifteen years old, is the founder and head of one of the most noted shipbuilding establishments in the world. He has superintended the construction of some of the swiftest torpedo boats and steam and sailing yachts afloat. He frequently takes his turn at the wheel in sailing his vessels on trial trips. He is aided greatly by his younger brother Nathaniel, but can plan vessels and conduct business without him. After examining a vessel's hull or a good model of it, he will give detailed instructions for building another just like it, and will make a more accurate duplicate than can most boat-builders whose sight is perfect.

The Rev. William H. Milburn, who lost his sight when a child, studied for the ministry, and was ordained before he attained his majority. In ten years he traveled about 200,000 miles in missionary work. He has written half a dozen books, among them a very careful history of the Mississippi Valley. He has long been chaplain of the lower house of Congress.

Blind Fanny Crosby, of New York, was a teacher of the blind for many years. She has written nearly three thousand hymns, among which are "Pass Me not, O Gentle Saviour," "Rescue the Perishing," "Saviour more than Life to Me," and "Jesus keep Me near the Cross."

Nor are these by any means the only examples of blind people now doing their full share of the world's work. In the United States alone there are engaged in musical occupation one hundred and fifty blind piano tuners, one hundred and fifty blind teachers of music in schools for the blind, five hundred blind private teachers, one hundred blind church organists, fifteen or more blind composers and publishers of music, and several blind dealers in musical instruments.

There is no open door to the temple of success. Every one who enters makes his own door, which closes behind him to all others, not even permitting his own children to pass.

Nearly forty years ago, on a rainy, dreary day in November, a young widow in Philadelphia sat wondering how she could feed and clothe three little ones left dependent by the death of her husband, a naval officer. Happening to think of a box of which her husband had spoken, she opened it, and found therein an envelope containing directions for a code of colored light signals to be used at night on the ocean. The system was not complete, but she perfected it, went to Washington, and induced the Secretary of the Navy to give it a trial. An admiral soon wrote that the signals were good for nothing, although the idea was valuable. For months and years she worked, succeeding at last in producing brilliant lights of different colors. She was paid $20,000 for the right to manufacture them in our navy. Nearly all the blockade runners captured in the Civil War were taken by the aid of the Coston signals, which are also considered invaluable in the Life Saving Service. Mrs. Coston introduced them into several European navies, and became wealthy.

A modern writer says that it is one of the mysteries of our life that genius, that noblest gift of God to man, is nourished by poverty. Its greatest works have been achieved by the sorrowing ones of the world in tears and despair. Not in the brilliant salon, not in the tapestried library, not in ease and competence, is genius usually born and nurtured; but often in adversity and destitution, amidst the harassing cares of a straitened household, in bare and fireless garrets, with the noise of squalid children, in the turbulence of domestic contentions, and in the deep gloom of uncheered despair. This is its most frequent birthplace, and amid scenes like these unpropitious, repulsive, wretched surroundings, have men labored, studied, and trained themselves, until they have at last emanated from the gloom of that obscurity the shining lights of their times; have become the companions of kings, the guides and teachers of their kind, and exercised an influence upon the thought of the world amounting to a species of intellectual legislation.

Chauncey Jerome's education was limited to three months in the district school each year until he was ten, when his father took him into his blacksmith shop at Plymouth, Conn., to make nails. Money was a scarce article with young Chauncey. He once chopped a load of wood for one cent, and often chopped by moonlight for neighbors at less than a dime a load. His father died when he was eleven, and his mother was forced to send Chauncey out, with tears in his eyes and a little bundle of clothes in his hand, to earn a living on a farm. His new employer kept him at work early and late chopping down trees all day, his shoes sometimes full of snow, for he had no boots until he was nearly twenty-one. At fourteen he was apprenticed for seven years to a carpenter, who gave him only board and clothes. Several times during his apprenticeship he carried his tools thirty miles on his back to his work at different places. After he had learned his trade he frequently walked thirty miles to a job with his kit upon his back. One day he heard people talking of Eli Terry, of Plymouth, who had undertaken to make two hundred clocks in one lot. "He'll never live long enough to finish them," said one. "If he should," said another, "he could not possibly sell so many. The very idea is ridiculous." Chauncey pondered long over this rumor, for it had long been his dream to become a great clock-maker. He tried his hand at the first opportunity, and soon learned to make a wooden clock. When he got an order to make twelve at twelve dollars apiece he thought his fortune was made. One night he happened to think that a cheap clock could be made of brass as well as of wood, and would not shrink, swell, or warp appreciably in any climate. He acted on the idea, and became the first great manufacturer of brass clocks. He made millions at the rate of six hundred a day, exporting them to all parts of the globe.

"The History of the English People" was written while J. R. Green was struggling against a mortal illness. He had collected a vast store of materials, and had begun to write, when his disease made a sudden and startling progress, and his physicians said they could do nothing to arrest it. In the extremity of ruin and defeat he applied himself with greater fidelity to his work. The time that might still be left to him for work must henceforth be wrested, day by day, from the grasp of death. The writing occupied five months, while from hour to hour and day to day his life was prolonged, his doctors said, by the sheer force of his own will and his inflexible determination to finish the "Making of England." He lay, too weak to lift a book, or to hold a pen, dictating every word, sometimes through hours of intense suffering. Yet so conscientious was he that, driven by death as he was, the greater part of the book was rewritten five times. When it was done he began the "Conquest of England," wrote it, reviewed it, and then, dissatisfied with it, rejected it all and began again. As death laid its cold fingers on his heart, he said: "I still have some work to do that I know is good. I will try to win but one week more to write it down." It was not until he was actually dying that he said, "I can work no more."

"What does he know," said a sage, "who has not suffered?" Schiller produced his greatest tragedies in the midst of physical suffering almost amounting to torture. Handel was never greater than when, warned by palsy of the approach of death, and struggling with distress and suffering, he sat down to compose the great works which have made his name immortal in music. Mozart composed his great operas, and last of all his "Requiem," when oppressed by debt and struggling with a fatal disease. Beethoven produced his greatest works amidst gloomy sorrow, when oppressed by almost total deafness.

Perhaps no one ever battled harder to overcome obstacles which would have disheartened most men than Demosthenes. He had such a weak voice, and such an impediment in his speech, and was so short of breath, that he could scarcely get through a single sentence without stopping to rest. All his first attempts were nearly drowned by the hisses, jeers, and scoffs of his audiences. His first effort that met with success was against his guardian, who had defrauded him, and whom he compelled to refund a part of his fortune. He was so discouraged by his defeats that he determined to give up forever all attempts at oratory. One of his auditors, however, believed the young man had something in him, and encouraged him to persevere. He accordingly appeared again in public, but was hissed down as before. As he withdrew, hanging his head in great confusion, a noted actor, Satyrus, encouraged him still further to try to overcome his impediment. He stammered so much that he could not pronounce some of the letters at all, and his breath would give out before he could get through a sentence. Finally, he determined to be an orator cost what it might. He went to the seashore and practiced amid the roar of the breakers with small pebbles in his mouth, in order to overcome his stammering, and at the same time accustom himself to the hisses and tumults of his audience. He overcame his short breath by practicing speaking while running up steep and difficult places on the shore. His awkward gestures were also corrected by long and determined drill before a mirror.

Disheartened by the expense of removing the troublesome seeds, Southern planters were seriously considering the abandonment of cotton culture. To clean a pound of cotton required the labor of a slave for a day. Eli Whitney, a young man from New England, teaching school in Georgia, saw the state of affairs, and determined to invent a machine to do the work. He worked in secret for many months in a cellar, and at last made a machine which cleaned the cotton perfectly and rapidly. Just as success crowned his long labor thieves broke into the cellar and stole his model. He recovered the model, but the principle was stolen, and other machines were made without his consent. In vain he tried to protect his right in the courts, for Southern juries would almost invariably decide against him. He had started the South in a great industry, and added millions to her wealth, yet the courts united with the men who had infringed his patents to rob him of the reward of his ingenuity and industry. At last he abandoned the whole thing in disgust, and turned his attention to making improvements in firearms, and with such success that he accumulated a fortune.

Robert Collyer, who brought his bride in the steerage when he came to America at the age of twenty-seven, worked at the anvil nine years in Pennsylvania, and then became a preacher, soon winning national renown.

A shrewd observer says of John Chinaman: "No sooner does he put his foot among strangers than he begins to work. No office is too menial or too laborious for him. He has come to make money, and he will make it. His frugality requires but little: he barely lives, but he saves what he gets; commences trade in the smallest possible way, and is continually adding to his store. The native scorns such drudgery, and remains poor; the Chinaman toils patiently on, and grows rich. A few years pass by, and he has warehouses; becomes a contractor for produce; buys foreign goods by the cargo; and employs his newly imported countrymen, who have come to seek their fortune as he did. He is not particularly scrupulous in matters of opinion. He never meddles with politics, for they are dangerous and not profitable; but he will adopt any creed, and carefully follow any observances, if, by so doing, he can confirm or improve his position. He thrives with the Spaniard, and works while the latter sleeps. He is too quick for the Dutchman, and can smoke and bargain at the same time. He has harder work with the Englishman, but still he is too much for him, and succeeds. Climate has no effect on him: it cannot stop his hands, unless it kills him; and if it does, he dies in harness, battling for money till his last breath. Whoever he may be, and in whatever position, whether in his own or a foreign country, he is diligent, temperate, and uncomplaining. He keeps the word he pledges, pays his debts, and is capable of noble and generous actions. It has been customary to speak lightly of him, and to judge a whole people by a few vagabonds in a provincial seaport, whose morals and manners have not been improved by foreign society."

Columbus was dismissed as a fool from court after court, but he pushed his suit against an incredulous and ridiculing world. Rebuffed by kings, scorned by queens, he did not swerve a hair's breadth from the overmastering purpose which dominated his soul. The words "New World" were graven upon his heart; and reputation, ease, pleasure, position, life itself if need be, must be sacrificed. Threats, ridicule, ostracism, storms, leaky vessels, mutiny of sailors, could not shake his mighty purpose.

You cannot keep a determined man from success. Place stumbling-blocks in his way and he takes them for stepping-stones, and on them will climb to greatness. Take away his money, and he makes spurs of his poverty to urge him on. Cripple him, and he writes the Waverley Novels. Lock him up in a dungeon, and he composes the immortal "Pilgrim's Progress." Put him in a cradle in a log cabin in the wilderness of America, and in a few years you will find him in the Capitol at the head of the greatest nation on the globe.

Would it were possible to convince the struggling youth of to-day that all that is great and noble and true in the history of the world is the result of infinite pains-taking, perpetual plodding, of common every-day industry!

When Lavoisier the chemist asked that his execution might be postponed for a few days in order to ascertain the results of the experiments he was conducting in prison, the communists refused to grant the request, saying: "The Republic has no need of philosophers." Dr. Priestley's house was burned and his chemical library destroyed by a mob shouting: "No philosophers," and he was forced to flee from his country. Bruno was burned in Rome for revealing the heavens, and Versalius [Transcriber's note: Vesalius?] was condemned for dissecting the human body; but their names shall live as long as time shall last. Kossuth was two years in prison at Buda, but he kept on working, undaunted. John Hunter said: "The few things I have been enabled to do have been accomplished under the greatest difficulties, and have encountered the greatest opposition."

Roger Bacon, one of the profoundest thinkers the world has produced, was terribly persecuted for his studies in natural philosophy, yet he persevered and won success. He was accused of dealing in magic, his books were burned in public, and he was kept in prison for ten years. Even our own revered Washington was mobbed in the streets because he would not pander to the clamor of the people and reject the treaty which Mr. Jay had arranged with Great Britain. But he remained firm, and the people adopted his opinion. The Duke of Wellington was mobbed in the streets of London and his windows were broken while his wife lay dead in the house; but the "Iron Duke" never faltered in his course, or swerved a hair's breadth from his purpose.

William Phips, when a young man, heard some sailors on the street, in Boston, talking about a Spanish ship, wrecked off the Bahama Islands, which was supposed to have money on board. Young Phips determined to find it. He set out at once, and, after many hardships, discovered the lost treasure. He then heard of another ship, wrecked off Port De La Plata many years before. He set sail for England and importuned Charles II. for aid. To his delight the king fitted up the ship Rose Algier for him. He searched and searched for a long time in vain. He had to return to England to repair his vessel. James II. was then on the throne, and he had to wait for four years before he could raise money to return. His crew mutinied and threatened to throw him overboard, but he turned the ship's guns on them. One day an Indian diver went down for a curious sea plant and saw several cannon lying on the bottom. They proved to belong to the wreck for which he was looking, sunk fifty years before. He had nothing but dim traditions to guide him, but he returned to England with $1,500,000. The King made him High Sheriff of New England, and he was afterward made Governor of Massachusetts Bay Colony.

Ben Jonson, when following his trade of a mason, worked on Lincoln's Inn in London with trowel in hand and a book in his pocket. Joseph Hunter was a carpenter in youth, Robert Burns a plowman, Keats a druggist, Thomas Carlyle and Hugh Miller masons. Dante and Descartes were soldiers. Andrew Johnson was a tailor. Cardinal Wolsey, Defoe, and Kirke White were butchers' sons. Faraday was the son of a blacksmith, and his teacher, Humphry Davy, was an apprentice to an apothecary. Kepler was a waiter boy in a German hotel, Bunyan a tinker, Copernicus the son of a Polish baker. The boy Herschel played the oboe for his meals. Marshal Ney, the "bravest of the brave," rose from the ranks. His great industry gained for him the name of "The

Indefatigable." Soult served fourteen years before he was made a sergeant. When made Foreign Minister of France he knew very little of geography, even. Richard Cobden was a boy in a London warehouse. His first speech in Parliament was a complete failure; but he was not afraid of defeat, and soon became one of the greatest orators of his day. Seven shoemakers sat in Congress during the first century of our government: Roger Sherman, Henry Wilson, Gideon Lee, William Graham, John Halley, H. P. Baldwin, and Daniel Sheffey.

A constant struggle, a ceaseless battle to bring success from inhospitable surroundings, is the price of all great achievements.

The man who has not fought his way up to his own loaf, and does not bear the scar of desperate conflict, does not know the highest meaning of success.

The money acquired by those who have thus struggled upward to success is not their only, or indeed their chief reward. When, after years of toil, of opposition, of ridicule, of repeated failure, Cyrus W. Field placed his hand upon the telegraph instrument ticking a message under the sea, think you that the electric thrill passed no further than the tips of his fingers? When Thomas A. Edison demonstrated in Menlo Park that the electric light had at last been developed into a commercial success, do you suppose those bright rays failed to illuminate the inmost recesses of his soul? Edward Everett said: "There are occasions in life in which a great mind lives years of enjoyment in a single moment. I can fancy the emotion of Galileo when, first raising the newly constructed telescope to the heavens, he saw fulfilled the grand prophecy of Copernicus, and beheld the planet Venus crescent like the moon. It was such another moment as that when the immortal printers of Mentz and Strasburg received the first copy of the Bible into their hands, the work of their divine art; like that when Columbus, through the gray dawn of the 12th of October, 1492, beheld the shores of San Salvador; like that when the law of gravitation first revealed itself to the intellect of Newton; like that when Franklin saw, by the stiffening fibres of the hemp cord of his kite, that he held the lightning in his grasp, like that when Leverrier received back from Berlin the tidings that the predicted planet was found."

"Observe yon tree in your neighbor's garden," says Zanoni to Viola in Bulwer's novel. "Look how it grows up, crooked and distorted. Some wind scattered the germ, from which it sprung, in the clefts of the rock. Choked up and walled round by crags and buildings, by nature and man, its life has been one struggle for the light. You see how it has writhed and twisted,—how, meeting the barrier in one spot, it has labored and worked, stem and branch, towards the clear skies at last. What has preserved it through each disfavor of birth and circumstances—why are its leaves as green and fair as those of the vine behind you, which, with all its arms, can embrace the open sunshine? My child, because of the very instinct that impelled the struggle,—because the labor for the light won to the light at length. So with a gallant heart, through every adverse accident of sorrow, and of fate, to turn to the sun, to strive for the heaven; this it is that gives knowledge to the strong and happiness to the weak."

"Each petty hand
Can steer a ship becalmed; but he that will
Govern her and carry her to her ends, must know
His tides, his currents; how to shift his sails;

What she will bear in foul, what in fair weathers;
What her springs are, her leaks, and how to stop them;
What strands, what shelves, what rocks to threaten her;
The forces and the natures of all winds,
Gusts, storms, and tempests; when her keel plows hell,
And deck knocks heaven; then to manage her
Becomes the name and office of a pilot."

CHAPTER V. USES OF OBSTACLES.

Nature, when she adds difficulties, adds brains.—EMERSON.

Many men owe the grandeur of their lives to their tremendous difficulties.—SPURGEON.

The good are better made by ill,
As odors crushed are sweeter still.
ROGERS.
Aromatic plants bestow
No spicy fragrance while they grow;
But crushed or trodden to the ground,
Diffuse their balmy sweets around.
GOLDSMITH.
As night to stars, woe lustre gives to man.—YOUNG.

There is no possible success without some opposition as a fulcrum: force is always aggressive and crowds something.—HOLMES.

The more difficulties one has to encounter, within and without, the more significant and the higher in inspiration his life will be.—HORACE BUSHMILL.

Adversity has the effect of eliciting talents which in prosperous circumstances would have lain dormant.—HORACE.

For gold is tried in the fire and acceptable men in the furnace of adversity.—SIRACH.

Though losses and crosses be lessons right severe,
There's wit there ye'll get there, ye'll find no other where.
BURNS.
Possession pampers the mind; privation trains and strengthens it.—HAZLITT.

"Adversity is the prosperity of the great."

No man ever worked his way in a dead calm.—JOHN NEAL.

"Kites rise against, not with, the wind."

"Many and many a time since," said Harriet Martineau, referring to her father's failure in business, "have we said that, but for that loss of money, we might have lived on in the ordinary provincial method of ladies with small means, sewing and economizing and growing narrower every year; whereas, by being thrown, while it was yet time, on our own resources, we have worked hard and usefully, won friends, reputation, and independence, seen the world abundantly, abroad and at home; in short, have truly lived instead of vegetating."

"I do believe God wanted a grand poem of that man," said George Macdonald of Milton, "and so blinded him that he might be able to write it."

Two of the three greatest epic poets of the world were blind,—Homer and Milton; while the third, Dante, was in his later years nearly, if not altogether, blind. It almost seems as though some great characters had been physically crippled in certain respects so that they would not dissipate their energy, but concentrate it all in one direction.

"I have been beaten, but not cast down," said Thiers, after making a complete failure of his first speech in the Chamber of Deputies. "I am making my first essay in arms. In the tribune, as under fire, a defeat is as useful as a victory."

A distinguished investigator in science said that when he encountered an apparently insuperable obstacle, he usually found himself upon the brink of some discovery.

"Returned with thanks" has made many an author. Failure often leads a man to success by arousing his latent energy, by firing a dormant purpose, by awakening powers which were sleeping. Men of mettle turn disappointments into helps as the oyster turns into pearl the sand which annoys it.

"Let the adverse breath of criticism be to you only what the blast of the storm wind is to the eagle,—a force against him that lifts him higher."

A kite would not fly unless it had a string tying it down. It is just so in life. The man who is tied down by half a dozen blooming responsibilities and their mother will make a higher and stronger flight than the bachelor who, having nothing to keep him steady, is always floundering in the mud. If you want to ascend in the world tie yourself to somebody.

"It was the severe preparation for the subsequent harvest," said Pemberton Leigh, the eminent English lawyer, speaking of his early poverty and hard work. "I learned to consider indefatigable labor as the indispensable condition of success, pecuniary independence as essential alike to virtue and happiness, and no sacrifice too great to avoid the misery of debt."

When Napoleon's companions made sport of him on account of his humble origin and poverty he devoted himself entirely to books, and soon rising above them in scholarship, commanded their respect. Soon he was regarded as the brightest ornament of the class.

"To make his way at the bar," said an eminent jurist, "a young man must live like a hermit and work like a horse. There is nothing that does a young lawyer so much good as to be half starved."

Thousands of men of great native ability have been lost to the world because they have not had to wrestle with obstacles, and to struggle under difficulties sufficient to stimulate into activity their dormant powers. No effort is too dear which helps us along the line of our proper career.

Poverty and obscurity of origin may impede our progress, but it is only like the obstruction of ice or debris in the river temporarily forcing the water into eddies, where it accumulates strength and a mighty reserve which ultimately sweeps the obstruction impetuously to the sea. Poverty and obscurity are not insurmountable obstacles, but they often act as a stimulus to the naturally indolent, and develop a firmer fibre of mind, a stronger muscle and stamina of body. If the germ of the seed has to struggle to push its way up through the stones and hard sod, to fight its way up to sunlight and air, and then to wrestle with storm and tempest, with snow and frost, the fibre of its timber will be all the tougher and stronger.

"Do you wish to live without a trial?" asks a modern teacher. "Then you wish to die but half a man. Without trial you cannot guess at your own strength. Men do not learn to swim on a table. They must go into deep water and buffet the waves. Hardship is the native soil of manhood and self-reliance. Trials are rough teachers, but rugged schoolmasters make rugged pupils. A man who goes through life prosperous, and comes to his grave without a wrinkle, is not half a man. Difficulties are God's errands. And when we are sent upon them we should esteem it a proof of God's confidence. We should reach after the highest good."

"If you wish to rise," said Talleyrand, "make enemies."

There is good philosophy in the injunction to love our enemies, for they are often our best friends in disguise. They tell us the truth when friends flatter. Their biting sarcasm and scathing rebuke are often mirrors which reveal us to ourselves. These unkind stings and thrusts are spurs which urge us on to grander success and nobler endeavor. Friends cover our faults and rarely rebuke; enemies drag out to the light all our weaknesses without mercy. We dread these thrusts and exposures as we do the surgeon's knife, but are the better for them. They reach depths before untouched, and we are led to resolve to redeem ourselves from scorn and inferiority.

We are the victors of our opponents. They have developed in us the very power by which we overcome them. Without their opposition we could never have braced and anchored and fortified ourselves, as the oak is braced and anchored for its thousand battles with the tempests. Our trials, our sorrows, and our griefs develop us in a similar way.

The man who has triumphed over difficulties bears the signs of victory in his face. An air of triumph is seen in every movement.

John Calvin, who made a theology for the seventeenth and eighteenth centuries, was tortured with disease for many years, and so was Robert Hall. The great men who have lifted the world to a higher level were not developed in easy circumstances, but were rocked in the cradle of difficulties and pillowed on hardships.

"The gods look on no grander sight than an honest man struggling with adversity."

"Then I must learn to sing better," said Anaximander, when told that the very boys laughed at his singing. Strong characters, like the palm-tree, seem to thrive best when most abused. Men who have stood up bravely under great misfortune for years are often unable to bear prosperity. Their good fortune takes the spring out of their energy, as the torrid zone enervates races accustomed to a vigorous climate. Some people never come to themselves until baffled, rebuffed, thwarted, defeated, crushed, in the opinion of those around them. Trials unlock their virtues; defeat is the threshold of their victory.

It is defeat that turns bone to flint; it is defeat that turns gristle to muscle; it is defeat that makes men invincible; it is defeat that has made those heroic natures that are now in the ascendency, and that has given the sweet law of liberty instead of the bitter law of oppression.

Difficulties call out great qualities, and make greatness possible. How many centuries of peace would have developed a Grant? Few knew Lincoln until the great weight of the war showed his character. A century of peace would never have produced a Bismarck. Perhaps Phillips and Garrison would never have been known to history had it not been for slavery.

"Will he not make a great painter?" was asked in regard to an artist fresh from his Italian tour. "No, never," replied Northcote. "Why not?" "Because he has an income of six thousand pounds a year." In the sunshine of wealth a man is, as a rule, warped too much to become an artist of high merit. A drenching shower of adversity would straighten his fibres out again. He should have some great thwarting difficulty to struggle against.

The best tools receive their temper from fire, their edge from grinding; the noblest characters are developed in a similar way. The harder the diamond, the more brilliant the lustre, and the greater the friction necessary to bring it out. Only its own dust is hard enough to make this most precious stone reveal its full beauty.

The spark in the flint would sleep forever but for friction; the fire in man would never blaze but for antagonism. The friction which retards a train upon the track, robbing the engine of a fourth of its power, is the very secret of locomotion. Oil the track, remove the friction, and the train will not move an inch. The moment man is relieved of opposition or friction, and the track of his life is oiled with inherited wealth or other aids, that moment he often ceases to struggle and therefore ceases to grow.

"It is this scantiness of means, this continual deficiency, this constant hitch, this perpetual struggle to keep the head above water and the wolf from the door, that keeps society from falling to pieces. Let every man have a few more dollars than he wants, and anarchy would follow."

Suddenly, with much jarring and jolting, an electric car came to a standstill just in front of a heavy truck that was headed in an opposite direction. The huge truck wheels were sliding uselessly round on the car tracks that were wet and slippery from rain. All the urging of the teamster and the straining of the horses in vain,—until the motorman quietly tossed a shovelful of sand on the track under the heavy wheels, then the truck lumbered on its way. "Friction is a very good thing," remarked a passenger.

The philosopher Kant observes that a dove, inasmuch as the only obstacle it has to overcome is the resistance of the air, might suppose that if only the air were out of the way it could fly with greater rapidity and ease. Yet if the air were withdrawn, and the bird should try to fly in a vacuum, it would fall instantly to the ground unable to fly at all. The very element that offers the opposition to flying is at the same time the condition of any flight whatever.

Rough seas and storms make sailors. Emergencies make giant men. But for our Civil War the names of its grand heroes would not be written among the greatest of our time.

The effort or struggle to climb to a higher place in life has strength and dignity in it, and cannot fail to leave us stronger for the struggle, even though we miss the prize.

From an aimless, idle, and useless brain, emergencies often call out powers and virtues before unknown and suspected. How often we see a young man develop astounding ability and energy after the death of a parent, or the loss of a fortune, or after some other calamity has knocked the props and crutches from under him. The prison has roused the slumbering fire in many a noble mind. "Robinson Crusoe" was written in prison. The "Pilgrim's Progress" appeared in Bedford Jail. The "Life and Times" of Baxter, Eliot's "Monarchia of Man," and Penn's "No Cross, No Crown," were written by prisoners. Sir Walter Raleigh wrote "The History of the World" during his imprisonment of thirteen years. Luther translated the Bible while confined in the Castle of Wartburg. For twenty years Dante worked in exile, and even under sentence of death. His works were burned in public after his death; but genius will not burn.

Take two acorns from the same tree, as nearly alike as possible; plant one on a hill by itself, and the other in the dense forest, and watch them grow. The oak standing alone is exposed to every storm. Its roots reach out in every direction, clutching the rocks and piercing deep into the earth. Every rootlet lends itself to steady the growing giant, as if in anticipation of fierce conflict with the elements. Sometimes its upward growth seems checked for years, but all the while it has been expending its energy in pushing a root across a large rock to gain a firmer anchorage. Then it shoots proudly aloft again, prepared to defy the hurricane. The gales which sport so rudely with its wide branches find more than their match, and only serve still further to toughen every minutest fibre from pith to bark.

The acorn planted in the deep forest shoots up a weak, slender sapling. Shielded by its neighbors, it feels no need of spreading its roots far and wide for support.

Take two boys, as nearly alike as possible. Place one in the country away from the hothouse culture and refinements of the city, with only the district school, the Sunday-school, and a few books. Remove wealth and props of every kind; and, if he has the right kind of material in him, he will thrive. Every obstacle overcome lends him strength for the next conflict. If he falls, he rises with more determination than before. Like a rubber ball, the harder the obstacle he meets the higher he rebounds. Obstacles and opposition are but apparatus of the gymnasium in which the fibres of his manhood are developed. He compels respect and recognition from those who have ridiculed his poverty. Put the other boy in a Vanderbilt family. Give him French and German nurses; gratify every wish. Place him under the tutelage of great masters and send him to Harvard. Give him thousands a year for spending money, and let him travel extensively.

The two meet. The city lad is ashamed of his country brother. The plain, threadbare clothes, hard hands, tawny face, and awkward manner of the country boy make sorry contrast with the genteel appearance of the other. The poor boy bemoans his hard lot, regrets that he has "no chance in life," and envies the city youth. He thinks that it is a cruel Providence that places such a wide gulf between them. They meet again as men, but how changed! It is as easy to distinguish the sturdy, self-made man from the one who has been propped up all his life by wealth, position, and family influence, as it is for the shipbuilder to tell the difference between the plank from the rugged mountain oak and one from the sapling of the forest. If you think there is no difference, place each plank in the bottom of a ship, and test them in a hurricane at sea.

When God wants to educate a man, he does not send him to school to the Graces, but to the Necessities. Through the pit and the dungeon Joseph came to a throne. We are not conscious of the mighty cravings of our half divine humanity; we are not aware of the god within us until some chasm yawns which must be filled, or till the rending asunder of our affections forces us to become conscious of a need. Paul in his Roman cell; John Huss led to the stake at Constance; Tyndale dying in his prison at Amsterdam; Milton, amid the incipient earthquake throes of revolution, teaching two little boys in Aldgate Street; David Livingstone, worn to a shadow, dying in a negro hut in Central Africa, alone,—what failures they might all to themselves have seemed to be, yet what mighty purposes was God working out by their apparent humiliations!

Two highwaymen chancing once to pass a gibbet, one of them exclaimed: "What a fine profession ours would be if there were no gibbets!" "Tut, you blockhead," replied the other, "gibbets are the making of us; for, if there were no gibbets, every one would be a highwayman." Just so with every art, trade, or pursuit; it is the difficulties that scare and keep out unworthy competitors.

"Success grows out of struggles to overcome difficulties," says Smiles. "If there were no difficulties, there would be no success. In this necessity for exertion we find the chief source of human advancement,—the advancement of individuals as of nations. It has led to most of the mechanical inventions and improvements of the age."

"Stick your claws into me," said Mendelssohn to his critics when entering the Birmingham orchestra. "Don't tell me what you like but what you don't like."

John Hunter said that the art of surgery would never advance until professional men had the courage to publish their failures as well as their successes.

"Young men need to be taught not to expect a perfectly smooth and easy way to the objects of their endeavor or ambition," says Dr. Peabody. "Seldom does one reach a position with which he has reason to be satisfied without encountering difficulties and what might seem discouragements. But if they are properly met, they are not what they seem, and may prove to be helps, not hindrances. There is no more helpful and profiting exercise than surmounting obstacles."

It is said that but for the disappointments of Dante, Florence would have had another prosperous Lord Mayor; and the ten dumb centuries continued voiceless, and the ten other listening centuries (for there will be ten of them, and more) would have had no "Divina Commedia" to hear!

It was in the Madrid jail that Cervantes wrote "Don Quixote." He was so poor that he could not even get paper during the last of his writing, and had to write on scraps of leather. A rich Spaniard was asked to help him, but the rich man replied: "Heaven forbid that his necessities should be relieved, it is his poverty that makes the world rich."

"A constant struggle, a ceaseless battle to bring success from inhospitable surroundings, is the price of all great achievements."

"She sings well," said a great musician of a promising but passionless cantatrice, "but she wants something, and in that something, everything. If I were single, I would court her, I would marry her; I would maltreat her; I would break her heart, and in six months she would be the greatest singer in Europe."

"He has the stuff in him to make a good musician," said Beethoven of Rossini, "if he had only been well flogged when a boy; but he is spoiled by the ease with which he composes."

We do our best while fighting desperately to attain what the heart covets. Martin Luther did his greatest work, and built up his best character, while engaged in sharp controversy with the Pope. Later in life his wife asks, "Doctor, how is it that whilst subject to Papacy we prayed so often and with such fervor, whilst now we pray with the utmost coldness and very seldom?"

When Lord Eldon was poor, Lord Thurlow withheld a promised commissionership of bankruptcy, saying that it was a favor not to give it then. "What he meant was," said Eldon, "that he had learned I was by nature very indolent, and it was only want that could make me very industrious."

Waters says that the struggle to obtain knowledge and to advance one's self in the world strengthens the mind, disciplines the faculties, matures the judgment, promotes self-reliance, and gives one independence of thought and force of character.

"The gods in bounty work up storms about us," says Addison, "that give mankind occasion to exert their hidden strength, and throw out into practice virtues that shun the day, and lie concealed in the smooth seasons and the calms of life."

The hothouse plant may tempt a pampered appetite or shed a languid odor, but the working world gets its food from fields of grain and orchards waving in the sun and free air, from cattle that wrestle on the plains, from fishes that struggle with currents of river or ocean; its choicest perfumes from flowers that bloom unheeded, and in wind-tossed forests finds its timber for temples and for ships.

"I do not see," says Emerson, "how any man can afford, for the sake of his nerves and his nap, to spare any action in which he can partake. It is pearls and rubies to his discourse. Drudgery, calamity, exasperation, want, are instructors in eloquence and wisdom. The true scholar grudges every opportunity of action passed by as a loss of power."

Kossuth called himself "a tempest-tossed soul, whose eyes have been sharpened by affliction."

Benjamin Franklin ran away, and George Law was turned out of doors. Thrown upon their own resources, they early acquired the energy and skill to overcome difficulties.

As soon as young eagles can fly the old birds tumble them out and tear the down and feathers from their nest. The rude and rough experience of the eaglet fits him to become the bold king of birds, fierce and expert in pursuing his prey.

Boys who are bound out, crowded out, kicked out, usually "turn out," while those who do not have these disadvantages frequently fail to "come out."

"It was not the victories but the defeats of my life which have strengthened me," said the aged Sidenham Poyntz.

Almost from the dawn of history, oppression has been the lot of the Hebrews, yet they have given the world its noblest songs, its wisest proverbs, its sweetest music. With them persecution seems to bring prosperity. They thrive where others would starve. They hold the purse-strings of many nations. To them hardship has been "like spring mornings, frosty but kindly, the cold of which will kill the vermin, but will let the plant live."

In one of the battles of the Crimea a cannon-ball struck inside the fort, crashing through a beautiful garden. But from the ugly chasm there burst forth a spring of water which ever afterward flowed a living fountain. From the ugly gashes which misfortunes and sorrows make in our hearts, perennial fountains of rich experience and new joys often spring.

Don't lament and grieve over lost wealth. The Creator may see something grand and mighty which even He cannot bring out as long as your wealth stands in the way. You must throw away the crutches of riches and stand upon your own feet, and develop the long unused muscles of manhood. God may see a rough diamond in you which only the hard hits of poverty can polish.

God knows where the richest melodies of our lives are, and what drill and what discipline are necessary to bring them out. The frost, the snows, the tempests, the lightnings, are the rough teachers that bring the tiny acorn to the sturdy oak. Fierce winters are as necessary to it as long summers. It is its half-century's struggle with the elements for existence, wrestling with the storm, fighting for its life from the moment that it leaves the acorn until it goes into the ship, that gives it value. Without this struggle it would have been character-less, stamina-less, nerve-less, and its grain would have never been susceptible of high polish. The most beautiful as well as the strongest woods are found not in tropical climates, but in the severe climates, where they have to fight the frosts and the winter's cold.

Many a man has never found himself until he has lost his all. Adversity stripped him only to discover him. Obstacles, hardships are the chisel and mallet which shape the strong life into beauty. The rough ledge on the hillside complains of the drill, of the blasting powder which disturbs its peace of centuries: it is not pleasant to be rent with powder, to be hammered and squared by the quarryman. But look again: behold the magnificent statue, the monument, chiseled into grace and beauty, telling its grand story of valor in the public square for centuries.

The statue would have slept in the marble forever but for the blasting, the chiseling, and the polishing. The angel of our higher and nobler selves would remain forever unknown in the rough quarries of our lives but for the blastings of affliction, the chiseling of obstacles, and the sand-papering of a thousand annoyances.

Who has not observed the patience, the calm endurance, the sweet loveliness chiseled out of some rough life by the reversal of fortune or by some terrible affliction.

How many business men have made their greatest strides toward manhood, have developed their greatest virtues, when the reverses of fortune have swept away everything they had in the world; when disease had robbed them of all they held dear in life. Often we cannot see the angel in the quarry of our lives, the statue of manhood, until the blasts of misfortune have rent the ledge, and difficulties and obstacles have squared and chiseled the granite blocks into grace and beauty.

Many a man has been ruined into salvation. The lightning which smote his dearest hopes opened up a new rift in his dark life, and gave him glimpses of himself which, until then, he had never seen.

The grave buried his dearest hopes, but uncovered possibilities in his nature of patience, endurance, and hope which he never dreamed he possessed before.

"Adversity is a severe instructor," says Edmund Burke, "set over us by one who knows us better than we do ourselves, as he loves us better too. He that wrestles with us strengthens our nerves and sharpens our skill. Our antagonist is our helper. This conflict with difficulty makes us acquainted with our object, and compels us to consider it in all its relations. It will not suffer us to be superficial."

Men who have the right kind of material in them will assert their personality, and rise in spite of a thousand adverse circumstances. You cannot keep them down. Every obstacle seems only to add to their ability to get on.

"Under different circumstances," says Castelar, "Savonarola would undoubtedly have been a good husband, a tender father, a man unknown to history, utterly powerless to print upon the sands of time and upon the human soul the deep trace which he has left, but misfortune came to visit him, to crush his heart, and to impart that marked melancholy which characterizes a soul in grief, and the grief that circled his brows with a crown of thorns was also that which wreathed them with the splendor of immortality. His hopes were centred in the woman he loved, his life was set upon the possession of her, and when her family finally rejected him, partly on account of his profession, and partly on account of his person, he believed that it was death that had come upon him, when in truth it was immortality."

The greatest men will ever be those who have risen from the ranks. It is said that there are ten thousand chances to one that genius, talent, and virtue shall issue from a farmhouse rather than from a palace.

The youth Opie earned his bread by sawing wood, but he reached a professorship in the Royal Academy. When but ten years old he showed the material he was made of by a beautiful drawing on a shingle. Antonio Canova was the son of a day laborer. Thorwaldsen's parents were poor, but, like hundreds of others, they did with their might what their hands found to do, and ennobled their work. They rose by being greater than their calling, as Arkwright rose above mere barbering, Bunyan above tinkering, Wilson above shoemaking, Lincoln above rail-splitting, and Grant above tanning. By being first-class barbers, tinkers, shoemakers, rail-splitters, tanners, they acquired the power which enabled them to become great inventors, authors, statesmen, generals.

Adversity exasperates fools, dejects cowards, draws out the faculties of the wise and industrious, puts the modest to the necessity of trying their skill, awes the opulent, and makes the idle industrious. Neither do uninterrupted success and prosperity qualify men for usefulness and happiness. The storms of adversity, like those of the ocean, rouse the faculties, and excite the invention, prudence, skill, and fortitude of the voyager. The martyrs of ancient times, in bracing their minds to outward calamities, acquired a loftiness of purpose and a moral heroism worth a lifetime of softness and security. A man upon whom continuous sunshine falls is like the earth in August: he becomes parched and dry and hard and close-grained. Men have drawn from adversity the elements of greatness. If you have the blues, go and see the poorest and sickest families within your knowledge. The darker the setting, the brighter the diamond. Don't run about and tell acquaintances that you have been unfortunate; people do not like to have unfortunate men for acquaintances.

Beethoven was almost totally deaf and burdened with sorrow when he produced his greatest works. Schiller wrote his best books in great bodily suffering. He was not free from pain for fifteen years. Milton wrote his leading productions when blind, poor, and sick. "Who best can suffer," said he, "best can do." Bunyan said that, if it were lawful, he could even pray for greater trouble, for the greater comfort's sake.

"Do you know what God puts us on our backs for?" asked Dr. Payson, smiling, as he lay sick in bed. "No," replied the visitor. "In order that we may look upward." "I am not come to condole but to rejoice with you," said the friend, "for it seems to me that this is no time for mourning." "Well, I am glad to hear that," said Dr. Payson, "it is not often I am addressed in such a way. The fact is I never had less need of condolence, and yet everybody persists in offering it; whereas, when I was prosperous and well, and a successful preacher, and really needed condolence, they flattered and congratulated me."

A German knight undertook to make an immense Aeolian harp by stretching wires from tower to tower of his castle. When he finished the harp it was silent; but when the breezes began to blow he heard faint strains like the murmuring of distant music. At last a tempest arose and swept with fury over his castle, and then rich and grand music came from the wires. Ordinary experiences do not seem to touch some lives—to bring out any poetry, any higher manhood.

Not until the breath of the plague had blasted a hundred thousand lives, and the great fire had licked up cheap, shabby, wicked London, did she arise, phoenix-like, from her ashes and ruin, a grand and mighty city.

True salamanders live best in the furnace of persecution.

"Every man who makes a fortune has been more than once a bankrupt, if the truth were known," said Albion Tourgée. "Grant's failure as a subaltern made him commander-in-chief, and for myself, my failure to accomplish what I set out to do led me to what I never had aspired to."

The appeal for volunteers in the great battle of life, in exterminating ignorance and error, and planting high on an everlasting foundation the banner of intelligence and right, is directed to you. Burst the trammels that impede your progress, and cling to hope. Place high thy standard, and with a firm tread and fearless eye press steadily onward.

Not ease, but effort, not facility, but difficulty, makes men. Toilsome culture is the price of great success, and the slow growth of a great character is one of its special necessities. Many of our best poets

"Are cradled into poetry by wrong,
And learn in suffering what they teach in song."

Byron was stung into a determination to go to the top by a scathing criticism of his first book, "Hours of Idleness," published when he was but nineteen years of age. Macaulay said, "There is scarce an instance in history of so sudden a rise to so dizzy an eminence as Byron reached." In a few years he stood by the side of such men as Scott, Southey, and Campbell, and died at thirty-seven, that age so fatal to genius. Many an orator like "stuttering Jack Curran," or "Orator Mum," as he was once called, has been spurred into eloquence by ridicule and abuse.

This is the crutch age. "Helps" and "aids" are advertised everywhere. We have institutes, colleges, universities, teachers, books, libraries, newspapers, magazines. Our thinking is done for us. Our problems are all worked out in "explanations" and "keys." Our boys are too often tutored through college with very little study. "Short roads" and "abridged methods" are characteristic of the century. Ingenious methods are used everywhere to get the drudgery out of the college course. Newspapers give us our politics, and preachers our religion. Self-help and self-reliance are getting old fashioned. Nature, as if conscious of delayed blessings, has rushed to man's relief with her wondrous forces, and undertakes to do the world's drudgery and emancipate him from Eden's curse.

But do not misinterpret her edict. She emancipates from the lower only to call to the higher. She does not bid the world go and play while she does the work. She emancipates the muscles only to employ the brain and heart.

The most beautiful as well as the strongest characters are not developed in warm climates, where man finds his bread ready made on trees, and where exertion is a great effort, but rather in a trying climate and on a stubborn soil. It is no chance that returns to the Hindoo ryot a penny and to the American laborer a dollar for his daily toil; that makes Mexico with its mineral wealth poor, and New England with its granite and ice rich. It is rugged necessity, it is the struggle to obtain, it is poverty the priceless spur, that develops the stamina of manhood, and calls the race out of barbarism. Labor found the world a wilderness and has made it a garden.

As the sculptor thinks only of the angel imprisoned in the marble block, so Nature cares only for the man or woman shut up in the human being. The sculptor cares nothing for the block as such; Nature has little regard for the mere lump of breathing clay. The sculptor will chip off all unnecessary material to set free the angel. Nature will chip and pound us remorselessly to bring out our possibilities. She will strip us of wealth, humble our pride, humiliate our ambition, let us down from the ladder of fame, will discipline us in a thousand ways, if she can develop a little character. Everything must give way to that. Wealth is nothing, position is nothing, fame is nothing, manhood is everything.

Not ease, not pleasure, not happiness, but a man, Nature is after. In every great painting of the masters there is one idea or figure which stands out boldly beyond everything else. Every other idea or figure on the canvas is subordinate to it, but pointing to the central idea, finds its true expression there. So in the vast universe of God, every object of creation is but a guideboard with an index-finger pointing to the central figure of the created universe—Man. Nature writes this thought upon every leaf, she thunders it in every creation. It is exhaled from every flower; it twinkles in every star.

Oh, what price will Nature not pay for a man! Ages and aeons were nothing for her to spend in preparing for his coming, or to make his existence possible. She has rifled the centuries for his development, and placed the universe at his disposal. The world is but his kindergarten, and every created thing but an object-lesson from the unseen universe. Nature resorts to a thousand expedients to develop a perfect type of her grandest creation. To do this she must induce him to fight his way up to his own loaf. She never allows him once to lose sight of the fact that it is the struggle to attain that develops the man. The moment we put our hand upon that which looks so attractive at a distance, and which we struggled so hard to reach, Nature robs it of its charm by holding up before us another prize still more attractive.

"Life," says a philosopher, "refuses to be so adjusted as to eliminate from it all strife and conflict and pain. There are a thousand tasks that, in larger interests than ours, must be done, whether we want them or no. The world refuses to walk upon tiptoe, so that we may be able to sleep. It gets up very early and stays up very late, and all the while there is the conflict of myriads of hammers and saws and axes with the stubborn material that in no other way can be made to serve its use and do its work for man. And then, too, these hammers and axes are not wielded without strain or pang, but swung by the millions of toilers who labor with their cries and groans and tears. Nay, our temple-building, whether it be for God or man, exacts its bitter toll, and fills life with cries and blows. The thousand rivalries of our daily business, the fiercer animosities when we are beaten, the even fiercer exultation when we have beaten, the crashing blows of disaster, the piercing scream of defeat,—these things we have not yet gotten rid of, nor in this life ever will. Why should we wish to get rid of them? We are here, my brother, to be hewed and hammered and planed in God's quarry and on God's anvil for a nobler life to come." Only the muscle that is used is developed.

The constantly cheerful man, who survives his blighted hopes and disappointments, who takes them just for what they are, lessons, and perhaps blessings in disguise, is the true hero.

There is a strength
Deep bedded in our hearts of which we reck
But little, till the shafts of heaven have pierced
Its fragile dwelling. Must not earth be rent
Before her gems are found?
MRS. HEMANS.
"If what shone afar so grand
Turns to ashes in the hand,
On again, the virtue lies
In the struggle, not the prize."
"The hero is not fed on sweets,
Daily his own heart he eats;
Chambers of the great are jails,
And head-winds right for royal sails."
"So many great
Illustrious spirits have conversed with woe,
Have in her school been taught, as are enough
To consecrate distress, and make ambition
Even wish the frown beyond the smile of fortune."
Then welcome each rebuff,
That turns earth's smoothness rough,
Each sting, that bids not sit nor stand but go.
BROWNING.

CHAPTER VI. ONE UNWAVERING AIM.

Life is an arrow—therefore you must know
What mark to aim at, how to use the bow—
Then draw it to the head and let it go.
HENRY VAN DYKE.
The important thing in life is to have a great aim, and to possess the aptitude and perseverance to attain it.—GOETHE.

Concentration alone conquers.—C. BUXTON.

"He who follows two hares is sure to catch neither."

"A double-minded man is unstable in all his ways."

Let every one ascertain his special business and calling, and then stick to it if he would be successful.—FRANKLIN.

"Digression is as dangerous as stagnation in the career of a young man in business."

Every man who observes vigilantly and resolves steadfastly grows unconsciously into genius.—BULWER.

Genius is intensity.—BALZAC.

"Why do you lead such a solitary life?" asked a friend of Michael Angelo. "Art is a jealous mistress," replied the artist; "she requires the whole man." During his labors at the Sistine Chapel, according to Disraeli, he refused to meet any one, even at his own house.

"That day we sailed westward, which was our course," were the simple but grand words which Columbus wrote in his journal day after day. Hope might rise and fall, terror and dismay might seize upon the crew at the mysterious variations of the compass, but Columbus, unappalled, pushed due west and nightly added to his record the above words.

"Cut an inch deeper," said a member of the Old Guard to the surgeon probing his wound, "and you will find the Emperor,"—meaning his heart. By the marvelous power of concentrated purpose Napoleon had left his name on the very stones of the capital, had burned it indelibly into the heart of every Frenchman, and had left it written in living letters all over Europe. France to-day has not shaken off the spell of that name. In the fair city on the Seine the mystic "N" confronts you everywhere.

Oh, the power of a great purpose to work miracles! It has changed the face of the world.

Napoleon knew that there were plenty of great men in France, but they did not know the might of the unwavering aim by which he was changing the destinies of Europe. He saw that what was called the "balance of power" was only an idle dream; that, unless some master-mind could be found which was a match for events, the millions would rule in anarchy. His iron will grasped the situation; and like William Pitt, he did not loiter around balancing the probabilities of failure or success, or dally with his purpose. There was no turning to the right nor to the left; no dreaming away time, nor building air-castles; but one look and purpose, forward, upward and onward, straight to his goal. He always hit the bull's-eye. His great success in war was due largely to his definiteness of aim. He was like a great burning-glass, concentrating the rays of the sun upon a single spot; he burned a hole wherever he went. The secret of his power lay in his ability to concentrate his forces upon a single point. After finding the weak place in the enemy's ranks, he would mass his men and hurl them like an avalanche upon the critical point, crowding volley upon volley, charge upon charge, till he made a breach. What a lesson of the power of concentration there is in this man's life! He was able to focus all his faculties upon the smallest detail, as well as upon an empire. But, alas! Napoleon was himself defeated by violation of his own tactics,—the constantly repeated crushing force of heavy battalions upon one point.

To succeed to-day a man must concentrate all the faculties of his mind upon one unwavering aim, and have a tenacity of purpose which means death or victory. Every other inclination which tempts him from his aim must be suppressed.

New Jersey has many ports, but they are so shallow and narrow that the shipping of the entire state amounts to but little. On the other hand, New York has but one ocean port, and yet it is so broad, deep, and grand, that it leads America in its enormous shipping trade. She sends her vessels into every port of the world, while the ships of her neighbor are restricted to local voyages.

A man may starve on a dozen half-learned trades or occupations; he may grow rich and famous upon one trade thoroughly mastered, even though it be the humblest.

Even Gladstone, with his ponderous yet active brain, says he cannot do two things at once; he throws his entire strength upon whatever he does. The intensest energy characterizes everything he undertakes, even his recreation. If such concentration of energy is necessary for the success of a Gladstone, what can we common mortals hope to accomplish by "scatteration?"

All great men have been noted for their power of concentration which makes them oblivious of everything outside their aim. Victor Hugo wrote his "Notre Dame" during the revolution of 1830, while the bullets were whistling across his garden. He shut himself up in one room, locking his clothes up, lest they should tempt him to go out into the street, and spent most of that winter wrapped in a big gray comforter, pouring his very life into his work.

Genius is intensity. Abraham Lincoln possessed such power of concentration that he could repeat quite correctly a sermon to which he had listened in his boyhood. Dr. O. W. Holmes, when an Andover student, riveted his eyes on the book he was studying as though he were reading a will that made him heir to a million.

A New York sportsman, in answer to an advertisement, sent twenty-five cents for a sure receipt to prevent a shotgun from scattering, and received the following; "Dear Sir: To keep a gun from scattering put in but a single shot."

It is the men who do one thing in this world who come to the front. Who is the favorite actor? It is a Jefferson, who devotes a lifetime to a "Rip Van Winkle," a Booth, an Irving, a Kean, who plays one character until he can play it better than any other man living, and not the shallow players who impersonate all parts. It is the man who never steps outside of his specialty or dissipates his individuality. It is an Edison, a Morse, a Bell, a Howe, a Stephenson, a Watt. It is Adam Smith, spending ten years on the "Wealth of Nations." It is Gibbon, giving twenty years to his "Decline and Fall of the Roman Empire." It is a Hume, writing thirteen hours a day on his "History of England." It is a Webster, spending thirty-six years on his dictionary. It is a Bancroft, working twenty-six years on his "History of the United States." It is a Field, crossing the ocean fifty times to lay a cable, while the world ridicules. It is a Newton, writing his "Chronology of Ancient Nations" sixteen times. It is a Grant, who proposes to "fight it out on this line if it takes all summer." These are the men who have written their names prominently in the history of the world.

A one-talent man who decides upon a definite object accomplishes more than the ten-talent man who scatters his energies and never knows exactly what he will do. The weakest living creature, by concentrating his powers upon one thing, can accomplish something; the strongest, by dispersing his over many, may fail to accomplish anything. Drop after drop, continually falling, wears a passage through the hardest rock. The hasty tempest, as Carlyle points out, rushes over it with hideous uproar and leaves no trace behind.

A great purpose is cumulative; and, like a great magnet, it attracts all that is kindred along the stream of life.

A Yankee can splice a rope in many different ways; an English sailor only knows one way, but that is the best one. It is the one-sided man, the sharp-edged man, the man of single and intense purpose, the man of one idea, who turns neither to the right nor to the left, though a paradise tempt him, who cuts his way through obstacles and forges to the front. The time has gone forever when a Bacon can span universal knowledge; or when, absorbing all the knowledge of the times, a Dante can sustain arguments against fourteen disputants in the University of Paris, and conquer in them all. The day when a man can successfully drive a dozen callings abreast is a thing of the past. Concentration is the keynote of the century.

Scientists estimate that there is energy enough in less than fifty acres of sunshine to run all the machinery in the world, if it could be concentrated. But the sun might blaze out upon the earth forever without setting anything on fire; although these rays focused by a burning-glass would melt solid granite, or even change a diamond into vapor. There are plenty of men who have ability enough; the rays of their faculties, taken separately, are all right, but they are powerless to collect them, to bring them all to bear upon a single spot. Versatile men, universal geniuses, are usually weak, because they have no power to concentrate their talents upon one point, and this makes all the difference between success and failure.

Chiseled upon the tomb of a disappointed, heart-broken king, Joseph II. of Austria, in the Royal Cemetery at Vienna, a traveler tells us, is this epitaph: "Here lies a monarch who, with the best of intentions, never carried out a single plan."

Sir James Mackintosh was a man of remarkable ability. He excited in every one who knew him the greatest expectations. Many watched his career with much interest, expecting that he would dazzle the world. But there was no purpose in his life. He had intermittent attacks of enthusiasm for doing great things, but his zeal all evaporated before he could decide what to do. This fatal defect in his character kept him balancing between conflicting motives; and his whole life was almost thrown away. He lacked power to choose one object and persevere with a single aim, sacrificing every interfering inclination. He vacillated for weeks trying to determine whether to use "usefulness" or "utility" in a composition.

One talent utilized in a single direction will do infinitely more than ten talents scattered. A thimbleful of powder behind a ball in a rifle will do more execution than a carload of powder unconfined. The rifle-barrel is the purpose that gives direct aim to the powder, which otherwise, no matter how good it might be, would be powerless. The poorest scholar in school or college often, in practical life, far outstrips the class leader or senior wrangler, simply because what little ability he has he employs for a definite object, while the other, depending upon his general ability and brilliant prospects, never concentrates his powers.

"A sublime self-confidence," says E. P. Whipple, "springing not from self-conceit, but from an intense identification of the man with his object, lifts him altogether above the fear of danger and death, and communicates an almost superhuman audacity to his will."

What a sublime spectacle is that of a man going straight to his goal, cutting his way through difficulties, and surmounting obstacles which dishearten others, as though they were stepping-stones.

It is fashionable to ridicule the man of one idea, but the men who have changed the front of the world have been men of a single aim. No man can make his mark on this age of specialties who is not a man of one idea, one supreme aim, one master passion. The man who would make himself felt on this bustling planet, who would make a breach in the compact conservatism of our civilization, must play all his guns on one point. A wavering aim, a faltering purpose, has no place in the nineteenth century. "Mental shiftlessness" is the cause of many a failure. The world is full of unsuccessful men who spend their lives letting empty buckets down into empty wells.

"Mr. A. often laughs at me," said a young American chemist, "because I have but one idea. He talks about everything, aims to excel in many things; but I have learned that, if I ever wish to make a breach, I must play my guns continually upon one point." This great chemist, when an obscure schoolmaster, used to study by the light of a pine knot in a log cabin. Not many years later he was performing experiments in electro-magnetism before English earls, and subsequently he was at the head of one of the largest scientific institutes of this country. This man was the late Professor Henry, of the Smithsonian Institution, Washington.

Douglas Jerrold once knew a man who was familiar with twenty-four languages but could not express a thought in one of them.

We should guard against a talent which we cannot hope to practice in perfection, says Goethe. Improve it as we may, we shall always, in the end, when the merit of the matter has become apparent to us, painfully lament the loss of time and strength devoted to such botching. An old proverb says: "The master of one trade will support a wife and seven children, and the master of seven will not support himself."

It is the single aim that wins. Men with monopolizing ambitions rarely live in history. They do not focus their powers long enough to burn their names indelibly into the roll of honor. Edward Everett, even with his magnificent powers, disappointed the expectations of his friends. He spread himself over the whole field of knowledge and elegant culture; but the mention of the name of Everett does not call up any one great achievement as does that of names like Garrison and Phillips. Voltaire called the Frenchman La Harpe an oven which was always heating, but which never cooked anything. Hartley Coleridge was splendidly endowed with talent, like Sir James Mackintosh, but there was one fatal lack in his character—he had no definite purpose, and his life was a failure. Unstable as water, he could not excel. Southey, his uncle, says:

"Coleridge has two left hands." He was so morbidly shy from living alone in his dreamland that he could not open a letter without trembling. He would often rally from his purposeless life, and resolve to redeem himself from the oblivion he saw staring him in the face; but, like Mackintosh, he remained a man of promise merely to the end of his life.

The world always makes way for the man with a purpose in him, like Bismarck or Grant. Look at Rufus Choate, concentrating all his attention first on one juryman, then on another, going back over the whole line again and again, until he has burned his arguments into their souls; until he has hypnotized them with his purpose; until they see with his eyes, think his thoughts, feel his sensations. He never stopped until he had projected his mind into theirs, and permeated their lives with his individuality. There was no escape from his concentration of purpose, his persuasive rhetoric, his convincing logic. "Carry the jury at all hazards," he used to say to young lawyers; "move heaven and earth to carry the jury, and then fight it out with the judge on the law questions as best you can."

The man who succeeds has a programme. He fixes his course and adheres to it. He lays his plans and executes them. He goes straight to his goal. He is not pushed this way and that every time a difficulty is thrown in his path; if he can't get over it he goes through it. Constant and steady use of the faculties under a central purpose gives strength and power, while the use of faculties without an aim or end only weakens them. The mind must be focused on a definite end, or, like machinery without a balance-wheel, it will rack itself to pieces.

This age of concentration calls, not for educated men merely, not for talented men, not for geniuses, not for jacks-of-all-trades, but for men who are trained to do one thing as well as it can be done. Napoleon could go through the drill of his soldiers better than any one of his men.

Stick to your aim. The constant changing of one's occupation is fatal to all success. After a young man has spent five or six years in a dry goods store, he concludes that he would rather sell groceries, thereby throwing away five years of valuable experience which will be of very little use to him in the grocery business; and so he spends a large part of his life drifting around from one kind of employment to another, learning part of each, but all of none, forgetting that experience is worth more to him than money, and that the years devoted to learning his trade or occupation are the most valuable. Half-learned trades, no matter if a man has twenty, will never give him a good living, much less a competency, while wealth is absolutely out of the question.

How many young men fail to reach the point of efficiency in one line of work before they get discouraged and venture into something else. How easy to see the thorns in one's own profession or vocation, and only the roses in that of another. A young man in business, for instance, seeing a physician riding about town in his carriage, visiting his patients, imagines that a doctor must have an easy, ideal life, and wonders that he himself should have embarked in an occupation so full of disagreeable drudgery and hardships. He does not know of the years of dry, tedious study which the physician has consumed, the months and perhaps years of waiting for patients, the dry detail of anatomy, the endless names of drugs and technical terms.

Scientists tell us that there is nothing in nature so ugly and disagreeable but intense light will make it beautiful. The complete mastery of one profession will render even the driest details interesting. The consciousness of thorough knowledge, the habit of doing everything to a finish, gives a feeling of strength, of superiority, which takes the drudgery out of an occupation. The more completely we master a vocation the more thoroughly we enjoy it. In fact, the man who has found his place and become master in it could scarcely be induced, even though he be a farmer, or a carpenter, or grocer, to exchange places with a governor or congressman. To be successful is to find your sphere and fill it, to get into your place and master it.

There is a sense of great power in a vocation after a man has reached the point of efficiency in it, the point of productiveness, the point where his skill begins to tell and bring in returns. Up to this point of efficiency, while he is learning his trade, the time seems to have been almost thrown away. But he has been storing up a vast reserve of knowledge of detail, laying foundations, forming his acquaintances, gaining his reputation for truthfulness, trustworthiness, and integrity, and in establishing his credit. When he reaches this point of efficiency, all the knowledge and skill, character, influence, and credit thus gained come to his aid, and he soon finds that in what seemed almost thrown away lies the secret of his prosperity. The credit he established as a clerk, the confidence, the integrity, the friendships formed, he finds equal to a large capital when he starts out for himself and takes the highway to fortune; while the young man who half learned several trades, and got discouraged and stopped just short of the point of efficiency, just this side of success, is a failure because he didn't go far enough; he did not press on to the point at which his acquisition would have been profitable.

In spite of the fact that nearly all very successful men have made a life work of one thing, we see on every hand hundreds of young men and women flitting about from occupation to occupation, trade to trade, in one thing to-day and another to-morrow,—just as though they could go from one thing to another by turning a switch, as if they could run as well on another track as on the one they have left, regardless of the fact that no two careers have the same gauge, that every man builds his own road upon which another's engine cannot run either with speed or safety. This fickleness, this disposition to shift about from one occupation to another, seems to be peculiar to

American life, so much so that, when a young man meets a friend whom he has not seen for some time, the commonest question to ask is, "What are you doing now?" showing the improbability or uncertainty that he is doing to-day what he was doing when they last met.

Some people think that if they "keep everlastingly at it" they will succeed, but this is not so. Working without a plan is as foolish as going to sea without a compass. A ship which has broken its rudder in mid-ocean may "keep everlastingly at it," may keep on a full head of steam, driving about all the time, but it never arrives anywhere, it never reaches any port unless by accident, and if it does find a haven, its cargo may not be suited to the people, the climate, or conditions among which it has accidentally drifted. The ship must be directed to a definite port, for which its cargo is adapted, and where there is a demand for it, and it must aim steadily for that port through sunshine and storm, through tempest and fog. So a man who would succeed must not drift about rudderless on the ocean of life. He must not only steer straight toward his destined port when the ocean is smooth, when the currents and winds serve, but he must keep his course in the very teeth of the wind and the tempest, and even when enveloped in the fogs of disappointment and mists of opposition. The Cunarders do not stop for fogs or storms; they plow straight through the rough seas with only one thing in view, their destined port, and no matter what the weather is, no matter what obstacles they encounter, their arrival in port can be predicted to within a few hours. It is practically certain, too, that the ship destined for Boston will not turn up at Fort Sumter or at Sandy Hook.

On the prairies of South America there grows a flower that always inclines in the same direction. If a traveler loses his way and has neither compass nor chart, by turning to this flower he will find a guide on which he can implicitly rely; for no matter how the rains descend or the winds blow, its leaves point to the north. So there are many men whose purposes are so well known, whose aims are so constant, that no matter what difficulties they may encounter, or what opposition they may meet, you can tell almost to a certainty where they will come out. They may be delayed by head winds and counter currents, but they will always head for the port and will steer straight towards the harbor. You know to a certainty that whatever else they may lose, they will not lose their compass or rudder.

Whatever may happen to a man of this stamp, even though his sails may be swept away and his mast stripped to the deck, though he may be wrecked by the storms of life, the needle of his compass will still point to the North Star of his hope. Whatever comes, his life will not be purposeless. Even a wreck that makes its port is a greater success than a full-rigged ship with all its sails flying, with every mast and rope intact; which merely drifts into an accidental harbor.

To fix a wandering life and give it direction is not an easy task, but a life which has no definite aim is sure to be frittered away in empty and purposeless dreams. "Listless triflers," "busy idlers," "purposeless busybodies," are seen everywhere. A healthy, definite purpose is a remedy for a thousand ills which attend aimless lives. Discontent, dissatisfaction, flee before a definite purpose. An aim takes the drudgery out of life, scatters doubts to the winds, and clears up the gloomiest creeds. What we do without a purpose begrudgingly, with a purpose becomes a delight, and no work is well done nor healthily done which is not enthusiastically done. It is just that added element which makes work immortal.

Mere energy is not enough, it must be concentrated on some steady, unwavering aim. What is more common than "unsuccessful geniuses," or failures with "commanding talents"? Indeed, "unrewarded genius" has become a proverb. Every town has unsuccessful educated and talented men. But education is of no value, talent is worthless, unless it can do something, achieve something. Men who can do something at everything, and a very little at anything, are not wanted in this age. In Paris, a certain Monsieur Kenard announced himself as a "public scribe, who digests accounts, explains the language of flowers, and sells fried potatoes." Jacks-at-all-trades are at war with the genius of the times.

What this age wants is young men and women who can do one thing without losing their identity or individuality, or becoming narrow, cramped, or dwarfed. Nothing can take the place of an all-absorbing purpose; education will not, genius will not, talent will not, industry will not, will-power will not. The purposeless life must ever be a failure. What good are powers, faculties, unless we can use them for a purpose? What good would a chest of tools do a carpenter unless he could use them? A college education, a head full of knowledge, are worth little to the men who cannot use them to some definite end.

The man without a purpose never leaves his mark upon the world. He has no individuality; he is absorbed in the mass, lost in the crowd, weak, wavering, incompetent. His outlines of individuality and angles of character have been worn off, planed down to suit the common thought until he has, as a man, been lost in the throng of humanity.

"He who would do some great thing in this short life must apply himself to the work with such a concentration of his forces as, to idle spectators, who live only to amuse themselves, looks like insanity."

What a great directness of purpose may be traced in the career of Pitt, who lived—ay, and died—for the sake of political supremacy. From a child, the idea was drilled into him that he must accomplish a public career worthy of his illustrious father. Even from boyhood he bent all his energy to this one great purpose. He went straight from college to the House of Commons. In one year he was Chancellor of the Exchequer; two years later he was Prime Minister of England, and reigned virtually king for a quarter of a century. He was utterly oblivious of everything outside his aim; insensible to the claims of love, art, literature, living and steadily working for the sole purpose of wielding the governing power of the nation. His whole soul was absorbed in the overmastering passion for political power.

"Consider, my lord," said Rowland Hill to the Prime Minister of England, "that a letter to Ireland and the answer back would cost thousands upon thousands of my affectionate countrymen more than a fifth of their week's wages. If you shut the post office to them, which you do now, you shut out warm hearts and generous affections from home, kindred, and friends." The lad learned that it cost to carry a letter from London to Edinburgh, four hundred and four miles, one eighteenth of a cent, while the government charged for a simple folded sheet of paper twenty-eight cents, and twice as much if there was the smallest inclosure. Against the opposition and contempt of the post-office department he at length carried his point, and on January 10, 1840, penny postage was established throughout Great Britain. Mr. Hill was chosen to introduce the system, at a salary of fifteen hundred pounds a year. His success was most encouraging, but at the end of two years a Tory minister dismissed him without paying for his services, as agreed. The public was indignant, and at once contributed sixty-five thousand dollars; and, at the request of Queen Victoria, Parliament voted him one hundred thousand dollars and ten thousand dollars a year for life.

Christ knew that one affection rules in man's life when he said, "No man can serve two masters." One affection, one object, will be supreme in us. Everything else will be neglected and done with half a heart. One may have subordinate plans, but he can have but one supreme aim, and from this aim all others will take their character.

It is a great purpose which gives meaning to life, it unifies all our powers, binds them together in one cable; makes strong and united what was weak, separated, scattered.

"Painting is my wife and my works are my children," replied Michael Angelo when asked why he did not marry.

"Smatterers" are weak and superficial. Of what use is a man who knows a little of everything and not much of anything? It is the momentum of constantly repeated acts that tells the story. "Let thine eyes look straight before thee. Ponder the path of thy feet and let all thy ways be established. Turn not to the right hand nor to the left." One great secret of St. Paul's power lay in his strong purpose. Nothing could daunt him, nothing intimidate. The Roman Emperor could not muzzle him, the dungeon could not appall him, no prison suppress him, obstacles could not discourage him. "This one thing I do" was written all over his work. The quenchless zeal of his mighty purpose burned its way down through the centuries, and its contagion will never cease to fire the hearts of men.

"Try and come home somebody," said the fond mother to Gambetta as she sent him off to Paris to school. Poverty pinched this lad hard in his little garret study and his clothes were shabby, but what of that? He had made up his mind to get on in the world. For years this youth was chained to his desk and worked like a hero. At last his opportunity came. Jules Favre was to plead a great cause on a certain day; but, being ill, he chose this young man, absolutely unknown, rough and uncouth, to take his place. For many years Gambetta had been preparing for such an opportunity, and he was equal to it, for he made one of the greatest speeches that up to that time had ever been made in France. That night all the papers in Paris were sounding the praises of this ragged, uncouth Bohemian, and soon all France recognized him as the Republican leader. This sudden rise was not due to luck or accident. He had been steadfastly working and fighting his way up against opposition and poverty for just such an occasion. Had he not been equal to it, it would only have made him ridiculous. What a stride; yesterday, poor and unknown, living in a garret, to-day, deputy elect, in the city of Marseilles, and the great Republican leader! The gossipers of France had never heard his name before. He had been expelled from the priest-making seminary as totally unfit for a priest and an utterly undisciplinable character. In two weeks, this ragged son of an Italian grocer arose in the Chamber, and moved that the Napoleon dynasty be disposed of and the Republic be declared established.

When Louis Napoleon had been defeated at Sedan and had delivered his sword to William of Prussia, and when the Prussian army was marching on Paris, the brave Gambetta went out of the besieged city in a balloon barely grazed by the Prussian guns, landed in Amiens, and by almost superhuman skill raised three armies of 800,000 men, provided for their maintenance, and directed their military operations. A German officer said, "This colossal energy is the most remarkable event of modern history, and will carry down Gambetta's name to remote posterity." This youth who was poring over his books in an attic while other youths were promenading the Champs Élysées, although but thirty-two years old, was now virtually dictator of France, and the greatest orator in the Republic. What a striking example of the great reserve of personal power, which, even in dissolute lives, is sometimes called out by a great emergency or sudden sorrow, and ever after leads the life to victory! When Gambetta found that his first speech had electrified all France, his great reserve rushed to the front, he was suddenly weaned from dissipation, and resolved to make his mark in the world. Nor did he lose his head in his quick leap into fame. He still lived in the upper room in the musty Latin quarter, and remained a poor man, without stain of dishonor, though he might easily have made himself a millionaire. When Gambetta died the "Figaro" said, "The Republic has lost its greatest man." American boys should study this great man, for he loved our country, and made our Republic the pattern for France.

There is no grander sight in the world than that of a young man fired with a great purpose, dominated by one unwavering aim. He is bound to win; the world stands one side and lets him pass; it always makes way for the man with a will in him. He does not have one half the opposition to overcome that the undecided, purposeless man has who, like driftwood, runs against all sorts of snags to which he must yield, because he has no momentum to force them out of his way. What a sublime spectacle it is to see a youth going straight to his goal, cutting his way through difficulties, and surmounting obstacles, which dishearten others, as though they were but stepping-stones! Defeat, like a gymnasium, only gives him new power; opposition only doubles his exertions, dangers only increase his courage. No matter what comes to him, sickness, poverty, disaster, he never turns his eye from his goal.

"Duos qui sequitur lepores, neutrum capit."

CHAPTER VII. SOWING AND REAPING.

Be not deceived; God is not mocked: for whatsoever a man soweth, that shall he also reap.—GALATIANS.

Sow an act, and you reap a habit; sow a habit, and you reap a character; sow a character, and you reap a destiny.—G. D. BOARDMAN.

Just as the twig is bent the tree's inclined.—POPE.

How use doth breed a habit in a man.—SHAKESPEARE.

All habits gather, by unseen degrees,
As brooks make rivers, rivers run to seas.
DRYDEN.
Infinite good comes from good habits which must result from the common influence of example, intercourse, knowledge, and actual experience—morality taught by good morals.—PLATO.

The chains of habit are generally too small to be felt till they are too strong to be broken.—SAMUEL JOHNSON.

Man is first startled by sin; then it becomes pleasing, then easy, then delightful, then frequent, then habitual, then confirmed. Then man is impenitent, then obstinate, then he is damned.—JEREMY TAYLOR.

"Rogues differ little. Each began as a disobedient son."

In the great majority of things, habit is a greater plague than ever afflicted Egypt.—JOHN FOSTER.

You cannot in any given case, by any sudden and single effort, will to be true if the habit of your life has been insincere.—F. W. ROBERTSON.

The tissue of the life to be,
We weave with colors all our own;
And in the field of destiny,
We reap as we have sown.
WHITTIER.

"Gentlemen of the jury, you will now consider your verdict," said the great lawyer, Lord Tenterden, as he roused from his lethargy a moment, and then closed his eyes forever. "Tête d'armée" (head of the army), murmured Napoleon faintly; and then, "on the wings of a tempest that raged with unwonted fury, up to the throne of the only power that controlled him while he lived, went the fiery soul of that wonderful warrior." "Give Dayrolles a chair," said the dying Chesterfield with his old-time courtesy, and the next moment his spirit spread its wings. "Young man, keep your record clean," thrilled from the lips of John B. Gough as he sank to rise no more. What power over the mind of man is exercised by the dominant idea of his life "that parts not quite with parting breath!" It has shaped his purpose throughout his earthly career, and he passes into the Great Unknown, moving in the direction of his ideal; impelled still, amid the utter retrocession of the vital force, by all the momentum resulting from his weight of character and singleness of aim.

It is a beautiful arrangement in the mental and
moral economy of our nature, that that which is performed as a duty may, by frequent repetitions, become a habit, and the habit of stern virtue, so repulsive to others, may hang around the neck like a wreath of flowers."

Cholera appeared mysteriously in Toulon, and, after a careful examination, the medical inspectors learned that the first victims were two sailors on the Montebello, a government transport, long out of service, anchored at the entrance to the port. For many years the vessel had been used for storing old, disused military equipments. Some of these had belonged to French soldiers who had died before Sebastopol. The doctors learned that the two poor sailors were seized, suddenly and mortally, a few days after displacing a pile of equipments stored deep in the hold of the Montebello. The cholera of Toulon came in a direct line from the hospital of Varna. It went to sleep, apparently gorged, on a heap of the cast-off garments of its victims, to awaken thirty years later to victorious and venomous life.

Professor Bonelli, of Turin, punctured an animal with the tooth of a rattlesnake. The head of this serpent had lain in a dry state for sixteen years exposed to the air and dust, and, moreover, had previously been preserved more than thirty years in spirits of wine. To his great astonishment an hour afterward the animal died. So habits, good or bad, that have been lost sight of for years will spring into a new life to aid or injure us at some critical moment, as kernels of wheat which had been clasped in a mummy's hand four thousand years sprang into life when planted. They only awaited moisture, heat, sunlight, and air to develop them.

In Jefferson's play, Rip Van Winkle, after he had "sworn off," at every invitation to drink said, "Well, this time don't count." True, as Professor James says, he may not have counted it, as thousands of others have not counted it, and a kind heaven may not count it, but it is being counted none the less. Down among his nerve cells and fibres the molecules are counting it, registering and storing it up to be used against him when the next temptation comes. Nothing we ever do is in strict scientific literalness wiped out. There is a tendency in the nervous system to repeat the same mode of action at regularly recurring intervals. Dr. Combe says that all nervous diseases have a marked tendency to observe regular periods. "If we repeat any kind of mental effort at the same hour daily, we at length find ourselves entering upon it without premeditation when the time approaches."

"The great thing in all education is to make our nervous system our ally instead of our enemy. It is to fund and capitalize our acquisition, and live at ease upon the interest of the fund. For this we must make automatic and habitual, as soon as possible, as many useful actions as we can, and guard against the growing into ways that are likely to be disadvantageous to us, as we would guard against the plague."

The nervous system is a living phonograph, infinitely more marvelous than that of Edison. No sound, however feeble, however slight, can escape being recorded in its wonderful mechanism. Although the molecules of this living machine may all be entirely changed many times during a lifetime, yet these impressions are never erased or lost. They become forever fixed in the character. Like Rip Van Winkle, the youth may say to himself, I will do this just once "just to see what it is like," no one will ever know it, and "I won't count this time." The country youth says it when he goes to the city. The young man says it when he drinks "just to be social." Americans, who are good church people at home, say it when in Paris and Vienna. Yes, "just to see what it is like" has ruined many a noble life. Many a man has lost his balance and fallen over the precipice into the sink of iniquity while just attempting "to see what it was like." "If you have been pilot on these waters twenty-five years," said a young man to the captain of a steamer, "you must know every rock and sandbank in the river." "No, I don't, but I know where the deep water is."

Just one little lie to help me out of this difficulty; "I won't count this." Just one little embezzlement; no one will know it, and I can return the money before it will be needed. Just one little indulgence; I won't count it, and a good night's sleep will make me all right again. Just one small part of my work slighted; it won't make any great difference, and, besides, I am usually so careful that a little thing like this ought not to be counted.

But, my young friend, it will be counted, whether you will or not; the deed has been recorded with an iron pen, even to the smallest detail. The Recording Angel is no myth; it is found in ourselves. Its name is Memory, and it holds everything. We think we have forgotten thousands of things until mortal danger, fever, or some other great stimulus reproduces them to the consciousness with all the fidelity of photographs. Sometimes all one's past life will seem to pass before him in an instant; but at all times it is really, although unconsciously, passing before him in the sentiments he feels, in the thoughts he thinks, in the impulses that move him apparently without cause.

"Our acts our angels are, or good or ill,
Our fatal shadows that walk by us still."

In a fable one of the Fates spun filaments so fine that they were invisible, and she became a victim of her cunning, for she was bound to the spot by these very threads.

Father Schoenmaker, missionary to the Indians, tried for years to implant civilization among the wild tribes. After fifteen years' labor he induced a chief to lay aside his blanket, the token of savagery; but he goes on to say, "It took fifteen years to get it off, and just fifteen minutes to get it on him again."

Physiologists say that dark-colored stripes similar to those on the zebra reappear, after a hundred or a thousand generations, on the legs and shoulders of horses, asses, and mules. Large birds on sea islands where there are no beasts to molest them lose the power of flight.

After a criminal's head had been cut off his breast was irritated, and he raised his hands several times as if to brush away the exciting cause. It was said that the cheek of Charlotte Corday blushed on being struck by a rude soldier after the head had been severed from the body.

Humboldt found in South America a parrot which was the only living creature that could speak a word of the language of a lost tribe. The bird retained the habit of speech after his teachers had died.

Caspar Hauser was confined, probably from birth, in a dungeon where no light or sound from the outer world, could reach him. At seventeen he was still a mental infant, crying and chattering without much apparent intelligence. When released, the light was disagreeable to his eyes; and, after the babbling youth had been taught to speak a few words, he begged to be taken back to the dungeon. Only cold and dismal silence seemed to satisfy him. All that gave pleasure to others gave his perverted senses only pain. The sweetest music was a source of anguish to him, and he could eat only his black crust without violent vomiting.

Deep in the very nature of animate existence is that principle of facility and inclination, acquired by repetition, which we call habit. Man becomes a slave to his constantly repeated acts. In spite of the protests of his weakened will the trained nerves continue to repeat the acts even when the doer abhors them. What he at first chooses, at last compels. Man is as irrevocably chained to his deeds as the atoms are chained by gravitation. You can as easily snatch a pebble from gravitation's grasp as you can separate the minutest act of life from its inevitable effect upon character and destiny. "Children may be strangled," says George Eliot, "but deeds never, they have an indestructible life." The smirched youth becomes the tainted man.

Practically all the achievements of the human race are but the accomplishments of habit. We speak of the power of Gladstone to accomplish so much in a day as something marvelous; but when we analyze that power we find it composed very largely of the results of habit. His mighty momentum has been rendered possible only by the law of the power of habit. He is now a great bundle of habits, which all his life have been forming. His habit of industry no doubt was irksome and tedious at first, but, practiced so conscientiously and persistently, it has gained such momentum as to astonish the world. His habit of thinking, close, persistent, and strong, has made him a power. He formed the habit of accurate, keen observation, allowing nothing to escape his attention, until he could observe more in half a day in London than a score of men who have eyes but see not. Thus he has multiplied himself many times. By this habit of accuracy he has avoided many a repetition; and so, during his lifetime, he has saved years of precious time, which many others, who marvel at his achievements, have thrown away.

Gladstone early formed the habit of cheerfulness, of looking on the bright side of things, which, Sydney Smith says, "is worth a thousand pounds a year." This again has saved him enormous waste of energy, as he tells us he has never yet been kept awake a single hour by any debate or business in Parliament. This loss of energy has wasted years of many a useful life, which might have been saved by forming the economizing habit of cheerfulness.

The habit of happy thought would transform the commonest life into harmony and beauty. The will is almost omnipotent to determine habits which virtually are omnipotent. The habit of directing a firm and steady will upon those things which tend to produce harmony of thought would produce happiness and contentment even in the most lowly occupations. The will, rightly drilled, can drive out all discordant thoughts, and produce a reign of perpetual harmony. Our trouble is that we do not half will. After a man's habits are well set, about all he can do is to sit by and observe which way he is going. Regret it as he may, how helpless is a weak man bound by the mighty cable of habit, twisted from the tiny threads of single acts which he thought were absolutely within his control!

Drop a stone down a precipice. By the law of gravitation it sinks with rapidly increasing momentum. If it falls sixteen feet the first second, it will fall forty-eight feet the next second, and eighty feet the third second, and one hundred and forty-four feet the fifth second, and if it falls for ten seconds it will in the last second rush through three hundred and four feet till earth stops it. Habit is cumulative. After each act of our lives we are not the same person as before, but quite another, better or worse, but not the same. There has been something added to, or deducted from, our weight of character.

"There is no fault nor folly of my life," said Ruskin; "that does not rise against me and take away my joy, and shorten my power of possession, of sight, of understanding; and every past effort of my life, every gleam of righteousness or good in it, is with me now to help me in my grasp of this hour and its vision."

"Many men of genius have written worse scrawls than I do," said a boy at Rugby when his teacher remonstrated with him for his bad penmanship; "it is not worth while to worry about so trivial a fault." Ten years later, when he had become an officer in the Crimea, his illegible copy of an order caused the loss of many brave men.

"Resist beginning" was an ancient motto which is needed in our day. The folly of the child becomes the vice of the youth, and then the crime of the man.

In 1880 one hundred and forty-seven of the eight hundred and ninety-seven inmates of Auburn State Prison were there on a second visit. What brings the prisoner back the second, third, or fourth time? It is habit which drives him on to commit the deed which his heart abhors and which his very soul loathes. It is the momentum made up from a thousand deviations from the truth and right, for there is a great difference between going just right and a little wrong. It is the result of that mysterious power which the repeated act has of getting itself repeated again and again.

When a woman was dying from the effects of her husband's cruelty and debauchery from drink she asked him to come to her bedside, and pleaded with him again for the sake of their children to drink no more. Grasping his hand with her thin, long fingers, she made him promise her: "Mary, I will drink no more till I take it out of this hand which I hold in mine." That very night he poured out a tumbler of brandy, stole into the room where she lay cold in her coffin, put the tumbler into her withered hand, and then took it out and drained it to the bottom. John B. Gough told this as a true story. How powerless a man is in the presence of a mighty habit, which has robbed him of will-power, of self-respect, of everything manly, until he becomes its slave!

Walpole tells of a gambler who fell at the table in a fit of apoplexy, and his companions began to bet upon his chances of recovery. When the physician came they refused to let him bleed the man because they said it would affect the bet. When President Garfield was hanging between life and death men bet heavily upon the issue, and even sold pools.

No disease causes greater horror or dread than cholera; yet when it is once fastened upon a victim he is perfectly indifferent, and wonders at the solicitude of his friends. His tears are dried; he cannot weep if he would. His body is cold and clammy and feels like dead flesh, yet he tells you he is warm, and calls for ice water. Have you never seen similar insensibility to danger in those whose habits are already dragging them to everlasting death?

Etherized by the fascinations of pleasure, we are often unconscious of pain while the devil amputates the fingers, the feet and hands, or even the arms and legs of our character. But oh, the anguish that visits the sad heart when the lethe passes away, and the soul becomes conscious of virtue sacrificed, of manhood lost.

The leper is often the last to suspect his danger, for the disease is painless in its early stages. A leading lawyer and public official in the Sandwich Islands once overturned a lighted lamp on his hand, and was surprised to find that it caused no pain. At last it dawned upon his mind that he was a leper. He resigned his offices and went to the leper's island, where he died. So sin in its early stages is not only painless but often even pleasant.

The hardening, deadening power of depraving habits and customs was strikingly illustrated by the Romans.

Under Nero, the taste of the people had become so debauched and morbid that no mere representation of tragedy would satisfy them. Their cold-blooded selfishness, the hideous realism of "a refined, delicate, aesthetic age," demanded that the heroes should actually be killed on the stage. The debauched and sanguinary Romans reckoned life worthless without the most thrilling experiences of horror or delight. Tragedy must be genuine bloodshed, comedy, actual shame. When "The Conflagration" was represented on the stage they demanded that a house be actually burned and the furniture plundered. When "Laureolus" was played they demanded that the actor be really crucified and mangled by a bear, and he had to fling himself down and deluge the stage with his own blood. Prometheus must be really chained to his rock, and Dirce in very fact be tossed and gored by the wild bull, and Orpheus be torn to pieces by a real bear, and Icarus was compelled to fly, even though it was known he would be dashed to death. When the heroism of "Mucius Scaevola" was represented, a real criminal was compelled to thrust his hand into the flame without a murmur, and stand motionless while it was being burned. Hercules was compelled to ascend the funeral pyre, and there be burned alive. The poor slaves and criminals were compelled to play their parts heroically until the flames enveloped them.

The pirate Gibbs, who was executed in New York, said that when he robbed the first vessel his conscience made a hell in his bosom; but after he had sailed for years under the black flag, he could rob a vessel and murder all the crew, and lie down and sleep soundly. A man may so accustom himself to error as to become its most devoted slave, and be led to commit the most fearful crimes in order to defend it, or to propagate it.

When Gordon, the celebrated California stage-driver, was dying, he put his foot out of the bed and swung it to and fro. When asked why he did so, he replied, "I am on the down grade and cannot get my foot on the brake."

In our great museums you see stone slabs with the marks of rain that fell hundreds of years before Adam lived, and the footprint of some wild bird that passed across the beach in those olden times. The passing shower and the light foot left their prints on the soft sediment; then ages went on, and the sediment hardened into stone; and there the prints remain, and will remain forever. So the child, so soft, so susceptible to all impressions, so joyous to receive new ideas, treasures them all up, gathers them all into itself, and retains them forever.

A tribe of Indians attacked a white settlement and murdered the few inhabitants. A woman of the tribe, however, carried away a very young infant, and reared it as her own. The child grew up with the Indian children, different in complexion, but like them in everything else. To scalp the greatest possible number of enemies was, in his view, the most glorious thing in the world. While he was still a youth he was seen by some white traders, and by them conducted back to civilized life. He showed great relish for his new life, and especially a strong desire for knowledge and a sense of reverence which took the direction of religion, so that he desired to become a clergyman. He went through his college course with credit, and was ordained. He fulfilled his function well, and appeared happy and satisfied. After a few years he went to serve in a settlement somewhere near the seat of war which was then going on between Britain and the United States, and before long there was fighting not far off. He went forth in his usual dress— black coat and neat white shirt and neckcloth. When he returned he was met by a gentleman of his acquaintance, who was immediately struck by an extraordinary change in the expression of his face and the flush on his cheek, and also by his unusually shy and hurried manner. After asking news of the battle the gentleman observed, "But you are wounded?" "No." "Not wounded! Why, there is blood upon the bosom of your shirt!" The young man quickly crossed his hands firmly upon his breast; and his friend, supposing that he wished to conceal a wound which ought to be looked to, pulled open his shirt, and saw—what made the young man let fall his hands in despair. From between his shirt and his breast the friend took out—a bloody scalp! "I could not help it," said the poor victim of early habits, in an agonized voice. He turned and ran, too swiftly to be overtaken, betook himself to the Indians, and never more appeared among the whites.

An Indian once brought up a young lion, and finding him weak and harmless, did not attempt to control him. Every day the lion gained in strength and became more unmanageable, until at last, when excited by rage, he fell upon his master and tore him to pieces. So what seemed to be an "innocent" sin has grown until it strangled him who was once its easy master.

Beware of looking at sin, for at each view it is apt to become better looking.

Habit is practically, for a middle-aged person, fate; for is it not practically certain that what I have done for twenty years I shall repeat to-day? What are the chances for a man who has been lazy and indolent all his life starting in to-morrow morning to be industrious; or a spendthrift, frugal; a libertine, virtuous; a profane, foul-mouthed man, clean and chaste?

A Grecian flute-player charged double fees for pupils who had been taught by inferior masters, on the ground that it was much harder to undo than to form habits.

Habit tends to make us permanently what we are for the moment. We cannot possibly hear, see, feel, or experience anything which is not woven in the web of character. What we are this minute and what we do this minute, what we think this minute, will be read in the future character as plainly as words spoken into the phonograph can be reproduced in the future.

"The air itself," says Babbage, "is one vast library on whose pages are written forever all that man has ever said, whispered, or done." Every sin you ever committed becomes your boon companion. It rushes to your lips every time you speak, and drags its hideous form into your imagination every time you think. It throws its shadow across your path whichever way you turn. Like Banquo's ghost, it will not down. You are fastened to it for life, and it will cling to you in the vast forever. Do you think yourself free? You are a slave to every sin you ever committed. They follow your pen and work their own character into every word you write.

Rectitude is only the confirmed habit of doing what is right. Some men cannot tell a lie: the habit of truth telling is fixed, it has become incorporated with their nature. Their characters bear the indelible stamp of veracity. You and I know men whose slightest word is unimpeachable; nothing could shake our confidence in them. There are other men who cannot speak the truth: their habitual insincerity has made a twist in their characters, and this twist appears in their speech.

"I never in my life committed more than one act of folly," said Rulhière one day in the presence of Talleyrand. "But where will it end?" inquired the latter. It was lifelong. One mistake too many makes all the difference between safety and destruction.

How many men would like to go to sleep beggars and wake up Rothschilds or Astors? How many would fain go to bed dunces and wake up Solomons? You reap what you have sown. Those who have sown dunce-seed, vice-seed, laziness-seed, always get a crop. They that sow the wind shall reap the whirlwind.

Habit, like a child, repeats whatever is done before it. Oh, the power of a repeated act to get itself repeated again and again! But, like the wind, it is a power which we can use to force our way in its very teeth as does the ship, and thus multiply our strength, or we can drift with it without exertion upon the rocks and shoals of destruction.

What a great thing it is to "start right" in life. Every young man can see that the first steps lead to the last, with all except his own. No, his little prevarications and dodgings will not make him a liar, but he can see that they surely will in John Smith's case. He can see that others are idle and on the road to ruin, but cannot see it in his own case.

There is a wonderful relation between bad habits. They all belong to the same family. If you take in one, no matter how small or insignificant it may seem, you will soon have the whole. A man who has formed the habit of laziness or idleness will soon be late at his engagements; a man who does not meet his engagements will dodge, apologize, prevaricate, and lie. I have rarely known a perfectly truthful man who was always behind time.

You have seen a ship out in the bay swinging with the tide and the waves; the sails are all up, and you wonder why it does not move, but it cannot, for down beneath the water it is anchored. So we often see a young man apparently well equipped, well educated, and we wonder that he does not advance toward manhood and character. But, alas! we find that he is anchored to some secret vice, and he can never advance until he cuts loose.

"The first crime past compels us into more,
And guilt grows fate that was but choice before."
"Small habits, well pursued betimes,
May reach the dignity of crimes."

Thousands can sympathize with David when he cried, "My sins have taken such hold upon me that I am not able to look up; my heart faileth me." Like the damned spot of blood on Lady Macbeth's hand, these foul spots on the imagination will not out. What a penalty nature exacts for physical sins. The gods are just, and "of our pleasant vices make instruments to plague us."

Plato wrote over his door, "Let no one ignorant of geometry enter here." The greatest value of the study of the classics and mathematics comes from the habits of accurate and concise thought which it induces. The habit-forming portion of life is the dangerous period, and we need the discipline of close application to hold us outside of our studies.

Washington at thirteen wrote one hundred and ten maxims of civility and good behavior, and was most careful in the formation of all habits. Franklin, too, devised a plan of self-improvement and character building. No doubt the noble characters of these two men, almost superhuman in their excellence, are the natural result of their early care and earnest striving towards perfection.

Fielding, describing a game of cards between Jonathan Wild, of pilfering propensities, and a professional gambler, says: "Such was the power of habit over the minds of these illustrious persons, that Mr. Wild could not keep his hands out of the count's pockets, though he knew they were empty; nor could the count abstain from palming a card, though he was well aware Mr. Wild had no money to pay him."

"Habit," says Montaigne, "is a violent and treacherous schoolmistress. She, by little and little, slyly and unperceived, slips in the foot of her authority, but having by this gentle and humble beginning, with the aid of time, fixed and established it, she then unmasks a furious and tyrannic countenance against which we have no more the courage nor the power so much as to lift up our eyes." It led a New York man actually to cut off his hand with a cleaver under a test of what he would resort to, to get a glass of whiskey. It has led thousands of nature's noblemen to drunkards' and libertines' graves.

Gough's life is a startling illustration of the power of habit, and of the ability of one apparently a hopeless slave to break his fetters and walk a free man in the sunlight of heaven. He came to America when nine years old. Possessed of great powers of song, of mimicry, and of acting, and exceedingly social in his tastes, a thousand temptations

"Widened and strewed with flowers the way
Down to eternal ruin."

"I would give this right hand to redeem those terrible seven years of dissipation and death," he
would often say in after years when, with his soul still scarred and battered from his conflict with
blighting passion, he tearfully urged young men to free themselves from the chains of bestial
habits.

In the laboratory of Faraday a workman one day knocked into a jar of acid a silver cup; it
disappeared, was eaten up by the acid, and could not be found. The question came up whether it
could ever be found. The great chemist came in and put certain chemicals into the jar, and every
particle of the silver was precipitated to the bottom. The mass was then sent to a silversmith, and
the cup restored. So a precious youth who has fallen into the sink of iniquity, lost, dissolved in
sin, can only be restored by the Great Chemist.

What is put into the first of life is put into the whole of life. "Out of a church of twenty-seven
hundred members, I have never had to exclude a single one who was received while a child,"
said Spurgeon. It is the earliest sin that exercises the most influence for evil.

Benedict Arnold was the only general in the Revolution that disgraced his country. He had great
military talent, wonderful energy, and a courage equal to any emergency. But Arnold did not
start right. Even when a boy he was despised for his cruelty and his selfishness. He delighted in
torturing insects and birds that he might watch their sufferings. He scattered pieces of glass and
sharp tacks on the floor of the shop he was tending, to cut the feet of the barefooted boys. Even
in the army, in spite of his bravery, the soldiers hated him, and the officers dared not trust him.

Let no man trust the first false step
Of guilt; it hangs upon a precipice,
Whose steep descent in last perdition ends.
YOUNG

Years ago there was a district lying near Westminster Abbey, London, called the "Devil's
Acre,"—a school for vicious habits, where depravity was universal; where professional beggars
were fitted with all the appliances of imposture; where there was an agency for the hire of
children to be carried about by forlorn widows and deserted wives, to move the compassion of
street-giving benevolence; where young pickpockets were trained in the art and mystery which
was to conduct them in due course to an expensive voyage for the good of their country to
Botany Bay.

Victor Hugo describes a strange association of men in the seventeenth century who bought
children and distorted and made monstrosities of them to amuse the nobility with; and in cultured
Boston there is an association of so-called "respectable men," who have opened thousands of
"places of business" for deforming men, women, and children's souls. But we deform ourselves
with agencies so pleasant that we think we are having a good time, until we become so changed
and enslaved that we scarcely recognize ourselves. Vice, the pleasant guest which we first
invited into our heart's parlor, becomes vulgarly familiar, and intrenches herself deep in our very

being. We ask her to leave, but she simply laughs at us from the hideous wrinkles she has made in our faces, and refuses to go. Our secret sins defy us from the hideous furrows they have cut in our cheeks. Each impure thought has chiseled its autograph deep into the forehead, too deep for erasure, and the glassy, bleary eye adds its testimony to our ruined character.

The devil does not apply his match to the hard coal; but he first lights the shavings of "innocent sins," and the shavings the wood, and the wood the coal. Sin is gradual. It does not break out on a man until it has long circulated through his system. Murder, adultery, theft, are not committed in deed until they have been committed in thought again and again.

"Don't write there," said a man to a boy who was writing with a diamond pin on a pane of glass in the window of a hotel. "Why not?" inquired the boy. "Because you can't rub it out." Yet the glass might have been broken and all trace of the writing lost, but things written upon the human soul can never be removed, for the tablet is immortal.

"In all the wide range of accepted British maxims," said Thomas Hughes, "there is none, take it all in all, more thoroughly abominable than this one, as to the sowing of wild oats. Look at it on what side you will, and I defy you to make anything but a devil's maxim of it. What man, be he young, old, or middle-aged, sows, that, and nothing else, shall he reap. The only thing to do with wild oats is to put them carefully into the hottest part of the fire, and get them burnt to dust, every seed of them. If you sow them, no matter in what ground, up they will come with long, tough roots and luxuriant stalks and leaves, as sure as there is a sun in heaven. The devil, too, whose special crop they are, will see that they thrive, and you, and nobody else, will have to reap them."

We scatter seeds with careless hand,
And dream we ne'er shall see them more;
But for a thousand years
Their fruit appears,
In weeds that mar the land.
JOHN KEBLE.

Theodora boasted that she could draw Socrates' disciples away from him. "That may be," said the philosopher, "for you lead them down an easy descent whereas I am forcing them to mount to virtue—an arduous ascent and unknown to most men."

"When I am told of a sickly student," said Daniel Wise, "that he is 'studying himself to death,' or of a feeble young mechanic, or clerk, that his hard work is destroying him, I study his countenance, and there, too often, read the real, melancholy truth in his dull, averted, sunken eye, discolored skin, and timid manner. These signs proclaim that the young man is in some way violating the laws of his physical nature. He is secretly destroying himself. Yet, say his unconscious and admiring friends, 'He is falling a victim to his own diligence!' Most lame and impotent conclusion! He is sapping the very source of life, and erelong will be a mind in ruins or a heap of dust. Young man, beware of his example! 'Keep thyself pure;' observe the laws of your physical nature, and the most unrelaxing industry will never rob you of a month's health, nor shorten the thread of your life; for industry and health are companions, and long life is the heritage of diligence."

"How shall I a habit break?"
As you did that habit make.
As you gathered, you must lose;
As you yielded, now refuse.
Thread by thread the strands we twist
Till they bind us neck and wrist.
Thread by thread the patient hand
Must untwine ere free we stand.
As we builded, stone by stone,
We must toil, unhelped, alone,
Till the wall is overthrown.
But remember, as we try,
Lighter every test goes by;
Wading in, the stream grows deep
Toward the centre's downward sweep;
Backward turn, each step ashore
Shallower is than that before.
Ah, the precious years we waste
Leveling what we raised in haste;
Doing what must be undone,
Ere content or love be won!
First across the gulf we cast
Kite-borne threads till lines are passed,
And habit builds the bridge at last.
JOHN BOYLE O'REILLY.

CHAPTER VIII. SELF-HELP.

I learned that no man in God's wide earth is either willing or able to help any other man.—PESTALOZZI.

What I am I have made myself.—HUMPHRY DAVY.

Be sure, my son, and remember that the best men always make themselves.—PATRICK HENRY.

Hereditary bondsmen, know ye not
Who would be free themselves must strike the blow?
BYRON.
God gives every bird its food, but he does not throw it into the nest.—J. G. HOLLAND.

Never forget that others will depend upon you, and that you cannot depend upon them.—DUMAS, FILS.

Our remedies oft in ourselves do lie, which we ascribe to Heaven.—SHAKESPEARE.

The best education in the world is that got by struggling to obtain a living.—WENDELL PHILLIPS.

Every person has two educations, one which he receives from others, and one, more important, which he gives himself.—GIBBON.

What the superior man seeks is in himself: what the small man seeks is in others.—CONFUCIUS.

Who waits to have his task marked out,
Shall die and leave his errand unfulfilled.
LOWELL.
In battle or business, whatever the game,
In law, or in love, it's ever the same:
In the struggle for power, or scramble for pelf,
Let this be your motto, "Rely on yourself."
SAXE.
Let every eye negotiate for itself,
And trust no agent.
SHAKESPEARE.

"Colonel Crockett makes room for himself!" exclaimed a backwoods congressman in answer to the exclamation of the White House usher to "Make room for Colonel Crockett!" This remarkable man was not afraid to oppose the head of a great nation. He preferred being right to being president. Though rough, uncultured, and uncouth, Crockett was a man of great courage and determination.

Garfield was the youngest member of the House of Representatives when he entered, but he had not been in his seat sixty days before his ability was recognized and his place conceded. He stepped to the front with the confidence of one who belonged there. He succeeded because all the world in concert could not have kept him in the background, and because when once in the front he played his part with an intrepidity and a commanding ease that were but the outward evidences of the immense reserves of energy on which it was in his power to draw.

[Illustration: James A. Garfield (missing from book)]

"Take the place and attitude which belong to you," says Emerson, "and all men acquiesce. The world must be just. It leaves every man with profound unconcern to set his own rate."

Grant was no book soldier. Some of his victories were contrary to all instructions in military works. He did not dare to disclose his plan to invest Vicksburg, and he even cut off all communication on the Mississippi River for seven days that no orders could reach him from General Halleck, his superior officer; for he knew that Halleck went by books, and he was proceeding contrary to all military theories. He was making a greater military history than had ever been written up to that time. He was greater than all books of tactics. The consciousness of power is everything. That man is strongest who owes most to himself.

"Man, it is within yourself," says Pestalozzi, "it is in the inner sense of your power that resides nature's instrument for your development."

Richard Arkwright, the thirteenth child, in a hovel, with no education, no chance, gave his spinning model to the world, and put a sceptre in England's right hand such as the queen never wielded.

"A person under the firm persuasion that he can command resources virtually has them," says Livy.

Solario, a wandering gypsy tinker, fell deeply in love with the daughter of the painter Coll' Antonio del Fiore, but was told that no one but a painter as good as the father should wed the maiden. "Will you give me ten years to learn to paint, and so entitle myself to the hand of your daughter?" Consent was given, Coll' Antonio thinking that he would never be troubled further by the gypsy. About the time that the ten years were to end the king's sister showed Coll' Antonio a Madonna and Child, which the painter extolled in terms of the highest praise. Judge of his surprise on learning that Solario was the artist. But later, his son-in-law surprised him even more by his rare skill.

Louis Philippe said he was the only sovereign in Europe fit to govern, for he could black his own boots.

When asked to name his family coat-of-arms, a self-made President of the United States replied, "A pair of shirtsleeves."

"Poverty is uncomfortable, as I can testify," said James A. Garfield; "but nine times out of ten the best thing that can happen to a young man is to be tossed overboard and compelled to sink or swim for himself. In all my acquaintance I have never known a man to be drowned who was worth the saving."

It is not the men who have inherited most, except it be in nobility of soul and purpose, who have risen highest; but rather the men with no "start" who have won fortunes, and have made adverse circumstances a spur to goad them up the steep mount, where

"Fame's proud temple shines afar."
To such men, every possible goal is accessible, and honest ambition has no height that genius or talent may tread, which has not felt the impress of their feet.

You may leave your millions to your son, but have you really given him anything? You cannot transfer the discipline, the experience, the power which the acquisition has given you; you cannot transfer the delight of achieving, the joy felt only in growth, the pride of acquisition, the character which trained habits of accuracy, method, promptness, patience, dispatch, honesty of dealing, politeness of manner have developed. You cannot transfer the skill, sagacity, prudence, foresight, which lie concealed in your wealth. It meant a great deal for you, but means nothing to your heir. In climbing to your fortune, you developed the muscle, stamina, and strength which enabled you to maintain your lofty position, to keep your millions intact. You had the power which comes only from experience, and which alone enables you to stand firm on your dizzy height. Your fortune was experience to you, joy, growth, discipline, and character; to him it will be a temptation, an anxiety, which will probably dwarf him. It was wings to you, it will be a dead weight to him; it was education to you and expansion of your highest powers; to him it may mean inaction, lethargy, indolence, weakness, ignorance. You have taken the priceless spur—necessity—away from him, the spur which has goaded man to nearly all the great achievements in the history of the world.

You thought it a kindness to deprive yourself in order that your son might begin where you left off. You thought to spare him the drudgery, the hardships, the deprivations, the lack of opportunities, the meagre education, which you had on the old farm. But you have put a crutch into his hand instead of a staff; you have taken away from him the incentive to self-development, to self-elevation, to self-discipline and self-help, without which no real success, no real happiness, no great character is ever possible. His enthusiasm will evaporate, his energy will be dissipated, his ambition, not being stimulated by the struggle for self-elevation, will gradually die away. If you do everything for your son and fight his battles for him, you will have a weakling on your hands at twenty-one.

"My life is a wreck," said the dying Cyrus W. Field, "my fortune gone, my home dishonored. Oh, I was so unkind to Edward when I thought I was being kind. If I had only had firmness enough to compel my boys to earn their living, then they would have known the meaning of money." His table was covered with medals and certificates of honor from many nations, in recognition of his great work for civilization in mooring two continents side by side in thought, of the fame he had won and could never lose. But grief shook the sands of life as he thought only of the son who had brought disgrace upon a name before unsullied, the wounds were sharper than those of a serpent's tooth.

During the great financial crisis of 1857 Maria Mitchell, who was visiting England, asked an English lady what became of daughters when no property was left them. "They live on their brothers," was the reply. "But what becomes of the American daughters," asked the English lady, "when there is no money left?" "They earn it," was the reply.

Men who have been bolstered up all their lives are seldom good for anything in a crisis. When misfortune comes, they look around for somebody to lean upon. If the prop is not there down they go. Once down, they are as helpless as capsized turtles, or unhorsed men in armor. Many a frontier boy has succeeded beyond all his expectations simply because all props were knocked out from under him and he was obliged to stand upon his own feet.

"A man's best friends are his ten fingers," said Robert Collyer, who brought his wife to America in the steerage. Young men who are always looking for something to lean upon never amount to anything.

There is no manhood mill which takes in boys and turns out men. What you call "no chance" may be your "only chance." Don't wait for your place to be made for you; make it yourself. Don't wait for somebody to give you a lift; lift yourself. Henry Ward Beecher did not wait for a call to a big church with a large salary. He accepted the first pastorate offered him, in a little town near Cincinnati. He became literally the light of the church, for he trimmed the lamps, kindled the fires, swept the rooms, and rang the bell. His salary was only about $200 a year,—but he knew that a fine church and great salary cannot make a great man. It was work and opportunity that he wanted. He felt that if there was anything in him work would bring it out.

"Physiologists tell us," says Waters, "that it takes twenty-eight years for the brain to attain its full development. If this is so, why should not one be able, by his own efforts, to give this long-growing organ a particular bent, a peculiar character? Why should the will not be brought to bear upon the formation of the brain as well as of the backbone?" The will is merely our steam power, and we may put it to any work we please. It will do our bidding, whether it be building up a character, or tearing it down. It may be applied to building up a habit of truthfulness and honesty, or of falsehood and dishonor. It will help build up a man or a brute, a hero or a coward. It will brace up resolution until one may almost perform miracles, or it may be dissipated in irresolution and inaction until life is a wreck. It will hold you to your task until you have formed a powerful habit of industry and application, until idleness and inaction are painful, or it will lead you into indolence and listlessness until every effort will be disagreeable and success impossible.

"The first thing I have to impress upon you is," says J. T. Davidson, "that a good name must be the fruit of one's own exertion. You cannot possess it by patrimony; you cannot purchase it with money; you will not light on it by chance; it is independent of birth, station, talents, and wealth; it must be the outcome of your own endeavor, and the reward of good principles and honorable conduct. Of all the elements of success in life none is more vital than self-reliance,—a determination to be, under God, the creator of your own reputation and advancement. If difficulties stand in the way, if exceptional disadvantages oppose you, all the better, as long as you have pluck to fight through them. I want each young man here (you will not misunderstand me) to have faith in himself and, scorning props and buttresses, crutches and life-preservers, to take earnest hold of life. Many a lad has good stuff in him that never comes to anything because he slips too easily into some groove of life; it is commonly those who have a tough battle to begin with that make their mark upon their age."

When Beethoven was examining the work of Moscheles, he found written at the end "Finis, with God's help." He wrote under it "Man, help yourself."

A young man stood listlessly watching some anglers on a bridge. He was poor and dejected. At length, approaching a basket filled with fish, he sighed, "If now I had these I would be happy. I could sell them and buy food and lodgings." "I will give you just as many and just as good," said the owner, who chanced to overhear his words, "if you will do me a trifling favor." "And what is that?" asked the other. "Only to tend this line till I come back; I wish to go on a short errand." The proposal was gladly accepted. The old man was gone so long that the young man began to get impatient. Meanwhile the fish snapped greedily at the hook, and he lost all his depression in the excitement of pulling them in. When the owner returned he had caught a large number. Counting out from them as many as were in the basket, and presenting them to the youth, the old fisherman said, "I fulfill my promise from the fish you have caught, to teach you whenever you see others earning what you need to waste no time in foolish wishing, but cast a line for yourself."

A white squall caught a party of tourists on a lake in Scotland, and threatened to capsize the boat. When it seemed that the crisis was really come the largest and strongest man in the party, in a state of intense fear, said, "Let us pray." "No, no, my man," shouted the bluff old boatman; "let the little man pray. You take an oar." The greatest curse that can befall a young man is to lean.

The grandest fortunes ever accumulated or possessed on earth were and are the fruit of endeavor that had no capital to begin with save energy, intellect, and the will. From Croesus down to Rockefeller the story is the same, not only in the getting of wealth, but also in the acquirement of eminence; those men have won most who relied most upon themselves.

It has been said that one of the most disgusting sights in this world is that of a young man with healthy blood, broad shoulders, presentable calves, and a hundred and fifty pounds, more or less, of good bone and muscle, standing with his hands in his pockets longing for help.

"The male inhabitants in the Township of Loaferdom, in the County of Hatework," says a printer's squib, "found themselves laboring under great inconvenience for want of an easily traveled road between Poverty and Independence. They therefore petitioned the Powers that be to levy a tax upon the property of the entire county for the purpose of laying out a macadamized highway, broad and smooth, and all the way down hill to the latter place."

"It is interesting to notice how some minds seem almost to create themselves," says Irving, "springing up under every disadvantage, and working their solitary but irresistible way through a thousand obstacles."

"Every one is the artificer of his own fortune," says Sallust.

Man is not merely the architect of his own fortune, but he must lay the bricks himself. Bayard Taylor, at twenty-three, wrote: "I will become the sculptor of my own mind's statue." His biography shows how often the chisel and hammer were in his hands to shape himself into his ideal. "I have seen none, known none, of the celebrities of my time," said Samuel Cox. "All my energy was directed upon one end, to improve myself."

"Man exists for culture," says Goethe; "not for what he can accomplish, but for what can be accomplished in him."

When young Professor Tyndall was in the government service, he had no definite aim in life until one day a government official asked him how he employed his leisure time. "You have five hours a day at your disposal," said he, "and this ought to be devoted to systematic study. Had I at your age some one to advise me as I now advise you, instead of being in a subordinate position, I might have been at the head of my department." The very next day young Tyndall began a regular course of study, and went to the University of Marburg, where he became noted for his indomitable industry. He was so poor that he bought a cask, and cut it open for a bathtub. He often rose before daylight to study, while the world was slumbering about him.

Labor is the only legal tender in the world to true success. The gods sell everything for that, nothing without it. You will never find success "marked down." The door to the temple of success is never left open. Every one who enters makes his own door which closes behind him to all others.

Circumstances have rarely favored great men. They have fought their way to triumph over the road of difficulty and through all sorts of opposition. A lowly beginning and a humble origin are no bar to a great career. The farmers' boys fill many of the greatest places in legislatures, in syndicates, at the bar, in pulpits, in Congress, to-day. Boys of lowly origin have made many of the greatest discoveries, are presidents of our banks, of our colleges, of our universities. Our poor boys and girls have written many of our greatest books, and have filled the highest places as teachers and journalists. Ask almost any great man in our large cities where he was born, and he will tell you it was on a farm or in a small country village. Nearly all of the great capitalists of the city came from the country. "'T is better to be lowly born."

The founder of Boston University left Cape Cod for Boston to make his way with a capital of only four dollars. Like Horace Greeley, he could find no opening for a boy; but what of that? He made an opening. He found a board, and made it into an oyster stand on the street corner. He borrowed a wheelbarrow, and went three miles to an oyster smack, bought three bushels of oysters, and wheeled them to his stand. Soon his little savings amounted to $130, and then he bought a horse and cart. This poor boy with no chance kept right on till he became the millionaire Isaac Rich.

Chauncey Jerome, the inventor of machine-made clocks, started with two others on a tour through New Jersey, they to sell the clocks, and he to make cases for them. On his way to New York he went through New Haven in a lumber wagon, eating bread and cheese. He afterward lived in a fine mansion in New Haven.

Self-help has accomplished about all the great things of the world. How many young men falter, faint, and dally with their purpose because they have no capital to start with, and wait and wait for some good luck to give them a lift. But success is the child of drudgery and perseverance. It cannot be coaxed or bribed; pay the price and it is yours. Where is the boy to-day who has less chance to rise in the world than Elihu Burritt, apprenticed to a blacksmith, in whose shop he had to work at the forge all the daylight, and often by candle-light? Yet, he managed, by studying with a book before him at his meals, carrying it in his pocket that he might utilize every spare moment, and studying nights and holidays, to pick up an excellent education in the odds and ends of time which most boys throw away. While the rich boy and the idler were yawning and stretching and getting their eyes open, young Burritt had seized the opportunity and improved it. At thirty years of age he was master of every important language in Europe and was studying those of Asia.

What chance had such a boy for distinction? Probably not a single youth will read this book who has not a better opportunity for success. Yet he had a thirst for knowledge, and a desire for self-improvement, which overcame every obstacle in his pathway. A wealthy gentleman offered to pay his expenses at Harvard; but no, he said he could get his education himself, even though he had to work twelve or fourteen hours a day at the forge. Here was a determined boy. He snatched every spare moment at the anvil and forge as though it were gold. He believed, with Gladstone, that thrift of time would repay him in after years with usury, and that waste of it would make him dwindle. Think of a boy working nearly all the daylight in a blacksmith's shop, and yet finding time to study seven languages in a single year!

If the youth of America who are struggling against cruel circumstances, to do something and be somebody in the world, could only understand that ninety per cent. of what is called genius is merely the result of persistent, determined industry, is in most cases downright hard work, that it is the slavery to a single idea which has given to many a mediocre talent the reputation of being a genius, they would be inspired with new hope. It is interesting to note that the men who talk most about genius are the men who like to work the least. The lazier the man, the more he will have to say about great things being done by genius.

The greatest geniuses have been the greatest workers. Sheridan was considered a genius, but it was found that the "brilliants" and "off-hand sayings" with which he used to dazzle the House of Commons were elaborated, polished and repolished, and put down in his memorandum book ready for any emergency.

Genius has been well defined as the infinite capacity for taking pains. If men who have done great things could only reveal to the struggling youth of to-day how much of their reputations was due to downright hard digging and plodding, what an uplift of inspiration and encouragement they would give. How often I have wished that the discouraged, struggling youth could know of the heart-aches, the head-aches, the nerve-aches, the disheartening trials, the discouraged hours, the fears and despair involved in works which have gained the admiration of the world, but which have taxed the utmost powers of their authors. You can read in a few minutes or a few hours a poem or a book with only pleasure and delight, but the days and months of weary plodding over details and dreary drudgery often required to produce it would stagger belief.

The greatest works in literature have been elaborated and elaborated, line by line, paragraph by paragraph, often rewritten a dozen times. The drudgery which literary men have put into the productions which have stood the test of time is almost incredible. Lucretius worked nearly a lifetime on one poem. It completely absorbed his life. It is said that Bryant rewrote "Thanatopsis" a hundred times, and even then was not satisfied with it. John Foster would sometimes linger a week over a single sentence. He would hack, split, prune, pull up by the roots, or practice any other severity on whatever he wrote, till it gained his consent to exist. Chalmers was once asked what Foster was about in London. "Hard at it," he replied, "at the rate of a line a week." Dickens, one of the greatest writers of modern fiction, was so worn down by hard work that he looked as "haggard as a murderer." Even Lord Bacon, one of the greatest geniuses that ever lived, left large numbers of MSS. filled with "sudden thoughts set down for use." Hume toiled thirteen hours a day on his "History of England." Lord Eldon astonished the world with his great legal learning, but when he was a student too poor to buy books, he had actually borrowed and copied many hundreds of pages of large law books, such as Coke upon Littleton, thus saturating his mind with legal principles which afterward blossomed out into what the world called remarkable genius. Matthew Hale for years studied law sixteen hours a day. Speaking of Fox, some one declared that he wrote "drop by drop." Rousseau says of the labor involved in his smooth and lively style: "My manuscripts, blotted, scratched, interlined, and scarcely legible, attest the trouble they cost me. There is not one of them which I have not been obliged to transcribe four or five times before it went to press.... Some of my periods I have turned or returned in my head for five or six nights before they were fit to be put to paper."

It is said that Waller spent a whole summer over ten lines in one of his poems. Beethoven probably surpassed all other musicians in his painstaking fidelity and persistent application. There is scarcely a bar in his music that was not written and rewritten at least a dozen times. His favorite maxim was, "The barriers are not yet erected which can say to aspiring talent and industry 'thus far and no further.'" Gibbon wrote his autobiography nine times, and was in his study every morning, summer and winter, at six o'clock; and yet youth who waste their evenings wonder at the genius which can produce "The Decline and Fall of the Roman Empire," upon which Gibbon worked twenty years. Even Plato, one of the greatest writers that ever lived, wrote the first sentence in his "Republic" nine different ways before he was satisfied with it. Burke's famous "Letter to a Noble Lord," one of the finest things in the English language, was so completely blotted over with alterations when the proof was returned to the printing-office that the compositors refused to correct it as it was, and entirely reset it. Burke wrote the conclusion of his speech at the trial of Hastings sixteen times, and Butler wrote his famous "Analogy" twenty times. It took Virgil seven years to write his Georgics, and twelve years to write the Aeneid. He was so displeased with the latter that he attempted to rise from his deathbed to commit it to the flames.

Haydn was very poor; his father was a coachman and he, friendless and lonely, married a servant girl. He was sent away from home to act as errand boy for a music teacher. He absorbed a great deal of information, but he had a hard life of persecution until he became a barber in Vienna. Here he blacked boots for an influential man, who became a friend to him. In 1798 this poor boy's oratorio, "The Creation," came upon the musical world like the rising of a new sun which never set. He was courted by princes and dined with kings and queens; his reputation was made; there was no more barbering, no more poverty. But of his eight hundred compositions, "The Creation" eclipsed them all. He died while Napoleon's guns were bombarding Vienna, some of the shot falling in his garden. The greatest creations of musicians were written with an effort, to fill the "aching void" in the human heart.

Frederick Douglass, America's most representative colored man, born a slave, was reared in bondage, liberated by his own exertions, educated and advanced by sheer pluck and perseverance to distinguished positions in the service of his country, and to a high place in the respect and esteem of the whole world.

When a man like Lord Cavanagh, without arms or legs, manages to put himself into Parliament, when a man like Francis Joseph Campbell, a blind man, becomes a distinguished mathematician, a musician, and a great philanthropist, we get a hint as to what it means to make the most possible out of ourselves and opportunities. Perhaps ninety-nine out of a hundred under such unfortunate circumstances would be content to remain helpless objects of charity for life. If it is your call to acquire money power instead of brain power, to acquire business power instead of professional power, double your talent just the same, no matter what it may be.

A glover's apprentice of Glasgow, Scotland, who was too poor to afford even a candle or a fire, and who studied by the light of the shop windows in the streets, and when the shops were closed climbed the lamp-post, holding his book in one hand, and clinging to the lamp-post with the other,—this poor boy, with less chance than almost any boy in America, became the most eminent scholar of Scotland.

Francis Parkman, half blind, became one of America's greatest historians in spite of everything, because he made himself such. Personal value is a coin of one's own minting; one is taken at the worth he has put into himself. Franklin was but a poor printer's boy, whose highest luxury at one time was only a penny roll, eaten in the streets of Philadelphia. Richard Arkwright, a barber all his earlier life, as he rose from poverty to wealth and fame, felt the need of correcting the defects of his early education. After his fiftieth year he devoted two hours a day, snatched from his sleep, to improving himself in orthography, grammar, and writing.

Michael Faraday was a poor boy, son of a blacksmith, who apprenticed him at the age of thirteen to a bookbinder in London. Michael laid the foundations of his future greatness by making himself familiar with the contents of the books he bound. He remained at night, after others had gone, to read and study the precious volumes. Lord Tenterden was proud to point out to his son the shop where his father had shaved for a penny. A French doctor once taunted Fléchier, Bishop of Nismes, who had been a tallow-chandler in his youth, with the meanness of his origin, to which he replied, "If you had been born in the same condition that I was, you would still have been but a maker of candles."

The Duke of Argyle, walking in his garden, saw a Latin copy of Newton's "Principia" on the grass, and supposing that it had been taken from his library, called for some one to carry it back. Edmund Stone, however, the son of the duke's gardener, claimed it. "Yours?" asked the surprised nobleman. "Do you understand geometry, Latin, and Newton?" "I know a little of them," replied Edmund. "But how," asked the duke, "came you by the knowledge of all these things?" "A servant taught me to read ten years since," answered Stone. "Does one need to know anything more than the twenty-four letters, in order to learn everything else that one wishes?" The duke was astonished. "I first learned to read," said the lad; "the masons were then at work upon your house. I approached them one day and observed that the architect used a rule and compasses, and that he made calculations. I inquired what might be the meaning and use of these things, and I was informed that there was a science called arithmetic. I purchased a book of arithmetic and learned it. I was told that there was another science called geometry; I bought the necessary books and learned geometry. By reading I found that there were good books on these sciences in Latin, so I bought a dictionary and learned Latin. I understood, also, that there were good books of the same kind in French; I bought a dictionary, and learned French. This, my lord, is what I have done; it seems to me that we may learn everything when we know the twenty-four letters of the alphabet."

Edwin Chadwick, in his report to the British Parliament, stated that children, working on half time, that is, studying three hours a day and working the rest of their time out of doors, really made the greatest intellectual progress during the year. Business men have often accomplished wonders during the busiest lives by simply devoting one, two, three, or four hours daily to study or other literary work.

James Watt received only the rudiments of an education at school, for his attendance was irregular on account of delicate health. He more than made up for all deficiencies, however, by the diligence with which he pursued his studies at home. Alexander V. was a beggar; he was "born mud, and died marble." William Herschel, placed at the age of fourteen as a musician in the band of the Hanoverian Guards, devoted all his leisure to philosophical studies. He acquired a large fund of general knowledge, and in astronomy, a science in which he was wholly self-instructed, his discoveries entitle him to rank with the greatest astronomers of all time.

George Washington was the son of a widow, born under the roof of a Westmoreland farmer; almost from infancy his lot had been the lot of an orphan. No academy had welcomed him to its shade, no college crowned him with its honors; to read, to write, to cipher, these had been his degrees in knowledge. Shakespeare learned little more than reading and writing at school, but by self-culture he made himself the great master among literary men. Burns, too, enjoyed few advantages of education, and his youth was passed in almost abject poverty.

James Ferguson, the son of a half-starved peasant, learned to read by listening to the recitations of one of his elder brothers. While a mere boy he discovered several mechanical principles, made models of mills and spinning-wheels, and by means of beads on strings worked out an excellent map of the heavens. Ferguson made remarkable things with a common penknife. How many great men have mounted the hill of knowledge by out-of-the-way paths. Gifford worked his intricate problems with a shoemaker's awl on a bit of leather. Rittenhouse first calculated eclipses on his plow-handle. A will finds a way.

Julius Caesar, who has been unduly honored for those great military achievements in which he appears as the scourge of his race, is far more deserving of respect for those wonderful Commentaries, in which his military exploits are recorded. He attained distinction by his writings on astronomy, grammar, history, and several other subjects. He was one of the most learned men and one of the greatest orators of his time. Yet his life was spent amid the turmoil of a camp or the fierce struggle of politics. If he found abundant time for study, who may not? Frederick the Great, too, was busy in camp the greater part of his life, yet whenever a leisure moment came, it was sure to be devoted to study. He wrote to a friend, "I become every day more covetous of my time, I render an account of it to myself, and I lose none of it but with great regret."

Columbus, while leading the life of a sailor, managed to become the most accomplished geographer and astronomer of his time.

When Peter the Great, a boy of seventeen, became the absolute ruler of Russia, his subjects were little better than savages, and in himself, even, the passions and propensities of barbarism were so strong that they were frequently exhibited during his whole career. But he determined to transform himself and the Russians into civilized people. He instituted reforms with great energy, and at the age of twenty-six started on a visit to the other countries of Europe for the purpose of learning about their arts and institutions. At Saardam, Holland, he was so impressed with the sights of the great East India dockyard, that he apprenticed himself to a shipbuilder, and helped build the St. Peter, which he promptly purchased. Continuing his travels, after he had learned his trade, he worked in England in paper-mills, saw-mills, rope-yards, watchmaker's shops, and other manufactories, doing the work and receiving the treatment of a common laborer.

While traveling, his constant habit was to obtain as much information as he could beforehand with regard to every place he was to visit, and he would demand, "Let me see all." When setting out on his investigations, on such occasions, he carried his tablets in his hand, and whatever he deemed worthy of remembrance was carefully noted down. He would often leave his carriage, if he saw the country people at work by the wayside as he passed along, and not only enter into conversation with them, on agricultural affairs, but accompany them to their houses, examine their furniture, and take drawings of their implements of husbandry. Thus he obtained much minute and correct knowledge, which he would scarcely have acquired by other means, and which he afterward turned to admirable account in the improvement of his own country.

The ancients said, "Know thyself;" the nineteenth century says, "Help thyself." Self-culture gives a second birth to the soul. A liberal education is a true regeneration. When a man is once liberally educated, he will generally remain a man, not shrink to a manikin, nor dwindle to a brute. But if he is not properly educated, if he has merely been crammed and stuffed through college, if he has merely a broken-down memory from trying to hold crammed facts enough to pass the examination, he will continue to shrink and shrivel and dwindle, often below his original proportions, for he will lose both his confidence and self-respect, as his crammed facts, which never became a part of himself, evaporate from his distended memory. Many a youth has made his greatest effort in his graduating essay. But, alas! the beautiful flowers of rhetoric blossomed only to exhaust the parent stock, which blossoms no more forever.

In Strasburg geese are crammed with food several times a day by opening their mouths and forcing the pabulum down the throat with the finger. The geese are shut up in boxes just large enough to hold them, and are not allowed to take any exercise. This is done in order to increase enormously the liver for pâté de fois gras. So are our youth sometimes stuffed with education. What are the chances for success of students who "cut" recitations or lectures, and gad, lounge about, and dissipate in the cities at night until the last two or three weeks, sometimes the last few days, before examination, when they employ tutors at exorbitant prices with the money often earned by hard-working parents, to stuff their idle brains with the pabulum of knowledge; not to increase their grasp or power of brain, not to discipline it, not for assimilation into the mental tissue to develop personal power, but to fatten the memory, the liver of the brain; to fatten it with crammed facts until it is sufficiently expanded to insure fifty per cent. in the examination.

True teaching will create a thirst for knowledge, and the desire to quench this thirst will lead the eager student to the Pierian spring. "Man might be so educated that all his prepossessions would be truth, and all his feelings virtues."

Every bit of education or culture is of great advantage in the struggle for existence. The microscope does not create anything new, but it reveals marvels. To educate the eye adds to its magnifying power until it sees beauty where before it saw only ugliness. It reveals a world we never suspected, and finds the greatest beauty even in the commonest things. The eye of an Agassiz could see worlds which the uneducated eye never dreamed of. The cultured hand can do a thousand things the uneducated hand cannot do. It becomes graceful, steady of nerve, strong, skillful, indeed it almost seems to think, so animated is it with intelligence. The cultured will can seize, grasp, and hold the possessor, with irresistible power and nerve, to almost superhuman effort. The educated touch can almost perform miracles. The educated taste can achieve wonders almost past belief. What a contrast this, between the cultured, logical, profound, masterly reason of a Gladstone and that of the hod-carrier who has never developed or educated his reason beyond what is necessary to enable him to mix mortar and carry brick.

"Culture comes from the constant choice of the best within our reach," says Bulwer. "Continue to cultivate the mind, to sharpen by exercise the genius, to attempt to delight or instruct your race; and, even supposing you fall short of every model you set before you, supposing your name moulder with your dust, still you will have passed life more nobly than the unlaborious herd. Grant that you win not that glorious accident, 'a name below,' how can you tell but that you may have fitted yourself for high destiny and employ, not in the world of men, but of spirits? The powers of the mind cannot be less immortal than the mere sense of identity; their acquisitions accompany us through the Eternal Progress, and we may obtain a lower or a higher grade hereafter, in proportion as we are more or less fitted by the exercise of our intellect to comprehend and execute the solemn agencies of God."

But be careful to avoid that over-intellectual culture which is purchased at the expense of moral vigor. An observant professor of one of our colleges has remarked that "the mind may be so rounded and polished by education, so well balanced, as not to be energetic in any one faculty. In other men not thus trained, the sense of deficiency and of the sharp, jagged corners of their knowledge leads to efforts to fill up the chasms, rendering them at last far better educated men than the polished, easy-going graduate who has just knowledge enough to prevent consciousness of his ignorance. While all the faculties of the mind should be cultivated, it is yet desirable that it should have two or three rough-hewn features of massive strength. Young men are too apt to forget the great end of life which is to be and do, not to read and brood over what other men have been and done."

In a gymnasium you tug, you expand your chest, you push, pull, strike, run, in order to develop your physical self; so you can develop your moral and intellectual nature only by continued effort.

"I repeat that my object is not to give him knowledge but to teach him how to acquire it at need," said Rousseau.

All learning is self-teaching. It is upon the working of the pupil's own mind that his progress in knowledge depends. The great business of the master is to teach the pupil to teach himself.

"Thinking, not growth, makes manhood," says Isaac Taylor. "Accustom yourself, therefore, to thinking. Set yourself to understand whatever you see or read. To join thinking with reading is one of the first maxims, and one of the easiest operations."

"How few think justly of the thinking few:
How many never think who think they do."

CHAPTER IX. WORK AND WAIT.

What we do upon some great occasion will probably depend on what we already are; and what we are will be the result of previous years of self-discipline.—H. P. LIDDON.

In all matters, before beginning, a diligent preparation should be made.—CICERO.

I consider a human soul without education like marble in a quarry which shows none of its inherent beauties until the skill of the polisher sketches out the colors, makes the surface shine, and discovers every ornamental cloud, spot, and vein that runs throughout the body of it.—ADDISON.

Many a genius has been slow of growth. Oaks that flourish for a thousand years do not spring up into beauty like a reed.—GEORGE HENRY LEWES.

Use your gifts faithfully, and they shall be enlarged; practice what you know, and you shall attain to higher knowledge.—ARNOLD.

All good abides with him who waiteth wisely.—THOREAU.

The more haste, ever the worse speed.—CHURCHILL.

Haste trips up its own heels, fetters and stops itself.—SENECA.

"Wisely and slow; they stumble that run fast."

How can we expect a harvest of thought who have not had the seed-time of character?—THOREAU.

I call a complete and generous education that which fits a man to perform justly, skillfully, and magnanimously, all the offices, both public and private, of peace and war.—MILTON.

The safe path to excellence and success, in every calling, is that of appropriate preliminary education, diligent application to learn the art and assiduity in practicing it.—EDWARD EVERETT.

The more you know, the more you can save yourself and that which belongs to you, and do more work with less effort.—CHARLES KINGSLEY.

"I was a mere cipher in that vast sea of human enterprise," said Henry Bessemer, speaking of his arrival in London in 1831. Although but eighteen years old, and without an acquaintance in the city, he soon made work for himself by inventing a process of copying bas-reliefs on cardboard.

His method was so simple that one could learn in ten minutes how to make a die from an embossed stamp for a penny. Having ascertained later that in this way the raised stamps on all official papers in England could easily be forged, he set to work and invented a perforated stamp which could not be forged nor removed from a document. At the public stamp office he was told by the chief that the government was losing 100,000 pounds a year through the custom of removing stamps from old parchments and using them again. The chief also appreciated the new danger of easy counterfeiting. So he offered Bessemer a definite sum for his process of perforation, or an office for life at eight hundred pounds a year. Bessemer chose the office, and hastened to tell the good news to a young woman with whom he had agreed to share his fortune. In explaining his invention, he told how it would prevent any one from taking a valuable stamp from a document a hundred years old and using it a second time.

"Yes," said his betrothed, "I understand that; but, surely, if all stamps had a date put upon them they could not at a future time be used without detection."

This was a very short speech, and of no special importance if we omit a single word of four letters; but, like the schoolboy's pins which saved the lives of thousands of people annually by not getting swallowed, that little word, by keeping out of the ponderous minds of the British revenue officers, had for a long period saved the government the burden of caring for an additional income of 100,000 pounds a year. And the same little word, if published in its connection, would render Henry's perforation device of far less value than a last year's bird's nest. Henry felt proud of the young woman's ingenuity, and suggested the improvement at the stamp office. As a result his system of perforation was abandoned and he was deprived of his promised office, the government coolly making use from that day to this, without compensation, of the idea conveyed by that little insignificant word.

So Bessemer's financial prospects were not very encouraging; but, realizing that the best capital a young man can have is a capital wife, he at once entered into a partnership which placed at his command the combined ideas of two very level heads. The result, after years of thought and experiment, was the Bessemer process of making steel cheaply, which has revolutionized the iron industry throughout the world. His method consists simply in forcing hot air from below into several tons of melted pig-iron, so as to produce intense combustion; and then adding enough spiegel-eisen (looking-glass iron), an ore rich in carbon, to change the whole mass to steel. He discovered this simple process only after trying in vain much more difficult and expensive methods.

"All things come round to him who will but wait."

The great lack of the age is want of thoroughness. How seldom you find a young man or woman who is willing to take time to prepare for his life work. A little education is all they want, a little smattering of books, and then they are ready for business.

"Can't wait" is characteristic of the century, and is written on everything; on commerce, on schools, on society, on churches. Can't wait for a high school, seminary, or college. The boy can't wait to become a youth, nor the youth a man. Youth rush into business with no great reserve of education or drill; of course they do poor, feverish work, and break down in middle life, and many die of old age in the forties. Everybody is in a hurry. Buildings are rushed up so quickly that they will not stand, and everything is made "to sell."

Not long ago a professor in one of our universities had a letter from a young woman in the West, asking him if he did not think she could teach elocution if she could come to the university and take twelve lessons. Our young people of to-day want something, and want it quickly. They are not willing to lay broad, deep foundations. The weary years in preparatory school and college dishearten them. They only want a "smattering" of an education. But as Pope says,—

"A little learning is a dangerous thing;
Drink deep, or taste not the Pierian spring:
There shallow draughts intoxicate the brain,
And drinking largely sobers us again."

The shifts to cover up ignorance, and "the constant trembling lest some blunder should expose one's emptiness," are pitiable. Short cuts and abridged methods are the demand of the hour. But the way to shorten the road to success is to take plenty of time to lay in your reserve power. You can't stop to forage your provender as the army advances; if you do the enemy will get there first. Hard work, a definite aim, and faithfulness, will shorten the way. Don't risk a life's superstructure upon a day's foundation.

Unless you have prepared yourself to profit by your chance, the opportunity will only make you ridiculous. A great occasion is valuable to you just in proportion as you have educated yourself to make use of it. Beware of that fatal facility of thoughtless speech and superficial action which has misled many a young man into the belief that he could make a glib tongue or a deft hand take the place of deep study or hard work.

Patience is nature's motto. She works ages to bring a flower to perfection. What will she not do for the greatest of her creation? Ages and aeons are nothing to her, out of them she has been carving her great statue, a perfect man.

Johnson said a man must turn over half a library to write one book. When an authoress told Wordsworth she had spent six hours on a poem, he replied that he would have spent six weeks. Think of Bishop Hall spending thirty years on one of his works. Owens was working on the "Commentary to the Epistle to the Hebrews" for twenty years. Moore spent several weeks on one of his musical stanzas which reads as if it were a dash of genius. Carlyle wrote with the utmost difficulty, and never executed a page of his great histories till he had consulted every known authority, so that every sentence is the quintessence of many books, the product of many hours of drudging research in the great libraries. To-day, "Sartor Resartus" is everywhere. You can get it for a mere trifle at almost any bookseller's, and hundreds of thousands of copies are scattered over the world. But when Carlyle brought it to London in 1851, it was refused almost contemptuously by three prominent publishers. At last he managed to get it into "Fraser's Magazine," the editor of which conveyed to the author the pleasing information that his work had been received with "unqualified disapprobation." Henry Ward Beecher sent a half dozen articles to the publisher of a religious paper to pay for his subscription, but they were respectfully declined. The publishers of the "Atlantic Monthly" returned Miss Alcott's manuscript, suggesting that she had better stick to teaching. One of the leading magazines ridiculed Tennyson's first poems, and consigned the young poet to oblivion. Only one of Ralph Waldo Emerson's books had a remunerative sale. Washington Irving was nearly seventy years old before the income from his books paid the expenses of his household.

In some respects it is very unfortunate that the old system of binding boys out to a trade has been abandoned. To-day very few boys learn any trade. They pick up what they know, as they go along, just as a student crams for a particular examination, just to "get through," without any effort to see how much he may learn on any subject.

Think of an American youth spending twelve years with Michael Angelo, studying anatomy that he might create the masterpiece of all art; or with Da Vinci devoting ten years to the model of an equestrian statue that he might master the anatomy of the horse. Most young American artists would expect, in a quarter of that time, to sculpture an Apollo Belvidere. While Michael Angelo was painting the Sistine Chapel he would not allow himself time for meals or to dress or undress; but he kept bread within reach that he might eat when hunger impelled, and he slept in his clothes.

A rich man asked Howard Burnett to do a little thing for his album. Burnett complied and charged a thousand francs. "But it took you only five minutes," objected the rich man. "Yes, but it took me thirty years to learn how to do it in five minutes."

"I prepared that sermon," said a young sprig of divinity, "in half an hour, and preached it at once, and thought nothing of it." "In that," said an older minister, "your hearers are at one with you, for they also thought nothing of it."

What the age wants is men who have the nerve and the grit to work and wait, whether the world applaud or hiss. It wants a Bancroft, who can spend twenty-six years on the "History of the United States;" a Noah Webster, who can devote thirty-six years to a dictionary; a Gibbon, who can plod for twenty years on the "Decline and Fall of the Roman Empire;" a Mirabeau, who can struggle on for forty years before he has a chance to show his vast reserve, destined to shake an empire; a Farragut, a Von Moltke, who have the persistence to work and wait for half a century for their first great opportunities; a Garfield, burning his lamp fifteen minutes later than a rival student in his academy; a Grant, fighting on in heroic silence, when denounced by his brother generals and politicians everywhere; a Field's untiring perseverance, spending years and a fortune laying a cable when all the world called him a fool; a Michael Angelo, working seven long years decorating the Sistine Chapel with his matchless "Creation" and the "Last Judgment," refusing all remuneration therefor, lest his pencil might catch the taint of avarice; a Titian, spending seven years on the "Last Supper;" a Stephenson, working fifteen years on a locomotive; a Watt, twenty years on a condensing engine; a Lady Franklin, working incessantly for twelve long years to rescue her husband from the polar seas; a Thurlow Weed, walking two miles through the snow with rags tied around his feet for shoes, to borrow the history of the French Revolution, and eagerly devouring it before the sap-bush fire; a Milton, elaborating "Paradise Lost" in a world he could not see, and then selling it for fifteen pounds; a Thackeray, struggling on cheerfully after his "Vanity Fair" was refused by a dozen publishers; a Balzac, toiling and waiting in a lonely garret, whom neither poverty, debt, nor hunger could discourage or intimidate; not daunted by privations, not hindered by discouragements. It wants men who can work and wait.

When a young lawyer Daniel Webster once looked in vain through all the law libraries near him, and then ordered at an expense of fifty dollars the necessary books, to obtain authorities and precedents in a case in which his client was a poor blacksmith. He won his cause, but, on account of the poverty of his client, only charged fifteen dollars, thus losing heavily on the books bought, to say nothing of his time. Years after, as he was passing through New York city, he was consulted by Aaron Burr on an important but puzzling case then pending before the Supreme Court. He saw in a moment that it was just like the blacksmith's case, an intricate question of title, which he had solved so thoroughly that it was to him now as simple as the multiplication table. Going back to the time of Charles II. he gave the law and precedents involved with such readiness and accuracy of sequence that Burr asked in great surprise if he had been consulted before in the case. "Most certainly not," he replied, "I never heard of your case till this evening." "Very well," said Burr, "proceed," and, when he had finished, Webster received a fee that paid him liberally for all the time and trouble he had spent for his early client.

Albert Bierstadt first crossed the Rocky Mountains with a band of pioneers in 1859, making sketches for the paintings of western scenes for which he had become famous. As he followed the trail to Pike's Peak, he gazed in wonder upon the enormous herds of buffaloes which dotted the plains as far as the eye could reach, and thought of the time when they would have disappeared before the march of civilization. The thought haunted him and found its final embodiment in "The Last of the Buffaloes" in 1890. To perfect this great work he had spent twenty years.

Everything which endures, which will stand the test of time, must have a deep, solid foundation. In Rome the foundation is often the most expensive part of an edifice, so deep must they dig to build on the living rock.

Fifty feet of Bunker Hill Monument is under ground; unseen and unappreciated by those who tread about that historic shaft, but it is this foundation, apparently thrown away, which enables it to stand upright, true to the plumb-line through all the tempests that lash its granite sides. A large part of every successful life must be spent in laying foundation stones under ground. Success is the child of drudgery and perseverance and depends upon "knowing how long it takes to succeed." Havelock joined the army at twenty-eight, and for thirty-four years worked and waited for his opportunity; conscious of his power, "fretting as a subaltern while he saw drunkards and fools put above his head."

But during all these years he was fitting himself to lead that marvelous march to Lucknow.

It was many years of drudgery and reading a thousand volumes that enabled George Eliot to get fifty thousand dollars for "Daniel Deronda." How came writers to be famous? By writing for years without any pay at all; by writing hundreds of pages for mere practice work; by working like galley-slaves at literature for half a lifetime. It was working and waiting many long and weary years that put one hundred and twenty-five thousand dollars into "The Angelus." Millet's first attempts were mere daubs, the later were worth fortunes. Schiller "never could get done."

Dante sees himself "growing lean over his Divine Comedy." It is working and waiting that gives perfection.

"I do not remember," said Beecher, "a book in all the depths of learning, nor a scrap in literature, nor a work in all the schools of art, from which its author has derived a permanent renown, that is not known to have been long and patiently elaborated."

Endurance is a much better test of character than any one act of heroism, however noble.

The pianist Thalberg said he never ventured to perform one of his celebrated pieces in public until he had played it at least fifteen hundred times. He laid no claim whatever to genius; he said it was all a question of hard work. The accomplishments of such industry, such perseverance, would put to shame many a man who claims genius.

Before Edmund Kean would consent to appear in that character which he acted with such consummate skill, The Gentleman Villain, he practiced constantly before a glass, studying expression for a year and a half. When he appeared upon the stage, Byron, who went to see him with Moore, said he never looked upon so fearful and wicked a face. As the great actor went on to delineate the terrible consequences of sin, Byron fainted.

"For years I was in my place of business by sunrise," said a wealthy banker who had begun without a dollar, "and often I did not leave it for fifteen or eighteen hours."

Festina lente—hasten slowly—is a good Latin motto. Patience, it is said, changes the mulberry leaf to satin. The giant oak on the hillside was detained months or years in its upward growth while its roots took a great turn around some rock, in order to gain a hold by which the tree was anchored to withstand the storms of centuries. Da Vinci spent four years on the head of Mona Lisa, perhaps the most beautiful ever painted, but he left therein, an artistic thought for all time.

Said Captain Bingham: "You can have no idea of the wonderful machine that the German army is and how well it is prepared for war. A chart is made out which shows just what must be done in the case of wars with the different nations. And every officer's place in the scheme is laid out beforehand. There is a schedule of trains which will supersede all other schedules the moment war is declared, and this is so arranged that the commander of the army here could telegraph to any officer to take such a train and go to such a place at a moment's notice. When the Franco-Prussian war was declared, Von Moltke was awakened at midnight and told of the fact. He said coolly to the official who aroused him, 'Go to pigeonhole No. —— in my safe and take a paper from it and telegraph as there directed to the different troops of the empire.' He then turned over and went to sleep and awoke at his usual hour in the morning. Every one else in Berlin was excited about the war, but Von Moltke took his morning walk as usual, and a friend who met him said, 'General, you seem to be taking it very easy. Aren't you afraid of the situation? I should think you would be busy.' 'Ah,' replied Von Moltke, 'all of my work for this time has been done long beforehand and everything that can be done now has been done.'"

That is done soon enough which is done well. Soon ripe, soon rotten. He that would enjoy the fruit must not gather the flower. He who is impatient to become his own master is more likely to become his own slave. Better believe yourself a dunce and work away than a genius and be idle. One year of trained thinking is worth more than a whole college course of mental absorption of a vast series of undigested facts. The facility with which the world swallows up the ordinary college graduate who thought he was going to dazzle mankind should bid you pause and reflect. But just as certainly as man was created not to crawl on all fours in the depths of primeval forests, but to develop his mental and moral faculties, just so certainly he needs education, and only by means of it will he become what he ought to become,—man, in the highest sense of the word. Ignorance is not simply the negation of knowledge, it is the misdirection of the mind. "One step in knowledge," says Bulwer, "is one step from sin; one step from sin is one step nearer to Heaven."

A learned clergyman was thus accosted by an illiterate preacher who despised education: "Sir, you have been to college, I presume?" "Yes, sir," was the reply. "I am thankful," said the former, "that the Lord opened my mouth without any learning." "A similar event," retorted the clergyman, "happened in Balaam's time."

"If a cloth were drawn around the eyes of Praxiteles' statue of Love," says Bulwer, "the face looked grave and sad; but as the bandage was removed, a beautiful smile would overspread the countenance. Even so does the removal of the veil of ignorance from the eyes of the mind bring radiant happiness to the heart of man."

A young man just graduated told the President of Trinity College that he had completed his education, and had come to say good-by. "Indeed," said the President, "I have just begun my education."

Many an extraordinary man has been made out of a very ordinary boy; but in order to accomplish this we must begin with him while he is young. It is simply astonishing what training will do for a rough, uncouth, and even dull lad, if he has good material in him, and comes under the tutelage of a skilled educator before his habits have become confirmed. Even a few weeks' or months' drill of the rawest and roughest recruits in the late Civil War so straightened and dignified stooping and uncouth soldiers, and made them so manly, erect, and courteous in their bearing, that their own friends scarcely knew them. If this change is so marked in the youth who has grown to maturity, what a miracle is possible in the lad who is taken early and put under a course of drill and systematic training, both physical, mental, and moral. How many a man who is now in the penitentiary, in the poorhouse, or among the tramps, or living out a miserable existence in the slums of our cities, bent over, uncouth, rough, slovenly, has possibilities slumbering within the rags, which would have developed him into a magnificent man, an ornament to the human race instead of a foul blot and scar, had he only been fortunate enough early in life to have come under efficient and systematic training.

Laziness begins in cobwebs and ends in iron chains. The more business a man has, the more he can do, for he learns to economize his time.

The industry that acquired riches, according to a wise teacher, the patience that is required in obtaining them, the reserved self-control, the measuring of values, the sympathy felt for fellow-toilers, the knowledge of what a dollar costs to the average man, the memory of it—all these things are preservative. But woe to the young farmer who hates farming; does not like sowing and reaping; is impatient with the dilatory and slow path to a small though secure fortune in the neighborhood where he was born, and comes to the city, hoping to become suddenly rich, thinking that he can break into the palace of wealth and rob it of its golden treasures!

Edison described his repeated efforts to make the phonograph reproduce an aspirated sound, and added: "From eighteen to twenty hours a day for the last seven months I have worked on this single word 'specia.' I said into the phonograph 'specia, specia, specia,' but the instrument responded 'pecia, pecia, pecia.' It was enough to drive one mad. But I held firm, and I have succeeded."

The road to distinction must be paved with years of self-denial and hard work.

Horace Mann, the great author of the common school system of Massachusetts, was a remarkable example of that pluck and patience which can work and wait. His only inheritance was poverty and hard work. But he had an unquenchable thirst for knowledge and a determination to get on in the world. He braided straw to get money to buy books which his soul thirsted for.

To Jonas Chickering there were no trifles in the manufacture of a piano. Others might work for salaries, but he was working for fame and fortune. Neither time nor pains were of any account to him compared with accuracy and knowledge. He could afford to work and wait, for quality, not quantity, was his aim. Fifty years ago the piano was a miserable, instrument compared with the perfect mechanism of to-day. Chickering was determined to make a piano which would yield the fullest, richest volume of melody with the least exertion to the player, and one which would withstand atmospheric changes and preserve its purity and truthfulness of tone. And he strove patiently and persistently till he succeeded.

"Thy life, wert thou the pitifullest of all the sons of earth, is no idle dream, but a solemn reality," said Carlyle. "It is thy own. It is all thou hast to comfort eternity with. Work then like a star, unhasting, yet unresting."

Gladstone was bound to win; although he had spent many years of preparation for his life work, in spite of the consciousness of marvelous natural endowments which would have been deemed sufficient by many young men, and notwithstanding he had gained the coveted prize of a seat in Parliament, yet he decided to make himself master of the situation; and amid all his public and private duties, he not only spent eleven terms more in the study of the law, but he studied Greek constantly and read every well written book or paper he could obtain, so determined was he that his life should be rounded out to its fullest measure, and that his mind should have broad and liberal culture.

Emperor William I. was not a genius, but the secret of his power lay in tireless perseverance. A friend says of him, "When I passed the palace at Berlin night after night, however late, I always saw that grand imperial figure standing beside the green lamp, and I used to say to myself, 'That is how the imperial crown of Germany was won.'"

Ole Bull said, "If I practice one day, I can see the result. If I practice two days my friends can see it; if I practice three days the great public can see it."

The habit of seizing every bit of knowledge, no matter how insignificant it may seem at the time, every opportunity, every occasion, and grinding them all up into experience, cannot be overestimated. You will find use for all of it. Webster once repeated an anecdote with effect which he heard fourteen years before, and which he had not thought of in the mean time. It exactly fitted the occasion. "It is an ill mason that rejects any stone."

Webster was once urged to speak on a subject of great importance, but refused, saying he was very busy and had no time to master the subject. "But," replied his friend, "a very few words from you would do much to awaken public attention to it." Webster replied, "If there be so much weight in my words, it is because I do not allow myself to speak on any subject until my mind is imbued with it." On one occasion Webster made a remarkable speech before the Phi Beta Kappa Society at Harvard, when a book was presented to him, but after he had gone, his "impromptu" speech, carefully written out, was found in the book which he had forgotten to take away.

Demosthenes was once urged to speak on a great and sudden emergency, but replied, "I am not prepared." In fact, it was thought by many that Demosthenes did not possess any genius whatever, because he never allowed himself to speak on any subject without thorough preparation. In any meeting or assembly, when called upon, he would never rise, even to make remarks, it was said, without previously preparing himself.

Alexander Hamilton said, "Men give me credit for genius. All the genius I have lies just in this: when I have a subject in hand I study it profoundly. Day and night it is before me. I explore it in all its bearings. My mind becomes pervaded with it. Then the effort which I make the people are pleased to call the fruit of genius; it is the fruit of labor and thought." The law of labor is equally binding on genius and mediocrity.

Are the results so distant that you delay the preparation in the hope that fortuitous good luck may make it unnecessary? As well might the husbandman delay sowing his seed until the spring and summer are past and the ground hardened by the frosts of a rigorous winter. As well might one who is desirous of enjoying firm health inoculate his system with the seeds of disease, and expect at such time as he may see fit to recover from its effects, and banish the malady. Nelaton, the great surgeon, said that if he had four minutes in which to perform an operation, on which a life depended, he would take one minute to consider how best to do it.

"Many men," says Longfellow, "do not allow their principles to take root, but pull them up every now and then, as children do flowers they have planted, to see if they are growing." We must not only work, but wait.

"The spruce young spark," says Sizer, "who thinks chiefly of his mustache and boots and shiny hat, of getting along nicely and easily during the day, and talking about the theatre, the opera, or a fast horse, ridiculing the faithful young fellow who came to learn the business and make a man of himself, because he will not join in wasting his time in dissipation, will see the day, if his useless life is not earlier blasted by vicious indulgences, when he will be glad to accept a situation from his fellow-clerk whom he now ridicules and affects to despise, when the latter shall stand in the firm, dispensing benefits and acquiring fortune."

"I have been watching the careers of young men by the thousand in this busy city of New York for over thirty years," said Dr. Cuyler, "and I find that the chief difference between the successful and the failures lies in the single element of staying power. Permanent success is oftener won by holding on than by sudden dash, however brilliant. The easily discouraged, who are pushed back by a straw, are all the time dropping to the rear—to perish or to be carried along on the stretcher of charity. They who understand and practice Abraham Lincoln's homely maxim of 'pegging away' have achieved the solidest success."

"When a man has done his work," says Ruskin, "and nothing can any way be materially altered in his fate, let him forget his toil, and jest with his fate if he will, but what excuse can you find for willfulness of thought at the very lime when every crisis of fortune hangs on your decisions? A youth thoughtless, when all the happiness of his home forever depends on the chances or the passions of the hour! A youth thoughtless, when the career of all his days depends on the opportunity of a moment! A youth thoughtless, when his every action is a foundation-stone of future conduct, and every imagination a foundation of life or death! Be thoughtless in any after years, rather than now—though, indeed, there is only one place where a man may be nobly thoughtless, his deathbed. Nothing should ever be left to be done there."

The Duke of Wellington became so discouraged because he did not advance in the army that he applied for a much inferior position in the customs department, but was refused. Napoleon had applied for every vacant position for seven years before he was recognized, but meanwhile he studied with all his might, supplementing what was considered a thorough military education by researches and reflections which in later years enabled him easily to teach the art of war to veterans who had never dreamed of his novel combinations.

Reserves which carry us through great emergencies are the result of long working and long waiting. Collyer declares that reserves mean to a man also achievement,—"the power to do the grandest thing possible to your nature when you feel you must, or some precious thing will be lost,—to do well always, but best in the crisis on which all things turn; to stand the strain of a long fight, and still find you have something left, and so to never know you are beaten, because you never are beaten." Every defeat is a Waterloo to him who has no reserves.

He only is independent in action who has been earnest and thorough in preparation and self-culture. "Not for school, but for life, we learn;" and our habits—of promptness, earnestness, and thoroughness, or of tardiness, fickleness, and superficiality—are the things acquired most readily and longest retained.

"One who reads the chronicles of discoveries is struck with the prominent part that accident has played in such annals. For some of the most useful processes and machinery the world is indebted to apparently chance occurrences. Inventors in search of one object have failed in their quest, but have stumbled on something more valuable than that for which they were looking. Saul is not the only man who has gone in search of asses and found a kingdom. Astrologers sought to read from the heavens the fate of men and the fortune of nations, and they led to a knowledge of astronomy. Alchemists were seeking for the philosopher's stone, and from their efforts sprung the science of chemistry. Men explored the heavens for something to explain irregularities in the movements of the planets, and discovered a star other than the one for which they were looking. A careless glance at such facts might encourage the delusion that aimless straying in bypaths is quite as likely to be rewarded as is the steady pressing forward, with fixed purpose, towards some definite goal.

"But it is to be remembered that the men who made the accidental discoveries were men who were looking for something. The unexpected achievement was but the return for the toil after what was attained. Others might have encountered the same facts, but only the eye made eager by the strain of long watching would be quick to note the meaning. If vain search for hidden treasure has no other recompense, it at least gives ability to detect the first gleam of the true metal. Men may wake at times surprised to find themselves famous, but it was the work they did before going to sleep, and not the slumber, that gave the eminence. When the ledge has been drilled and loaded and the proper connections have been made, a child's touch on the electric key may be enough to annihilate the obstacle, but without the long preparation the pressure of a giant's hand would be without effect.

"In the search for truth and the shaping of character the principle remains the same as in science and literature. Trivial causes are followed by wonderful results, but it is only the merchantman who is on the watch for goodly pearls who is represented as finding the pearl of great price."

To vary the language of another, the three great essentials to success in mental and physical labor are Practice, Patience, and Perseverance, but the greatest of these is Perseverance.

Let us, then, be up and doing,
With a heart for any fate;
Still achieving, still pursuing,
Learn to labor and to wait.
LONGFELLOW.

CHAPTER X. CLEAR GRIT.

I shall show the cinders of my spirits
Through the ashes of my chance.
SHAKESPEARE.
What though ten thousand faint,
Desert, or yield, or in weak terror flee!
Heed not the panic of the multitude;
Thine be the captain's watchword,—Victory!
HORATIUS BONAR.
Better to stem with heart and hand
The roaring tide of life, than lie,
Unmindful, on its flowery strand,
Of God's occasions drifting by!
Better with naked nerve to hear
The needles of this goading air,
Than in the lap of sensual ease forego
The godlike power to do, the godlike aim to know.
WHITTIER.
Let fortune empty her whole quiver on me,
I have a soul that, like an ample shield,
Can take in all, and verge enough for more.
DRYDEN.
There's a brave fellow! There's a man of pluck!
A man who's not afraid to say his say,
Though a whole town's against him.
LONGFELLOW.
Our greatest glory is not in never falling, but in rising every time we fall.—GOLDSMITH.

Attempt the end and never stand to doubt;
Nothing's so hard but search will find it out.
HERRICK.
The barriers are not yet erected which shall say to aspiring talent, "Thus far and no farther."—
BEETHOVEN.

"Friends and comrades," said Pizarro, as he turned toward the south, after tracing with his sword upon the sand a line from east to west, "on that side are toil, hunger, nakedness, the drenching storm, desertion, and death; on this side, ease and pleasure. There lies Peru with its riches; here, Panama and its poverty. Choose, each man, what best becomes a brave Castilian. For my part, I go to the south." So saying, he crossed the line and was followed by thirteen Spaniards in armor. Thus, on the little island of Gallo in the Pacific, when his men were clamoring to return to Panama, did Pizarro and his few volunteers resolve to stake their lives upon the success of a desperate crusade against the powerful empire of the Incas. At the time they had not even a vessel to transport them to the country they wished to conquer. Is it necessary to add that all difficulties yielded at last to such resolute determination?

"Perseverance is a Roman virtue,
That wins each godlike act, and plucks success
E'en from the spear-proof crest of rugged danger."

At a time when abolitionists were dangerously unpopular, a crowd of brawny Cape Cod fishermen had made such riotous demonstrations that all the speakers announced, except Stephen Foster and Lucy Stone, had fled from an open-air platform. "You had better run, Stephen," said she, "they are coming." "But who will take care of you?" asked Foster. "This gentleman will take care of me," she replied, calmly laying her hand within the arm of a burly rioter with a club, who had just sprung upon the platform. "Wh—what did you say?" stammered the astonished rowdy, as he looked at the little woman; "yes, I'll take care of you, and no one shall touch a hair of your head." With this he forced a way for her through the crowd, and, at her earnest request, placed her upon a stump and stood guard with his club while she delivered an address so effective that the audience offered no further violence, and even took up a collection of twenty dollars to repay Mr. Foster for the damage his clothes had received when the riot was at its height.

"When you get into a tight place and everything goes against you, till it seems as if you could not hold on a minute longer," said Harriet Beecher Stowe, "never give up then, for that's just the place and time that the tide'll turn."

Charles Sumner said, "Three things are necessary: first, backbone; second, backbone; third, backbone."

While digging among the ruins of Pompeii, which was buried by the dust and ashes from an eruption of Vesuvius, A. D. 79, the workmen found the skeleton of a Roman soldier in the sentry-box at one of the city's gates. He might have found safety under sheltering rocks close by; but, in the face of certain death, he had remained at his post, a mute witness to the thorough discipline, the ceaseless vigilance and fidelity which made the Roman legionaries masters of the known world. Bulwer, describing the flight of a party amid the dust, and ashes, and streams of boiling water, and huge hurtling fragments of scoria, and gusty winds, and lurid lightnings, continues: "The air was now still for a few minutes; the lamp from the gate streamed out far and clear; the fugitives hurried on. They gained the gate. They passed by the Roman sentry. The lightning flashed over his livid face and polished helmet, but his stern features were composed even in their awe! He remained erect and motionless at his post. That hour itself had not animated the machine of the ruthless majesty of Rome into the reasoning and self-acting man. There he stood amidst the crashing elements; he had not received the permission to desert his station and escape."

The world admires the man who never flinches from unexpected difficulties, who calmly, patiently, and courageously grapples with his fate, who dies, if need be, at his post.

"Clear grit" always commands respect. It is that quality which achieves, and everybody admires achievement. In the strife of parties and principles, backbone without brains will carry against brains without backbone. "A politician weakly and amiably in the right is no match for a politician tenaciously and pugnaciously in the wrong." You cannot, by tying an opinion to a man's tongue, make him the representative of that opinion; at the close of any battle for principles, his name will be found neither among the dead nor among the wounded, but among the missing.

The "London Times" was an insignificant sheet published by Mr. Walter and was steadily losing money. John Walter, Jr., then only twenty-seven years old, begged his father to give him full control of the paper. After many misgivings, the father finally consented. The young journalist began to remodel the establishment and to introduce new ideas everywhere. The paper had not attempted to mould public opinion, and had no individuality or character of its own. The audacious young editor boldly attacked every wrong, even the government, when he thought it corrupt. Thereupon the public customs, printing, and the government advertisements were withdrawn. The father was in utter dismay. The son he was sure would ruin the paper and himself. But no remonstrance could swerve him from his purpose, to give the world a great journal which should have weight, character, individuality, and independence.

The public soon saw that a new power stood behind the "Times"; that its articles meant business; that new life and new blood and new ideas had been infused into the insignificant sheet; that a man with brains and push and tenacity of purpose stood at the helm,—a man who could make a way when he could not find one. Among other new features foreign dispatches were introduced, and they appeared in the "Times" several days before their appearance in the government organs. The "leading article" also was introduced to stay. But the aggressive editor antagonized the government, and his foreign dispatches were all stopped at the outpost, while those of the ministerial journalists were allowed to proceed. But nothing could daunt this resolute young spirit. At enormous expense he employed special couriers. Every obstacle put in his way, and all opposition from the government, only added to his determination to succeed. Enterprise, push, grit were behind the "Times," and nothing could stay its progress. Walter was the soul of the paper, and his personality pervaded every detail. In those days only three hundred copies of the "Times" could be struck off in an hour by the best presses, and Walter had duplicate and even triplicate types set. Then he set his brain to work, and finally the Walter Press, throwing off 17,000 copies, both sides printed, per hour, was the result. It was the 29th of November, 1814, that the first steam printed paper was given to the world. Walter's tenacity of purpose was remarkable. He shrank from no undertaking, and neglected no detail.

"Mean natures always feel a sort of terror before great natures, and many a base thought has been unuttered, many a sneaking vote withheld, through the fear inspired by the rebuking presence of one noble man." As a rule, pure grit, character, has the right of way. In the presence of men permeated with grit and sound in character, meanness and baseness slink out of sight. Mean men are uncomfortable, dishonesty trembles, hypocrisy is uncertain.

Lincoln, being asked by an anxious visitor what he would do after three or four years if the rebellion was not subdued, replied: "Oh, there is no alternative but to keep pegging away."

"It is in me and it shall come out," said Sheridan, when told that he would never make an orator, as he had failed in his first speech in Parliament. He became known as one of the foremost orators of his day.

When a boy Henry Clay was very bashful and diffident, and scarcely dared recite before his class at school, but he determined to become an orator. So he committed speeches and recited them in the cornfields, or in the barn with the horse and cows for an audience.

Look at Garrison reading this advertisement in a Southern paper: "Five thousand dollars will be paid for the head of W. L. Garrison by the Governor of Georgia." Behold him again; a broadcloth mob is leading him through the streets of Boston by a rope. He is hurried to jail. See him return calmly and unflinchingly to his work, beginning at the point at which he was interrupted. Note this heading in the "Liberator," the type of which he set himself in an attic on State Street, in Boston: "I am in earnest, I will not equivocate, I will not excuse, I will not retreat a single inch, and I will be heard." Was Garrison heard? Ask a race set free largely by his efforts. Even the gallows erected in front of his own door did not daunt him. He held the ear of an unwilling world with that burning word "freedom," which was destined never to cease its vibrations until it had breathed its sweet secret to the last slave.

If impossibilities ever exist, popularly speaking, they ought to have been found somewhere between the birth and the death of Kitto, that deaf pauper and master of Oriental learning. But Kitto did not find them there. In the presence of his decision and imperial energy they melted away. Kitto begged his father to take him out of the poorhouse, even if he had to subsist like the Hottentots. He told him that he would sell his books and pawn his handkerchief, by which he thought he could raise about twelve shillings. He said he could live upon blackberries, nuts, and field turnips, and was willing to sleep on a hayrick. Here was real grit. What were impossibilities to such a resolute will? Patrick Henry voiced that decision which characterized the great men of the Revolution when he said, "Is life so dear, or peace so sweet, as to be purchased at the price of chains and slavery? Forbid it, Almighty God! I know not what course others may take; but as for me, give me liberty or give me death!"

Grit is a permanent, solid quality, which enters into the very structure, the very tissues of the constitution. A weak man, a wavering, irresolute man, may be "spunky" upon occasion, he may be "plucky" in an emergency; but pure "grit" is a part of the very character of strong men alone. Lord Erskine was a plucky man; he even had flashes of heroism, and when he was with weaker men, he was thought to have nerve and even grit; but when he entered the House of Commons, although a hero at the bar, the imperiousness, the audacious scorn, and the intellectual supremacy of Pitt disturbed his equanimity and exposed the weak places in his armor. In Pitt's commanding presence he lost his equilibrium. His individuality seemed off its centre; he felt fluttered, weak, and uneasy.

Many of our generals in the late war exhibited heroism. They were "plucky," and often displayed great determination, but Grant had pure "grit" in the most concentrated form. He could not be moved from his base; he was self-centred, immovable. "If you try to wheedle out of him his plans for a campaign, he stolidly smokes; if you call him an imbecile and a blunderer, he blandly lights another cigar; if you praise him as the greatest general living, he placidly returns the puff from his regalia; and if you tell him he should run for the presidency, it does not disturb the equanimity with which he inhales and exhales the unsubstantial vapor which typifies the politician's promises. While you are wondering what kind of creature this man without a tongue is, you are suddenly electrified with the news of some splendid victory, proving that behind the cigar, and behind the face discharged of all tell-tale expression, is the best brain to plan and the strongest heart to dare among the generals of the Republic."

Demosthenes was a man who could rise to sublime heights of heroism, but his bravery was not his normal condition and depended upon his genius being aroused.

He had "pluck" and "spunk" on occasions, but Lincoln had pure "grit." When the illustrated papers everywhere were caricaturing him, when no epithet seemed too harsh to heap upon him, when his methods were criticised by his own party, and the generals in the war were denouncing his "foolish" confidence in Grant, and delegations were waiting upon him to ask for that general's removal, the great President sat with crossed legs, and was reminded of a story.

Lincoln and Grant both had that rare nerve which cares not for ridicule, is not swerved by public clamor, can bear abuse and hatred. There is a mighty force in truth and in the sublime conviction and supreme self-confidence behind it, in the knowledge that truth is mighty and the conviction and confidence that it will prevail.

Pure grit is that element of character which enables a man to clutch his aim with an iron grip, and keep the needle of his purpose pointing to the star of his hope. Through sunshine and storm, through hurricane and tempest, through sleet and rain, with a leaky ship, with a crew in mutiny, it perseveres; in fact, nothing but death can subdue it, and it dies still struggling.

The man of grit carries in his very presence a power which controls and commands. He is spared the necessity of declaring himself, for his grit speaks in his every act. It does not come by fits and starts, it is a part of his very life. It inspires a sublime audacity and a heroic courage. Many of the failures of life are due to the want of grit or business nerve. It is unfortunate for a young man to start out in business life with a weak, yielding disposition, with no resolution or backbone to mark his own course and stick to it, with no ability to say "No" with an emphasis, obliging this man by investing in hopeless speculation, and rather than offend a friend, indorsing a questionable note.

A little boy was asked how he learned to skate. "Oh, by getting up every time I fell down," he replied.

Whipple tells a story of Masséna which illustrates the masterful purpose that plucks victory out of the jaws of defeat. "After the defeat at Essling, the success of Napoleon's attempt to withdraw his beaten army depended on the character of Masséna, to whom the Emperor dispatched a messenger, telling him to keep his position for two hours longer at Aspern. This order, couched in the form of a request, required almost an impossibility; but Napoleon knew the indomitable tenacity of the man to whom he gave it. The messenger found Masséna seated on a heap of rubbish, his eyes bloodshot, his frame weakened by his unparalleled exertions during a contest of forty hours, and his whole appearance indicating a physical state better befitting the hospital than the field. But that steadfast soul seemed altogether unaffected by bodily prostration; half dead as he was with fatigue, he rose painfully and said, 'Tell the Emperor that I will hold out for two hours.' And he kept his word."

"Often defeated in battle," said Macaulay of Alexander the Great, "he was always successful in war." He might have said the same of Washington, and, with appropriate changes, of all who win great triumphs of any kind.

In the battle of Marengo, the Austrians considered the day won. The French army was inferior in numbers, and had given way. The Austrian army extended its wings on the right and on the left, to follow up the French. Then, though the French themselves thought the battle lost, and the Austrians were confident it was won, Napoleon gave the command to charge; and, the trumpet's blast being given, the Old Guard charged down into the weakened centre of the enemy, cut it in two, rolled the two wings up on either side, and the battle was won for France.

"Never despair," says Burke, "but if you do, work on in despair."

Once when Marshal Ney was going into battle, looking down at his knees which were smiting together, he said, "You may well shake; you would shake worse yet if you knew where I am going to take you."

It is victory after victory with the soldier, lesson after lesson with the scholar, blow after blow with the laborer, crop after crop with the farmer, picture after picture with the painter, and mile after mile with the traveler, that secures what all so much desire—SUCCESS.

A promising Harvard student was stricken with paralysis of both legs. Physicians said there was no hope for him. The lad determined to continue his college studies. The examiners heard him at his bedside, and in four years he took his degree. He resolved to make a critical study of Dante, to do which he had to learn Italian and German. He persevered in spite of repeated attacks of illness and partial loss of sight. He was competing for the university prize. Think of the paralytic lad, helpless in bed, competing for a prize, fighting death inch by inch. What a lesson! Before his book was published or the prize awarded, the brave student died, but the book was successful. He meant that his life should not be a burden or a failure, and he was not only graduated from the best college in America, but competed successfully for the university prize, and made a valuable contribution to literature.

Professor L. T. Townsend, the famous author of "Credo," is another triumph of grit over environment. He had a hard struggle as a boy, but succeeded in working his way through Amherst College, living on forty-five cents a week.

Orange Judd was a remarkable example of success through grit. He earned corn by working for farmers, carried it on his back to mill, brought back the meal to his room, cooked it himself, milked cows for his pint of milk per day, and lived on mush and milk for months together. He worked his way through Wesleyan University, and took a three years' post-graduate course at Yale.

Congressman William W. Crapo, while working his way through college, being too poor to buy a dictionary, actually copied one, walking from his home in the village of Dartmouth, Mass., to New Bedford to replenish his store of words and definitions from the town library.

Oh, the triumphs of this indomitable spirit of the conqueror! This it was that enabled Franklin to dine on a small loaf in the printing-office with a book in his hand. It helped Locke to live on bread and water in a Dutch garret. It enabled Gideon Lee to go barefoot in the snow, half starved and thinly clad. It sustained Lincoln and Garfield on their hard journeys from the log cabin to the White House.

President Chadbourne put grit in place of his lost lung, and worked thirty-five years after his funeral had been planned.

Lord Cavanagh put grit in the place of arms and legs, and went to Parliament in spite of his deformity.

Henry Fawcett put grit in place of eyesight, and became the greatest Postmaster-General England ever had.

Prescott also put grit in place of eyesight, and became one of America's greatest historians. Francis Parkman put grit in place of health and eyesight, and became the greatest historian of America in his line. Thousands of men have put grit in place of health, eyes, ears, hands, legs, and yet have achieved marvelous success. Indeed, most of the great things of the world have been accomplished by grit and pluck. You cannot keep a man down who has these qualities. He will make stepping-stones out of his stumbling-blocks, and lift himself to success.

At fifty, Barnum was a ruined man, owing thousands more than he possessed, yet he resolutely resumed business once more, fairly wringing success from adverse fortune, and paying his notes at the same time. Again and again he was ruined, but phoenix-like, he rose repeatedly from the ashes of his misfortune each time more determined than before.

It was the last three days of the first voyage of Columbus that told. All his years of struggle and study would have availed nothing if he had yielded to the mutiny. It was all in those three days. But what days!

"It is all very well," said Charles J. Fox, "to tell me that a young man has distinguished himself by a brilliant first speech. He may go on, or he may be satisfied with his first triumph; but show me a young man who has not succeeded at first, and nevertheless has gone on, and I will back that young man to do better than most of those who have succeeded at the first trial."

Cobden broke down completely the first time he appeared on a platform in Manchester, and the chairman apologized for him. But he did not give up speaking till every poor man in England had a larger, better, and cheaper loaf.

See young Disraeli, sprung from a hated and persecuted race; without opportunity, pushing his way up through the middle classes, up through the upper classes, until he stands self-poised upon the topmost round of political and social power. Scoffed, ridiculed, rebuffed, hissed from the

House of Commons, he simply says, "The time will come when you will hear me." The time did come, and the boy with no chance swayed the sceptre of England for a quarter of a century.

One of the most remarkable examples in history is Disraeli, forcing his leadership upon that very party whose prejudices were deepest against his race, and which had an utter contempt for self-made men and interlopers. Imagine England's surprise when she awoke to find this insignificant Hebrew actually Chancellor of the Exchequer. He was easily master of all the tortures supplied by the armory of rhetoric; he could exhaust the resources of the bitterest invective; he could sting Gladstone out of his self-control; he was absolute master of himself and his situation. You can see that this young man intends to make his way in the world. A determined audacity is in his very face. He is a gay fop. Handsome, with the hated Hebrew blood in his veins, after three defeats in parliamentary elections he was not the least daunted, for he knew his day would come, as it did. Lord Melbourne, the great Prime Minister, when this gay young fop was introduced to him, asked him what he wished to be. "Prime Minister of England," was his audacious reply.

One of the greatest preachers of modern times, Lacordaire, failed again and again. Everybody said he would never make a preacher, but he was determined to succeed, and in two years from his humiliating failures he was preaching in Notre Dame to immense congregations.

The boy Thorwaldsen, whose father died in the poor-house, and whose education was so scanty that he had to write his letters over many times before they could be posted, by his indomitable perseverance, tenacity, and grit, fascinated the world with the genius which neither his discouraging father, poverty, nor hardship could suppress.

William H. Seward was given a thousand dollars by his father to go to college with; this was all he was to have. The son returned at the end of the freshman year with extravagant habits and no money. His father refused to give him more, and told him he could not stay at home. When the youth found the props all taken out from under him, and that he must now sink or swim, he left home moneyless, returned to college, graduated at the head of his class, studied law, was elected Governor of New York, and became Lincoln's great Secretary of State during the Civil War.

Louisa M. Alcott wrote the conclusion to "An Old-Fashioned Girl" with her left hand in a sling, one foot up, head aching, and no voice. She proudly writes in her diary, "Twenty years ago I resolved to make the family independent if I could. At forty, that is done. Debts all paid, even the outlawed ones, and we have enough to be comfortable. It has cost me my health, perhaps." She earned two hundred thousand dollars by her pen.

Mrs. Frank Leslie often refers to the time she lived in her carpetless attic while striving to pay her husband's obligations. She has fought her way successfully through nine lawsuits, and has paid the entire debt. She manages her ten publications entirely herself, signs all checks and money-orders, makes all contracts, looks over all proofs, and approves the make-up of everything before it goes to press. She has developed great business ability, which no one dreamed she possessed.

Garfield said, "If the power to do hard work is not talent, it is the best possible substitute for it." The triumph of industry and grit over low birth and iron fortune in America, this land of opportunity, ought to be sufficient to put to shame all grumblers over their hard fortune and those who attempt to excuse aimless, shiftless, successless men because they have no chance.

The fear of ridicule and the dread of humiliation often hinder one from taking decisive steps when it is plainly a duty, so that courage is a very important element of decision. In a New England academy a pupil who was engaged to assist the teacher was unable to solve a problem in algebra. The class was approaching the problem, and he was mortified because, after many trials, he was obliged to take it to the teacher for solution. The teacher returned it unsolved. What could he do? He would not confess to the class that he could not solve it, so, after many futile attempts, he went to a distant town to seek the assistance of a friend who, he believed, could do the work. But, alas! his friend had gone away, and would not be back for a week. On his way back he said to himself, "What a fool! am I unable to perform a problem in algebra, and shall I go back to my class and confess my ignorance? I can solve it and I will." He shut himself in his room, determined not to sleep until he had mastered the problem, and finally he won success. Underneath the solution he wrote, "Obtained Monday evening, September 2, at half past eleven o'clock, after more than a dozen trials that have consumed more than twenty hours of time."

During a winter in the war of 1812, General Jackson's troops, unprovided for and starving, became mutinous and were going home. But the general set the example of living on acorns; then rode before the rebellious line and threatened with death the first mutineer that should try to leave.

The race is not always to the swift, the battle is not always to the strong. Horses are sometimes weighted or hampered in the race, and this is taken into account in the result. So in the race of life the distance alone does not determine the prize. We must take into consideration the hindrances, the weights we have carried, the disadvantages of education, of breeding, of training, of surroundings, of circumstances. How many young men are weighted down with debt, with poverty, with the support of invalid parents or brothers and sisters, or friends? How many are fettered with ignorance, hampered by inhospitable surroundings, with the opposition of parents who do not understand them? How many a round boy is hindered in the race by being forced into a square hole? How many are delayed in their course because nobody believes in them, because nobody encourages them, because they get no sympathy and are forever tortured for not doing that against which every fibre of their being protests, and every drop of their blood rebels? How many have to feel their way to the goal, through the blindness of ignorance and lack of experience? How many go bungling along from the lack of early discipline and drill in the vocation they have chosen? How many have to hobble along on crutches because they were never taught to help themselves, but to lean upon a father's wealth or a mother's indulgence? How many are weakened for the journey of life by self-indulgence, by dissipation, by "life-sappers;" how many are crippled by disease, by a weak constitution, by impaired eyesight or hearing?

When the prizes of life shall be awarded by the Supreme Judge, who knows our weaknesses and frailties, the distance we have run, the weights we have carried, the handicaps, will all be taken into account. Not the distance we have run, but the obstacles we have overcome, the disadvantages under which we have made the race, will decide the prizes. The poor wretch who has plodded along against unknown temptations, the poor woman who has buried her sorrows in her silent heart and sewed her weary way through life, those who have suffered abuse in silence, and who have been unrecognized or despised by their fellow-runners, will often receive the greater prize.

"The wise and active conquer difficulties,
By daring to attempt them: sloth and folly
Shiver and sink at sight of toil and hazard,
And make the impossibility they fear."
Tumble me down, and I will sit
Upon my ruins, smiling yet:
Tear me to tatters, yet I'll be
Patient in my necessity:
Laugh at my scraps of clothes, and shun
Me as a fear'd infection:
Yet scare-crow like I'll walk, as one
Neglecting thy derision.
ROBERT HERRICK.

CHAPTER XI. THE GRANDEST THING IN THE WORLD.

"One ruddy drop of manly blood the surging sea outweighs."

"Manhood overtops all titles."

The truest test of civilization is not the census, nor the size of cities, nor the crops; no, but the kind of man the country turns out.—EMERSON.

Hew the block off, and get out the man.—POPE.

Eternity alone will reveal to the human race its debt of gratitude to the peerless and immortal name of Washington.—JAMES A. GARFIELD.

Better not be at all
Than not be noble.
TENNYSON.
Be noble! and the nobleness that lies
In other men, sleeping, but never dead,
Will rise in majesty to meet thine own.
LOWELL.
Virtue alone out-builds the pyramids:
Her monuments shall last when Egypt's fall.
YOUNG.
Were one so tall to touch the pole,
Or grasp creation in his span,
He must be measured by his soul,
The mind's the measure of the man.
WATTS.
We live in deeds, not years; in thoughts, not breaths;
In feelings, not in figures on a dial.
We should count time by heart-throbs. He most lives
Who thinks most, feels the noblest, acts the best.
BAILEY.
"Good name in man or woman
Is the immediate jewel of their souls."
But this one thing I know, that these qualities did not now begin to exist, cannot be sick with my sickness, nor buried in my grave.—EMERSON.

A Moor was walking in his garden when a Spanish cavalier suddenly fell at his feet, pleading for concealment from pursuers who sought his life in revenge for the killing of a Moorish gentleman. The Moor promised aid, and locked his visitor in a summer-house until night should afford opportunity for his escape. Not long after the dead body of his son was brought home, and from the description given he knew the Spaniard was the murderer. He concealed his horror, however, and at midnight unlocked the summer-house, saying, "Christian, the youth whom you have murdered was my only son. Your crime deserves the severest punishment. But I have solemnly pledged my word not to betray you, and I disdain to violate a rash engagement even with a cruel enemy." Then, saddling one of his fleetest mules, he said, "Flee while the darkness of night conceals you. Your hands are polluted with blood; but God is just; and I humbly thank Him that my faith is unspotted, and that I have resigned judgment to Him."

[Illustration: John Greenleaf Whittier (missing from book)]

Character never dies. As Longfellow says:—

"Were a star quenched on high,
For ages would its light,
Still traveling downward from the sky,
Shine on our mortal sight.
"So when a great man dies,
For years beyond our ken,
The light he leaves behind him lies
Upon the paths of men."

The character of Socrates was mightier than the hemlock, and banished the fear and sting of death.

Who can estimate the power of a well-lived life? Character is power. Hang this motto in every school in the land, in every home, in every youth's room. Mothers, engrave it on every child's heart.

You cannot destroy one single atom of a Garrison, even though he were hanged. The mighty force of martyrs to truth lives; the candle burns more brilliantly than before it was snuffed. "No varnish or veneer of scholarship, no command of the tricks of logic or rhetoric, can ever make you a positive force in the world;" but your character can.

When the statue of George Peabody, erected in one of the thoroughfares of London, was unveiled, the sculptor Story was asked to speak. Twice he touched the statue with his hand, and said, "That is my speech. That is my speech." What could be more eloquent? Character needs no recommendation. It pleads its own cause.

"Show me," said Omar the Caliph to Amru the warrior, "the sword with which you have fought so many battles and slain so many infidels." "Ah!" replied Amru, "the sword without the arm of the master is no sharper nor heavier than the sword of Farezdak the poet." So one hundred and fifty pounds of flesh and blood without character is of no great value.

Napoleon was so much impressed with the courage and resources of Marshal Ney, that he said, "I have two hundred millions in my coffers, and I would give them all for Ney."

In Agra, India, stands the Taj Mahal, the acme of Oriental architecture, said to be the most beautiful building in the world. It was planned as a mausoleum for the favorite wife of Shah Jehan. When the latter was deposed by his son Aurungzebe, his daughter Jahanara chose to share his captivity and poverty rather than the guilty glory of her brother. On her tomb in Delhi were cut her dying words: "Let no rich coverlet adorn my grave; this grass is the best covering for the tomb of the poor in spirit, the humble, the transitory Jahanara, the disciple of the holy men of Christ, the daughter of the Emperor Shah Jehan." Travelers who visit the magnificent Taj linger long by the grass-green sarcophagus in Delhi, but give only passing notice to the beautiful Jamma Masjid, a mausoleum afterwards erected in her honor.

Some writer has well said that David of the throne we cannot always recall with pleasure, but David of the Psalms we never forget. The strong, sweet faith of the latter streams like sunlight through even the closed windows of the soul, long after the wearied eye has turned with disgust from all the gilded pomp and pride of the former.

Robertson says that when you have got to the lowest depths of your heart, you will find there not the mere desire of happiness, but a craving as natural to us as the desire for food,—the craving for nobler, higher life.

"Private Benjamin Owen, —— Regiment, Vermont Volunteers, was found asleep at his post while on picket duty last night. The court-martial has sentenced him to be shot in twenty-four hours, as the offense occurred at a critical time." "I thought when I gave Bennie to his country," said farmer Owen as he read the above telegram with dimming eyes, "that no other father in all this broad laud made so precious a gift. He only slept a minute,—just one little minute,—at his post, I know that was all, for Bennie never dozed over a duty. How prompt and trustworthy he was! He was as tall as I, and only eighteen! and now they shoot him because he was found asleep when doing sentinel duty!" Just then Bennie's little sister Blossom answered a tap at the door, and returned with a letter. "It is from him," was all she said.

DEAR FATHER,—For sleeping on sentinel duty I am to be shot. At first, it seemed awful to me; but I have thought about it so much now that it has no terror. They say that they will not bind me, nor blind me; but that I may meet my death like a man. I thought, father, that it might have been on the battlefield, for my country, and that, when I fell, it would be fighting gloriously; but to be shot down like a dog for nearly betraying it,—to die for neglect of duty! Oh, father, I wonder the very thought does not kill me! But I shall not disgrace you. I am going to write you all about it; and when I am gone, you may tell my comrades; I cannot now.

You know I promised Jemmie Carr's mother I would look after her boy; and, when he fell sick, I did all I could for him. He was not strong when he was ordered back into the ranks, and the day before that night I carried all his baggage, besides my own, on our march. Toward night we went in on double-quick, and the baggage began to feel very heavy. Everybody was tired; and as for Jemmie, if I had not lent him an arm now and then, he would have dropped by the way. I was all tired out when we came into camp; and then it was Jemmie's turn to be sentry, and I could take his place; but I was too tired, father. I could not have kept awake if a gun had been pointed at my head; but I did not know it until,—well, until it was too late.

They tell me to-day that I have a short reprieve,—given to me by circumstances,—"time to write to you," our good colonel says. Forgive him, father, he only does his duty; he would gladly save me if he could; and do not lay my death up against Jemmie. The poor boy is broken-hearted, and does nothing but beg and entreat them to let him die in my stead. I can't bear to think of mother and Blossom. Comfort them, father! Tell them I die as a brave boy should, and that, when the war is over, they will not be ashamed of me, as they must be now. God help me: it is very hard to bear! Good-by, father. To-night, in the early twilight, I shall see the cows all coming home from pasture, and precious little Blossom standing on the back stoop, waiting for me,—but I shall never, never come! God bless you all!

"God be thanked!" said Mr. Owen reverently; "I knew Bennie was not the boy to sleep carelessly."

Late that night a little figure glided out of the house and down the path. Two hours later the conductor of the southward mail lifted her into a car at Mill Depot. Next morning she was in New York, and the next she was admitted to the White House at Washington. "Well, my child," said the President in pleasant, cheerful tones, "what do you want so bright and early this morning?" "Bennie's life, please, sir," faltered Blossom. "Bennie? Who is Bennie?" asked Mr. Lincoln. "My brother, sir. They are going to shoot him for sleeping at his post," said the little girl. "I remember," said the President; "it was a fatal sleep. You see, child, it was a time of special danger. Thousands of lives might have been lost through his culpable negligence." "So my father said; but poor Bennie was so tired, sir, and Jemmie so weak. He did the work of two, sir, and it was Jemmie's night, not his; but Jemmie was too tired, and Bennie never thought about himself,—that he was tired, too." "What is that you say, child? Come here; I do not understand." He read Bennie's letter to his father, which Blossom held out, wrote a few lines, rang his bell, and said to the messenger who appeared, "Send this dispatch at once." Then, turning to Blossom, he continued: "Go home, my child, and tell that father of yours, who could approve his country's sentence, even when it took the life of a child like that, that Abraham Lincoln thinks the life far too precious to be lost. Go back, or—wait until to-morrow; Bennie will need a change after he has so bravely faced death, he shall go with you." "God bless you, sir," said Blossom. Not all the queens are crowned.

Two days later, when the young soldier came with his sister to thank the President, Mr. Lincoln fastened the strap of a lieutenant upon his shoulder, saying, "The soldier that could carry a sick comrade's baggage, and die for the act without complaining, deserves well of his country."

When telegrams poured in announcing terrible carnage upon battlefields in our late war, and when President Lincoln's heart-strings were nearly broken over the cruel treatment of our prisoners at Andersonville, Belle Isle, and Libby Prison, he never once departed from his famous motto, "With malice toward none, with charity for all." When it was reported that among those returned at Baltimore from Southern prisons, not one in ten could stand alone from hunger and neglect, and many were so eaten and covered by vermin as to resemble those pitted by smallpox, and so emaciated that they were living skeletons, not even these reports could move the great President to retaliate in kind upon the Southern prisoners.

Among the slain on the battlefield at Fredericksburg was the body of a youth upon which was found next the heart a photograph of Lincoln. Upon the back of it were these words: "God bless President Lincoln." The youth had been sentenced to death for sleeping at his post, but had been pardoned by the President.

David Dudley Field said he considered Lincoln the greatest man of his day. Webster, Clay, Calhoun, and others were great, each in one way, but Lincoln was great in many ways. There seemed to be hidden springs of greatness in this man that would gush forth in the most unexpected way. The men about him were at a loss to name the order of his genius. Horace Greeley was almost as many-sided, but was a wonderful combination of goodness and weakness, while Lincoln seemed strong in every way. After Lincoln had signed the Emancipation Proclamation he said, "The promise must now be kept; I shall never recall one word."

Bishop Hamilton, of Salisbury, bears the following testimony to the influence for good which Gladstone, when a school-fellow at Eton, exercised upon him. "I was a thoroughly idle boy; but I was saved from worse things by getting to know Gladstone." At Oxford we are told the effect of his example was so strong that men who followed him there ten years later declare "that undergraduates drank less in the forties because Gladstone had been so courageously abstemious in the thirties."

The Rev. John Newton said, "I see in this world two heaps of human happiness and misery; now if I can take but the smallest bit from one heap and add it to the other, I carry a point; if as I go home a child has dropped a half-penny, and by giving it another I can wipe away its tears, I feel I have done something."

A holy hermit, who had lived for six years in a cave of the Thebaid, fasting, praying, and performing severe penances, spending his whole life in trying to make himself of some account with God, that he might be sure of a seat in Paradise, prayed to be shown some saint greater than himself, in order that he might pattern after him to reach still greater heights of holiness. The same night an angel came to him and said, "If thou wouldst excel all others in virtue and sanctity, strive to imitate a certain minstrel who goes begging and singing from door to door." The hermit, much chagrined, sought the minstrel and asked him how he had managed to make himself so acceptable to God. The minstrel hung down his head and replied, "Do not mock me, holy father; I have performed no good works, and I am not worthy to pray. I only go from door to door to amuse people with my viol and my flute." The hermit insisted that he must have done some good deeds. The minstrel replied, "Nay, I know of nothing good that I have done." "But how hast thou become a beggar? Hast thou spent thy substance in riotous living?" "Nay, not so," replied the minstrel. "I met a poor woman running hither and thither, distracted, because her husband and children had been sold into slavery to pay a debt. I took her home and protected her from certain sons of Belial, for she was very beautiful. I gave her all I possessed to redeem her family and returned her to her husband and children. Is there any man who would not have done the same?" The hermit shed tears, and said in all his life he had not done as much as the poor minstrel.

"A good name is rather to be chosen than great riches, and loving favor than silver or gold."

A gentleman, traveling through West Virginia, went to a house, and procured food for himself and companion and their horses. He wanted to make payment, but the woman was ashamed to take pay for a mere act of kindness. He pressed the money upon her. Finally she said, "If you don't think I'm mean, I'll take one quarter of a dollar from you, so as to look at it now and then, for there has been no money in this house for a year."

Do not take the world's estimate of success. The real height of the Washington Monument is not measured between the capstone and the earth, but includes the fifty feet of solid masonry below. Many of the most successful lives are like the rivers of India which run under ground, unseen and unheard by the millions who tread above them. But have these rivers therefore no influence? Ask the rich harvest fields if they feel the flowing water beneath. The greatest worth is never measured. It is only the nearest stars whose distances we compute. That life whose influence can be measured by the world's tape-line of dollars and corn is not worth the measuring.

All the forces in nature that are the most powerful are the quietest. We speak of the rolling thunder as powerful; but gravitation, which makes no noise, yet keeps orbs in their orbits, and the whole system in harmony, binding every atom in each planet to the great centre of all attraction, is ten thousand times ten thousand times more powerful. We say the bright lightning is mighty; so it is when it rends the gnarled oak into splinters, or splits solid battlements into fragments; but it is not half so powerful as the gentle light that comes so softly from the skies that we do not feel it, that travels at an inconceivable speed, strikes and yet is not felt, but exercises an influence so great that the earth is clothed with verdure through its influence, and all nature beautified and blessed by its ceaseless action. The things that make no noise, make no pretension, may be really the strongest. The most conclusive logic that a preacher uses in the pulpit will never exercise the influence that the consistent piety of character will exercise over all the earth.

The old Sicilian story relates how Pythias, condemned to death through the hasty anger of Dionysius of Syracuse, asked that he might go to his native Greece, and arrange his affairs, promising to return before the time appointed for his execution. The tyrant laughed his request to scorn, saying that when he was once safe out of Sicily no one would answer for his reappearance. At this juncture, Damon, a friend of the doomed man, offered to become surety for him, and to die in his stead if he did not come back in time. Dionysius was surprised, but accepted the proposition. When the fatal day came, Pythias had not reached Syracuse, but Damon remained firm in his faith that his friend would not fail him. At the very last hour Pythias appeared and announced himself ready to die. But such touching loyalty moved even the iron heart of Dionysius; accordingly he ordered both to be spared, and asked to be allowed to make a third partner in such a noble friendship. It is a grander thing to be nobly remembered than to be nobly born.

When Attila, flushed with conquest, appeared with his barbarian horde before the gates of Rome in 452, Pope Leo alone of all the people dared go forth and try to turn his wrath aside. A single magistrate followed him. The Huns were awed by the fearless majesty of the unarmed old man, and led him before their chief, whose respect was so great that he agreed not to enter the city, provided a tribute should be paid to him.

Blackie thinks there is no kind of a sermon so effective as the example of a great man, where we see the thing done before us,—actually done,—the thing of which we were not even dreaming.

It was said that when Washington led the American forces as commanding officer, it "doubled the strength of the army."

When General Lee was in conversation with one of his officers in regard to a movement of his army, a plain farmer's boy overheard the general's remark that he had decided to march upon Gettysburg instead of Harrisburg. The boy telegraphed this fact to Governor Curtin. A special engine was sent for the boy. "I would give my right hand," said the governor, "to know if this boy tells the truth." A corporal replied, "Governor, I know that boy; it is impossible for him to lie; there is not a drop of false blood in his veins." In fifteen minutes the Union troops were marching to Gettysburg, where they gained a victory. Character is power. The great thing is to be a man, to have a high purpose, a noble aim, to be dead in earnest, to yearn for the good and the true.

"Your lordships," said Wellington in Parliament, "must all feel the high and honorable character of the late Sir Robert Peel. I was long connected with him in public life. We were both in the councils of our sovereign together, and I had long the honor to enjoy his private friendship. In all the course of my acquaintance with him, I never knew a man in whose truth and justice I had greater confidence, or in whom I saw a more invariable desire to promote the public service. In the whole course of my communication with him, I never knew an instance in which he did not show the strongest attachment to truth; and I never saw in the whole course of my life the smallest reason for suspecting that he stated anything which he did not firmly believe to be the fact."

"The Secretary stood alone," said Grattan of the elder Pitt. "Modern degeneracy had not reached him. Original and unaccommodating, the features of his character had the hardihood of antiquity. His august mind overawed majesty; and one of his sovereigns thought royalty so impaired in his presence, that he conspired to remove him, in order to be relieved from his superiority. No state chicanery, no narrow system of vicious politics, sunk him to the level of the vulgar great; but, overbearing, persuasive, and impracticable, his object was England, his ambition, fame. A character so exalted, so unsullied, so various, so authoritative, astonished a corrupt age, and the Treasury trembled at the name of Pitt through all the classes of venality. Corruption imagined, indeed, that she had found defects in this statesman, and talked much of the inconsistency of his policy, and much of the ruin of his victories; but the history of his country and the calamities of the enemy answered and refuted her. Upon the whole, there was in this man something that could create, subvert, or reform; an understanding, a spirit, and an eloquence to summon mankind to united exertion, or to break the bonds of slavery asunder, and to rule the wilderness of free minds with unbounded authority; something that could establish or overwhelm an empire, and strike a blow in the world that would resound through the universe."

Pitt was Paymaster-General for George II. When a subsidy was voted a foreign office, it was customary for the office to claim one half per cent. for honorarium. Pitt astonished the King of Sardinia by sending him the sum without any deduction, and further astonished him by refusing a present as a compliment to his integrity. He was a poor man.

Washington would take no pay as commander-in-chief of the Continental armies. He would keep a strict account of his expenses; and these, he doubted not, would be discharged.

Remember, the main business of life is not to do, but to become; an action itself has its finest and most enduring fruit in character.

In 1837, after George Peabody moved to London, there came a commercial crisis in the United States. Many banks suspended specie payments. Many mercantile houses went to the wall, and thousands more were in great distress. Edward Everett said, "The great sympathetic nerve of the commercial world, credit, as far as the United States were concerned, was for the time paralyzed." Probably not a half dozen men in Europe would have been listened to for a moment in the Bank of England upon the subject of American securities, but George Peabody was one of them. His name was already a tower of strength in the commercial world. In those dark days his integrity stood four-square in every business panic. Peabody retrieved the credit of the State of Maryland, and, it might almost be said, of the United States. His character was the magic wand which in many a case changed almost worthless paper into gold. Merchants on both sides of the Atlantic procured large advances from him, even before the goods consigned to him had been sold.

Thackeray says, "Nature has written a letter of credit upon some men's faces which is honored wherever presented. You cannot help trusting such men; their very presence gives confidence. There is a 'promise to pay' in their very faces which gives confidence, and you prefer it to another man's indorsement." Character is credit.

With most people, as with most nations, "things are worth what they will sell for," and the dollar is mightier than the sword. As good as gold has become a proverb—as though it were the highest standard of comparison.

Themistocles, having conceived the design of transferring the government of Greece from the hands of the Lacedaemonians into those of the Athenians, kept his thoughts continually fixed on this great project. Being at no time very nice or scrupulous in the choice of his measures, he thought anything which could tend to the accomplishment of the end he had in view just and lawful. Accordingly in an assembly of the people one day, he intimated that he had a very important design to propose; but he could not communicate it to the public at large, because the greatest secrecy was necessary to its success, and he therefore desired that they would appoint a person to whom he might explain himself on the subject. Aristides was unanimously selected by the assembly, which deferred entirely to his opinion. Themistocles, taking him aside, told him that the design he had conceived was to burn the fleet belonging to the rest of the Grecian states, which then lay in a neighboring port, when Athens would assuredly become mistress of all Greece. Aristides returned to the assembly, and declared to them that nothing could be more advantageous to the commonwealth than the project of Themistocles, but that, at the same time, nothing in the world could be more unfair. The assembly unanimously declared that, since such was the case, Themistocles should wholly abandon his project.

A tragedy by Aeschylus was once represented before the Athenians, in which it was said of one of the characters, "that he cared not more to be just than to appear so." At these words all eyes were instantly turned upon Aristides as the man who, of all the Greeks, most merited that distinguished reputation. Ever after he received, by universal consent, the surname of the Just,— a title, says Plutarch, truly royal, or rather truly divine. This remarkable distinction roused envy, and envy prevailed so far as to procure his banishment for years, upon the unjust suspicion that his influence with the people was dangerous to their freedom. When the sentence was passed by his countrymen, Aristides himself was present in the midst of them, and a stranger who stood near, and could not write, applied to him to write for him on his shell-ballot. "What name?" asked the philosopher. "Aristides," replied the stranger.

"Do you know him, then?" said Aristides, "or has he in any way injured you?" "Neither," said the other, "but it is for this very thing I would he were condemned. I can go nowhere but I hear of Aristides the Just." Aristides inquired no further, but took the shell, and wrote his name on it as desired. The absence of Aristides soon dissipated the apprehensions which his countrymen had so idly indulged. He was in a short time recalled, and for many years after took a leading part in the affairs of the republic, without showing the least resentment against his enemies, or seeking any other gratification than that of serving his countrymen with fidelity and honor. The virtues of Aristides did not pass without reward. He had two daughters, who were educated at the expense of the state, and to whom portions were allotted from the public treasury.

The strongest proof, however, of the justice and integrity of Aristides is, that notwithstanding he had possessed the highest employments in the republic, and had the absolute disposal of its treasures, yet he died so poor as not to leave money enough to defray the expenses of his funeral.

Men of character are the conscience of the society to which they belong; they, and not the police, guarantee the execution of the laws. Their influence is the bulwark of good government.

It was said of the first Emperor Alexander of Russia, that his personal character was equivalent to a constitution. Of Montaigne, it was said that his high reputation for integrity was a better protection for him than a regiment of horse would have been, he being the only man among the French gentry who, during the wars of the Fronde, kept his castle gates unbarred. There are men, fortunately for the world, who would rather be right than be President.

Fisher Ames, while in Congress, said of Roger Sherman, of Connecticut: "If I am absent during a discussion of a subject, and consequently know not on which side to vote, when I return I always look at Roger Sherman, for I am sure if I vote with him, I shall vote right."

Character gravitates upward, as with a celestial gravitation, while mere genius, without character, gravitates downward. How often we see in school or college young men, who are apparently dull and even stupid, rise gradually and surely above others who are without character, merely because the former have an upward tendency in their lives, a reaching-up principle, which gradually but surely unfolds, and elevates them to positions of honor and trust. There is something which everybody admires in an aspiring soul, one whose tendency is upward and onward, in spite of hindrances and in defiance of obstacles.

We may try to stifle the voice of the mysterious angel within, but it always says "yes" to right actions and "no" to wrong ones. No matter whether we heed it or not, no power can change its decision one iota. Through health, through disease, through prosperity and adversity, this faithful servant stands behind us in the shadow of ourselves, never intruding, but weighing every act we perform, every word we utter, pronouncing the verdict "right" or "wrong."

Francis Horner, of England, was a man of whom Sydney Smith said, that "the ten commandments were stamped upon his forehead." The valuable and peculiar light in which Horner's history is calculated to inspire every right-minded youth is this: he died at the age of thirty-eight, possessed of greater influence than any other private man, and admired, beloved, trusted, and deplored by all except the heartless and the base. No greater homage was ever paid in Parliament to any deceased member. How was this attained? By rank? He was the son of an Edinburgh merchant. By wealth? Neither he nor any of his relatives ever had a superfluous sixpence. By office? He held but one, and that for only a few years, of no influence, and with very little pay. By talents? His were not splendid, and he had no genius. Cautious and slow, his only ambition was to be right. By eloquence? He spoke in calm, good taste, without any of the oratory that either terrifies or seduces. By any fascination of manner? His was only correct and agreeable. By what was it, then? Merely by sense, industry, good principles and a good heart, qualities which no well constituted mind need ever despair of attaining. It was the force of his character that raised him; and this character was not impressed on him by nature, but formed, out of no peculiarly fine elements, by himself. There were many in the House of Commons of far greater ability and eloquence. But no one surpassed him in the combination of an adequate portion of these with moral worth. Horner was born to show what moderate powers, unaided by anything whatever except culture and goodness, may achieve, even when these powers are displayed amidst the competition and jealousies of public life.

"When it was reported in Paris that the great Napoleon was dead, I passed the Palais Royal," says a French writer, "where a public crier called, 'Here's your account of the death of Bonaparte.' This cry which once would have appalled all Europe fell perfectly flat. I entered," he adds, "several cafés, and found the same indifference,—coldness everywhere; no one seemed interested or troubled. This man, who had conquered Europe and awed the world, had inspired neither the love nor the admiration of even his own countrymen. He had impressed the world with his marvelousness, and had inspired astonishment but not love."

Emerson says that Napoleon did all that in him lay to live and thrive without moral principle. It was the nature of things, the eternal law of man and of the world, which balked and ruined him; and the result, in a million attempts of this kind, will be the same. His was an experiment, under the most favorable conditions, to test the powers of intellect without conscience. Never elsewhere was such a leader so endowed, and so weaponed; never has another leader found such aids and followers. And what was the result of this vast talent and power, of these immense armies, burned cities, squandered treasures, immolated millions of men, of this demoralized Europe? He left France smaller, poorer, feebler than he found her.

A hundred years hence what difference will it make whether you were rich or poor, a peer or a peasant? But what difference may it not make whether you did what was right or what was wrong?

"The 'Vicar of Wakefield,'" said George William Curtis, "was sold, through Dr. Johnson's mediation, for sixty pounds; and ten years after, the author died. With what love do we hang over its pages! What springs of feeling it has opened! Goldsmith's books are influences and friends forever, yet the five thousandth copy was never announced, and Oliver Goldsmith, M. D., often wanted a dinner! Horace Walpole, the coxcomb of literature, smiled at him contemptuously from his gilded carriage. Goldsmith struggled cheerfully with his adverse fate, and died. But then sad mourners, whom he had aided in their affliction, gathered around his bed, and a lady of distinction, whom he had only dared to admire at a distance, came and cut a lock of his hair for remembrance. When I see Goldsmith, thus carrying his heart in his hand like a palm branch, I look on him as a successful man, whom adversity could not bring down from the level of his lofty nature."

Dr. Maudsley tells us that the aims which chiefly predominate—riches, position, power, applause of men—are such as inevitably breed and foster many bad passions in the eager competition to attain them. Hence, in fact, come disappointed ambition, jealousy, grief from loss of fortune, all the torments of wounded self-love, and a thousand other mental sufferings,—the commonly enumerated moral causes of insanity. They are griefs of a kind to which a rightly developed nature should not fall a prey. There need be no envy nor jealousy, if a man were to consider that it mattered not whether he did a great thing or some one else did it, Nature's only concern being that it should be done; no grief from loss of fortune, if he were to estimate at its true value that which fortune can bring him, and that which fortune can never bring him; no wounded self-love, if he had learned well the eternal lesson of life,—self-renunciation.

Soon after his establishment in Philadelphia Franklin was offered a piece for publication in his newspaper. Being very busy, he begged the gentleman would leave it for consideration. The next day the author called and asked his opinion of it. "Well, sir," replied Franklin, "I am sorry to say I think it highly scurrilous and defamatory. But being at a loss on account of my poverty whether to reject it or not, I thought I would put it to this issue: At night, when my work was done, I bought a two-penny loaf, on which I supped heartily, and then, wrapping myself in my great coat, slept very soundly on the floor till morning, when another loaf and mug of water afforded a pleasant breakfast. Now, sir, since I can live very comfortably in this manner, why should I prostitute my press to personal hatred or party passion for a more luxurious living?"

One cannot read this anecdote of our American sage without thinking of Socrates' reply to King Archelaus, who had pressed him to give up preaching in the dirty streets of Athens, and come and live with him in his splendid courts: "Meal, please your Majesty, is a half-penny a peck at Athens, and water I get for nothing!"

During Alexander's march into Africa he found a people dwelling in peace, who knew neither war nor conquest. While he was interviewing the chief two of his subjects brought a case before him for judgment. The dispute was this: the one had bought of the other a piece of ground, which, after the purchase, was found to contain a treasure, for which he felt bound to pay. The other refused to receive anything, stating that when he sold the ground he sold it with all the advantages apparent or concealed which it might be found to afford. The king said, "One of you has a daughter and the other a son; let them be married and the treasure given to them as a dowry." Alexander was surprised, and said, "If this case had been in our country it would have been dismissed, and the king would have kept the treasure." The chief said, "Does the sun shine on your country, and the rain fall, and the grass grow?" Alexander replied, "Certainly." The chief then asked, "Are there any cattle?" "Certainly," was the reply. The chief replied, "Then it is for these innocent cattle that the Great Being permits the rain to fall and the grass to grow."

A good character is a precious thing, above rubies, gold, crowns, or kingdoms, and the work of making it is the noblest labor on earth.

Professor Blackie of the University of Edinburgh said to a class of young men: "Money is not needful; power is not needful; liberty is not needful; even health is not the one thing needful; but character alone is that which can truly save us, and if we are not saved in this sense, we certainly must be damned." It has been said that "when poverty is your inheritance, virtue must be your capital."

During the American Revolution, while General Reed was President of Congress, the British Commissioners offered him a bribe of ten thousand guineas to desert the cause of his country. His reply was, "Gentlemen, I am poor, very poor; but your king is not rich enough to buy me."

"When Le Père Bourdaloue preached at Rouen," said Père Arrius, "the tradesmen forsook their shops, lawyers their clients, physicians their sick, and tavern-keepers their bars; but when I preached the following year I set all things to rights,—every man minded his own business."

"I fear John Knox's prayers more than an army of ten thousand men," said Mary, Queen of Scotland.

When Pope Paul IV. heard of the death of Calvin he exclaimed with a sigh, "Ah, the strength of that proud heretic lay in—riches? No. Honors? No. But nothing could move him from his course. Holy Virgin! With two such servants, our church would soon be mistress of both worlds."

Garibaldi's power over his men amounted to fascination. Soldiers and officers were ready to die for him. His will power seemed to enslave them. In Rome he called for forty volunteers to go where half of them would be sure to be killed and the others probably wounded. The whole battalion rushed forward; and they had to draw lots, so eager were all to obey.

What power of magic lies in a great name! There was not a throne in Europe that could stand against Washington's character, and in comparison with it the millions of the Croesuses would look ridiculous. What are the works of avarice compared with the names of Lincoln, Grant, or Garfield? A few names have ever been the leaven which has preserved many a nation from premature decay.

"But strew his ashes to the wind
Whose sword or voice has served mankind—
And is he dead, whose glorious mind
Lifts thine on high?—
To live in hearts we leave behind
Is not to die."

Mr. Gladstone gave in Parliament, when announcing the death of Princess Alice, a touching story of sick-room ministration. The Princess' little boy was ill with diphtheria, the physician had cautioned her not to inhale the poisoned breath; the child was tossing in the delirium of fever. The mother took the little one in her lap and stroked his fevered brow; the boy threw his arms around her neck, and whispered, "Kiss me, mamma;" the mother's instinct was stronger than the physician's caution; she pressed her lips to the child's, but lost her life.

At a large dinner-party given by Lord Stratford after the Crimean War, it was proposed that every one should write on a slip of paper the name which appeared most likely to descend to posterity with renown. When the papers were opened every one of them contained the name of Florence Nightingale.

Leckey says that the first hospital ever established was opened by that noble Christian woman, Fabiola, in the fourth century. The two foremost names in modern philanthropy are those of John Howard and Florence Nightingale. Not a general of the Crimean War on either side can be named by one person in ten. The one name that rises instantly, when that carnival of pestilence and blood is suggested, is that of a young woman just recovering from a serious illness, Florence Nightingale. A soldier said, "Before she came there was such cussin' and swearin'; and after that it was as holy as a church." She robbed war of half its terrors. Since her time the hospital systems of all the nations during war have been changed. No soldier was braver and no patriot truer than Clara Barton, and wherever that noble company of Protestant women known as the Red Cross Society,—the cross, I suppose, pointing to Calvary, and the red to the blood of the Redeemer,— wherever those consecrated workers seek to alleviate the condition of those who suffer from plagues, cholera, fevers, flood, famine, there this tireless angel moves on her pathway of blessing. And of all heroes, what nobler ones than these, whose names shine from the pages of our missionary history? I never read of Mrs. Judson, Mrs. Snow, Miss Brittain, Miss West, without feeling that the heroic age of our race has just begun, the age which opens to woman the privilege of following her benevolent inspirations wheresoever she will, without thinking that our Christianity needs no other evidence.

"Duty is the cement without which all power, goodness, intellect, truth, happiness, and love itself can have no permanence, but all the fabric of existence crumbles away from under us and leaves us at last sitting in the midst of a ruin, astonished at our own desolation." A constant, abiding sense of duty is the last reason of culture.

"I slept and dreamed that life is beauty;
I woke and found that life is duty."

We have no more right to refuse to perform a duty than to refuse to pay a debt. Moral insolvency is certain to him who neglects and disregards his duty to his fellow-men. Nor can we hire another to perform our duty. The mere accident of having money does not release you from your duty to the world. Nay, it increases it, for it enables you to do a larger and nobler duty.

If your money is not clean, if there is a dirty dollar in your millions, you have not succeeded. If there is the blood of the poor and unfortunate, of orphans and widows, on your bank account, you have not succeeded. If your wealth has made others poorer, your life is a failure. If you have gained it in an occupation that kills, that shortens the lives of others, that poisons their blood, or engenders disease, if you have taken a day from a human life, if you have gained your money by that which has debauched other lives, you have failed.

Remember that a question will be asked you some time which you cannot evade, the right answer to which will fix your destiny forever: "How did you get that fortune?" Are other men's lives in it; are others' hope and happiness buried in it; are others' comforts sacrificed to it; are others' rights buried in it; are others' opportunities smothered in it; others' chances strangled by it; has their growth been stunted by it; their characters stained by it; have others a smaller loaf, a meaner home? If so, you have failed; all your millions cannot save you from the curse, "thou hast been weighed in the balance and found wanting."

When Walter Scott's publisher and printer failed and $600,000 of debt stared them in the face, friends came forward and offered to raise money enough to allow him to arrange with his creditors. "No," said he proudly, "this right hand shall work it all off; if we lose everything else, we will at least keep our honor unblemished." What a grand picture of manliness, of integrity in this noble man, working like a dray-horse to cancel that great debt, throwing off at white heat the "Life of Napoleon," "Woodstock," "The Tales of a Grandfather," articles for the "Quarterly," and so on, all written in the midst of great sorrow, pain, and ruin. "I could not have slept soundly," he writes, "as I now can under the comfortable impression of receiving the thanks of my creditors, and the conscious feeling of discharging my duty as a man of honesty. I see before me a long, tedious, and dark path, but it leads to stainless reputation. If I die in the harness, as is very likely, I shall die with honor."

One of the last things he uttered was, "I have been, perhaps, the most voluminous author of my day, and it is a comfort to me to think that I have tried to unsettle no man's faith, to corrupt no man's principles, and that I have written nothing which, on my deathbed, I would wish blotted out."

Although Agassiz refused to lecture even for a large sum of money, yet he left a greater legacy to the world, and left even more money to Harvard University ($300,000) than he would have left if he had taken the time to lecture for money.

Faraday had to choose between a fortune of nearly a million and a life of almost certain poverty if he pursued science. He chose poverty and science, and earned a name never to be erased from the book of fame.

Beecher says that we are all building a soul-house for eternity; yet with what differing architecture and what various care!

What if a man should see his neighbor getting workmen and building materials together, and should say to him, "What are you building?" and he should answer, "I don't exactly know. I am waiting to see what will come of it." And so walls are reared, and room is added to room, while the man looks idly on, and all the bystanders exclaim, "What a fool he is!" Yet this is the way many men are building their characters for eternity, adding room to room, without plan or aim, and thoughtlessly waiting to see what the effect will be. Such builders will never dwell in "the house of God, not made with hands, eternal in the heavens."

Some people build as cathedrals are built, the part nearest the ground finished; but that part which soars towards heaven, the turrets and the spires, forever incomplete.

Many men are mere warehouses full of merchandise—the head and heart are stuffed with goods. Like those houses in the lower streets of cities which were once family dwellings, but are now used for commercial purposes, there are apartments in their souls which were once tenanted by taste, and love, and joy, and worship; but they are all deserted now, and the rooms are filled with material things.

CHAPTER XII. WEALTH IN ECONOMY.

Economy is half the battle of life.—SPURGEON.

Economy is the parent of integrity, of liberty and ease, and the beauteous sister of temperance, of cheerfulness and health.—DR. JOHNSON.

Can anything be so elegant as to have few wants and to serve them one's self?

As much wisdom can be expended on a private economy as on an empire.—EMERSON.

Riches amassed in haste will diminish; but those collected by hand and little by little will multiply.—GOETHE.

No gain is so certain as that which proceeds from the economical use of what you have.—LATIN PROVERB.

Beware of little extravagances: a small leak will sink a big ship.—FRANKLIN.

Better go to bed supperless than rise with debts.—GERMAN PROVERB.

Debt is like any other trap, easy enough to get into, but hard enough to get out of.—H. W. SHAW.

Sense can support herself handsomely in most countries on some eighteen pence a day; but for phantasy, planets and solar systems will not suffice.—MACAULAY.

Economy, the poor man's mint.—TUPPER.

I can get no remedy against this consumption of the purse; borrowing only lingers and lingers it out; but the disease is incurable.—SHAKESPEARE.

Whatever be your talents, whatever be your prospects, never speculate away on the chance of a palace that which you may need as a provision against the workhouse.—BULWER.

Not for to hide it in a hedge,
Nor for a train attendant,
But for the glorious privilege
Of being independent.
BURNS.

"We shan't get much here," whispered a lady to her companion, as John Murray blew out one of the two candles by whose light he had been writing when they asked him to contribute to some benevolent object. He listened to their story and gave one hundred dollars. "Mr. Murray, I am very agreeably surprised," said the lady quoted; "I did not expect to get a cent from you." The old Quaker asked the reason for her opinion; and, when told, said, "That, ladies, is the reason I am able to let you have the hundred dollars. It is by practicing economy that I save up money with which to do charitable actions. One candle is enough to talk by."

Emerson relates the following anecdote: "An opulent merchant in Boston was called on by a friend in behalf of a charity. At that time he was admonishing his clerk for using whole wafers instead of halves; his friend thought the circumstance unpropitious; but to his surprise, on listening to the appeal, the merchant subscribed five hundred dollars. The applicant expressed his astonishment that any person who was so particular about half a wafer should present five hundred dollars to a charity; but the merchant said, "It is by saving half wafers, and attending to such little things, that I have now something to give."

"How did you acquire your great fortune?" asked a friend of Lampis, the shipowner. "My great fortune, easily," was the reply, "my small one, by dint of exertion."

Four years from the time Marshall Field left the rocky New England farm to seek his fortune in Chicago he was admitted as a partner in the firm of Coaley, Farwell & Co. The only reason the modest young man gave, to explain his promotion when he had neither backing, wealth, nor influence, was that he saved his money.

If a man will begin at the age of twenty and lay by twenty-six cents every working day, investing at seven per cent. compound interest, he will have thirty-two thousand dollars when he is seventy years old. Twenty cents a day is no unusual expenditure for beer or cigars, yet in fifty years it would easily amount to twenty thousand dollars. Even a saving of one dollar a week from the date of one's majority would give him one thousand dollars for each of the last ten of the allotted years of life. "What maintains one vice would bring up two children."

Such rigid economy, such high courage, enables one to surprise the world with gifts even if he is poor. In fact, the poor and the middle classes give most in the aggregate to missions and hospitals and to the poor. Only frugality enables them to outdo the rich on their own ground.

But miserliness or avariciousness is a different thing from economy. The miserly is the miserable man, who hoards money from a love of it. A miser who spends a cent upon himself where another would spend a quarter does it from parsimony, which is a subordinate characteristic of avarice. Of this the following is an illustration: "True, I should like some soup, but I have no appetite for the meat," said the dying Ostervalde; "what is to become of that? It will be a sad waste." And so the rich Paris banker would not let his servant buy meat for broth.

A writer on political economy tells of the mishaps resulting from a broken latch on a farmyard gate. Every one going through would shut the gate, but as the latch would not hold it, it would swing open with every breeze. One day a pig ran out into the woods. Every one on the farm went to help get him back. A gardener jumped over a ditch to stop the pig, and sprained his ankle so badly as to be confined to his bed for two weeks. When the cook returned, she found that her linen, left to dry at the fire, was all badly scorched. The dairymaid in her excitement left the cows untied, and one of them broke the leg of a colt. The gardener lost several hours of valuable time. Yet a new latch would not have cost five cents.

Guy, the London bookseller, and afterward the founder of the great hospital, was a great miser, living in the back part of his shop, eating upon an old bench, and using his counter for a table, with a newspaper for a cloth. He did not marry. One day he was visited by "Vulture" Hopkins, another well-known miser. "What is your business?" asked Guy, lighting a candle. "To discuss your methods of saving money," was the reply, alluding to the niggardly economy for which Guy was famous. On learning Hopkins's business he blew out the light, saying, "We can do that in the dark." "Sir, you are my master in the art," said the "Vulture;" "I need ask no further. I see where your secret lies."

Yet that kind of economy which verges on the niggardly is better than the extravagance that laughs at it. Either, when carried to excess, is not only apt to cause misery, but to ruin the character.

"Lay by something for a rainy day," said a gentleman to an Irishman in his service. Not long afterwards he asked Patrick how much he had added to his store. "Faith, nothing at all," was the reply; "I did as you bid me, but it rained very hard yesterday, and it all went—in drink."

"Wealth, a monster gorged
'Mid starving populations."

But nowhere and at no period were these contrasts more startling than in Imperial Rome. There a whole population might be trembling lest they should be starved by the delay of an Alexandrian corn-ship, while the upper classes were squandering fortunes at a single banquet, drinking out of myrrhine and jeweled vases worth hundreds of pounds, and feasting on the brains of peacocks and the tongues of nightingales. As a consequence, disease was rife, men were short-lived. At this time the dress of Roman ladies displayed an unheard-of splendor. The elder Pliny tells us that he himself saw Lollia Paulina dressed for a betrothal feast in a robe entirely covered with pearls and emeralds, which had cost 40,000,000 sesterces, and which was known to be less costly than some of her other dresses. Gluttony, caprice, extravagance, ostentation, impurity, rioted in the heart of a society which knew of no other means by which to break the monotony of its weariness or alleviate the anguish of its despair.

The expense ridiculously bestowed on the Roman feasts passes all belief. Suetonius mentions a supper given to Vitellius by his brother, in which, among other articles, there were two thousand of the choicest fishes, seven thousand of the most delicate birds, and one dish, from its size and capacity, named the aegis or shield of Minerva. It was filled chiefly with the liver of the scari, a delicate species of fish, the brains of pheasants and peacocks, and the tongues of parrots, considered desirable chiefly because of their great cost.

"I hope that there will not be another sale," exclaimed Horace Walpole, "for I have not an inch of room nor a farthing left." A woman once bought an old door-plate with "Thompson" on it because she thought it might come in handy some time. The habit of buying what you don't need because it is cheap encourages extravagance. "Many have been ruined by buying good pennyworths."

"Where there is no prudence," said Dr. Johnson, "there is no virtue."

The eccentric John Randolph once sprang from his seat in the House of Representatives, and exclaimed in his piercing voice, "Mr. Speaker, I have found it." And then, in the stillness which followed this strange outburst, he added, "I have found the Philosopher's Stone: it is Pay as you go."

Many a young man seems to think that when he sees his name on a sign he is on the highway to fortune, and he begins to live on a scale as though there was no possible chance of failure; as though he were already beyond the danger point. Unfortunately Congress can pass no law that will remedy the vice of living beyond one's means.

"The prosperity of fools shall destroy them." "However easy it may be to make money," said Barnum, "it is the most difficult thing in the world to keep it." Money often makes the mare—run away with you.

Very few men know how to use money properly. They can earn it, lavish it, hoard it, waste it, but to deal with it wisely, as a means to an end, is an education difficult of acquirement.

After a large stained-glass window had been constructed an artist picked up the discarded fragments and made one of the most exquisite windows in Europe for another cathedral. So one boy will pick up a splendid education out of the odds and ends of time which others carelessly throw away, or gain a fortune by saving what others waste.

It has become a part of the new political economy to argue that a debt on a church or a house or a firm is a desirable thing to develop character. When the young man starts out in life with the old-fashioned idea strong in his mind that debt is bondage and a disgrace, that a mortgage is to be shunned like the cholera, and that to owe a dollar that you cannot pay, unless overtaken by misfortune, is nothing more or less than stealing, then he is bound in so much at least to succeed, and save his old age from being a burden upon his friends or the state.

To do your best you must own every bit of yourself. If you are in debt, part of you belongs to your creditors. Nothing but actual sin is so paralyzing to a young man's energies as debt.

The "loose change" which many young men throw away carelessly, or worse, would often form the basis of a fortune and independence. The earnings of the people of the United States, rich and poor, old and young, male and female, amount to an average of less than fifty cents a day. But it is by economizing such savings that one must get his start in business. The man without a penny is practically helpless, from a business point of view, except so far as he can immediately utilize his powers of body and mind. Besides, when a man or woman is driven to the wall, the chance of goodness surviving self-respect and the loss of public esteem is frightfully diminished.

"Money goes as it comes." "A child and a fool imagine that twenty years and twenty shillings can never be spent."

Live between extravagance and meanness. Don't save money and starve your mind. "The very secret and essence of thrift consists in getting things into higher values. Spend upward, that is, for the higher faculties. Spend for the mind rather than for the body, for culture rather than for amusement. Some young men are too stingy to buy the daily papers, and are very ignorant and narrow." "There is that withholdeth more than is meet, but it tendeth to poverty." "Don't squeeze out of your life and comfort and family what you save."

Liberal, not lavish, is Nature's hand. Even God, it is said, cannot afford to be extravagant. When He increased the loaves and fishes, He commanded to gather up the fragments, that nothing be lost.

"Nature uses a grinding economy," says Emerson, "working up all that is wasted to-day into to-morrow's creation; not a superfluous grain of sand for all the ostentation she makes of expense and public works. She flung us out in her plenty, but we cannot shed a hair or a paring of a nail but instantly she snatches at the shred and appropriates it to her general stock." Last summer's flowers and foliage decayed in autumn only to enrich the earth this year for other forms of beauty. Nature will not even wait for our friends to see us, unless we die at home. The moment the breath has left the body she begins to take us to pieces, that the parts may be used again for other creations. Mark the following contrast:—

1772.	1822.
Man, to the plow;	Man, tally-ho;
Wife, to the cow;	Wife, piano;
Girl, to the sow;	Miss, silk and satin;
Boy, to the mow;	Boy, Greek and Latin;
And your rents will be netted.	And you'll all be gazetted.
Hone's Works.	The Times.

More than a lifetime has elapsed since the above was published, but instead of returning to the style of 1772, our farmers have out-Heroded Herod in the direction of the fashion, of 1822, and many a farmhouse, like the home of Artemas [Transcriber's note: Artemus?] Ward, may be known by the cupola and the mortgage with which it is decorated.

It is by the mysterious power of economy, it has been said, that the loaf is multiplied, that using does not waste, that little becomes much, that scattered fragments grow to unity, and that out of nothing or next to nothing comes the miracle of something. It is not merely saving, still less, parsimony. It is foresight and arrangement, insight and combination, causing inert things to labor, useless things to serve our necessities, perishing things to renew their vigor, and all things to exert themselves for human comfort.

English working men and women work very hard, seldom take a holiday, and though they get nearly double the wages of the same classes in France, yet save very little. The millions earned by them slip out of their hands almost as soon as obtained to satisfy the pleasures of the moment. In France every housekeeper is taught the art of making much out of little. "I am simply astonished," writes an American lady stopping in France, "at the number of good wholesome dishes which my friend here makes for her table from things, which at home, I always throw away. Dainty little dishes from scraps of cold meat, from hard crusts of bread, delicately prepared and seasoned, from almost everything and nothing. And yet there is no feeling of stinginess or want."

"I wish I could write all across the sky, in letters of gold," says Rev. William Marsh, "the one word, savings-bank."

Boston savings-banks have $130,000,000 on deposit, mostly saved in driblets. Josiah Quincy used to say that the servant girls built most of the palaces on Beacon Street.

"So apportion your wants that your means may exceed them," says Bulwer. "With one hundred pounds a year I may need no man's help; I may at least have 'my crust of bread and liberty.' But with five thousand pounds a year I may dread a ring at my bell; I may have my tyrannical master in servants whose wages I cannot pay; my exile may be at the fiat of the first long-suffering man who enters a judgment against me; for the flesh that lies nearest my heart some Shylock may be dusting his scales and whetting his knife. Every man is needy who spends more than he has; no man is needy who spends less. I may so ill manage, that with five thousand pounds a year I purchase the worst evils of poverty,—terror and shame; I may so well manage my money, that with one hundred pounds a year I purchase the best blessings of wealth,—safety and respect."

Edmund Burke, speaking on Economic Reform, quoted from Cicero: "Magnum vectigal est parsimonia," accenting the second word on the first syllable. Lord North whispered a correction, when Burke turned the mistake to advantage. "The noble lord hints that I have erred in the quantity of a principal word in my quotation; I rejoice at it, sir, because it gives me an opportunity of repeating the inestimable adage,—'Magnum vectigal est parsimonia.'" The sentiment, meaning "Thrift is a good income," is well worthy of emphatic repetition by us all.

Washington examined the minutest expenditures of his family, even when President of the United States. He understood that without economy none can be rich, and with it none need be poor.

"I make a point of paying my own bills," said Wellington.

John Jacob Astor said that the first thousand dollars cost him more effort than all of his millions. Boys who are careless with their dimes and quarters, just because they have so few, never get this first thousand, and without it no fortune is possible.

To find out uses for the persons or things which are now wasted in life is to be the glorious work of the men of the next generation, and that which will contribute most to their enrichment.

Economizing "in spots" or by freaks is no economy at all. It must be done by management.

Learn early in life to say "I can't afford it." It is an indication of power and courage and manliness. Dr. Franklin said, "It is not our own eyes, but other people's, that ruin us." "Fashion wears out more apparel than the man," says Shakespeare.

"Of what a hideous progeny of ill is debt the father," said Douglas Jerrold. "What meanness, what invasions of self-respect, what cares, what double-dealing! How in due season it will carve the frank, open face into wrinkles; how like a knife it will stab the honest heart. And then its transformations,—how it has been known to change a goodly face into a mask of brass; how with the evil custom of debt has the true man become a callous trickster! A freedom from debt, and what nourishing sweetness may be found in cold water; what toothsomeness in a dry crust; what ambrosial nourishment in a hard egg! Be sure of it, he who dines out of debt, though his meal be a biscuit and an onion, dines in 'The Apollo.' And then, for raiment, what warmth in a threadbare coat, if the tailor's receipt be in your pocket! What Tyrian purple in the faded waistcoat, the vest not owed for; how glossy the well-worn hat, if it covers not the aching head of a debtor! Next, the home sweets, the outdoor recreation of the free man. The street door falls not a knell in his heart, the foot on the staircase, though he lives on the third pair, sends no spasm through his anatomy; at the rap of his door he can crow 'come in,' and his pulse still beats healthfully. See him abroad! How he returns look for look with any passenger. Poverty is a bitter draught, yet may, and sometimes can with advantage, be gulped down. Though the drinker makes wry faces, there may, after all, be a wholesome goodness in the cup. But debt, however courteously it may be offered, is the Cup of Siren; and the wine, spiced and delicious though it be, is poison. My son, if poor, see Hyson in the running spring; see thy mouth water at a last week's roll; think a threadbare coat the only wear; and acknowledge a whitewashed garret the fittest housing-place for a gentleman; do this, and flee debt. So shall thy heart be at rest, and the sheriff confounded."

"Whoever has sixpence is sovereign over all men to the extent of that sixpence," says Carlyle; "commands cooks to feed him, philosophers to teach him, kings to mount guard over him,—to the extent of that sixpence."

If a man owes you a dollar, he is almost sure to owe you a grudge, too. If you owe another money, you will be apt to regard him with uncharitable eyes. Why not economize before getting into debt instead of pinching afterwards?

Communities which live wholly from hand to mouth never make much progress in the useful arts. Savings mean power. Comfort and independence abide with those who can postpone their desires.

"Hunger, rags, cold, hard work, contempt, suspicion, unjust reproach, are disagreeable," says Horace Greeley, "but debt is infinitely worse than them all."

Many a ruined man dates his downfall from the day when he began borrowing money. Debt demoralized Daniel Webster, and Theodore Hook, and Sheridan, and Fox, and Pitt. Mirabeau's life was made wretched by duns.

"Annual income," says Micawber, "twenty pounds; annual expenditure, nineteen six, result—happiness. Annual income, twenty pounds; annual expenditure, twenty pounds ought and six, result—misery."

"We are ruined," says Colton, "not by what we really want, but by what we think we do. Therefore never go abroad in search of your wants; if they be real wants, they will come home in search of you; for he that buys what he does not want will soon want what he cannot buy."

The honorable course is to give every man his due. It is better to starve than not to do this. It is better to do a small business on a cash basis than a large one on credit. Owe no man anything, wrote St. Paul. It is a good motto to place in every purse, in every counting-room, in every church, in every home.

Economy is of itself a great revenue.—CICERO.

CHAPTER XIII. RICH WITHOUT MONEY.

Let others plead for pensions; I can be rich without money, by endeavoring to be superior to everything poor. I would have my services to my country unstained by any interested motive.—LORD COLLINGWOOD.

Ill fares the land, to hastening ills a prey,
Where wealth accumulates and men decay.
GOLDSMITH.
Pennilessness is not poverty, and ownership is not possession; to be without is not always to lack, and to reach is not to attain; sunlight is for all eyes that look up, and color for those who choose.—HELEN HUNT.

I ought not to allow any man, because he has broad lands, to feel that he is rich in my presence. I ought to make him feel that I can do without his riches, that I cannot be bought,—neither by comfort, neither by pride,—and although I be utterly penniless, and receiving bread from him, that he is the poor man beside me.—EMERSON.

To be content with what we possess is the greatest and most secure of riches.—CICERO.

There is no riches above a sound body and no joy above the joy of the heart.—ECCLESIASTES.

Where, thy true treasure? Gold says, "Not in me;"
And "Not in me," the Diamond. Gold is poor;
India's insolvent: seek it in thyself.
YOUNG.
He is richest who is content with the least, for content is the wealth of nature.—SOCRATES.

A great heart in a little house is of all things here below that which has ever touched me most.—LACORDAIRE.

My crown is in my heart, not on my head,
Nor decked with diamonds and Indian stones,
Nor to be seen: my crown is called content;
A crown it is, that seldom kings enjoy.
SHAKESPEAKE.

Many a man is rich without money. Thousands of men with nothing in their pockets, and thousands without even a pocket, are rich.

A man born with a good, sound constitution, a good stomach, a good heart and good limbs, and a pretty good headpiece, is rich.

Good bones are better than gold, tough muscles than silver, and nerves that carry energy to every function are better than houses and land.

"Heart-life, soul-life, hope, joy, and love, are true riches," said Beecher.

Why should I scramble and struggle to get possession of a little portion of this earth? This is my world now; why should I envy others its mere legal possession? It belongs to him who can see it, enjoy it. I need not envy the so-called owners of estates in Boston and New York. They are merely taking care of my property and keeping it in excellent condition for me. For a few pennies for railroad fare whenever I wish I can see and possess the best of it all. It has cost me no effort, it gives me no care; yet the green grass, the shrubbery, and the statues on the lawns, the finer sculptures and the paintings within, are always ready for me whenever I feel a desire to look upon them. I do not wish to carry them home with me, for I could not give them half the care they now receive; besides, it would take too much of my valuable time, and I should be worrying continually lest they be spoiled or stolen. I have much of the wealth of the world now. It is all prepared for me without any pains on my part. All around me are working hard to get things that will please me, and competing to see who can give them the cheapest. The little I pay for the use of libraries, railroads, galleries, parks, is less than it would cost to care for the least of all I use. Life and landscape are mine, the stars and flowers, the sea and air, the birds and trees. What more do I want? All the ages have been working for me; all mankind are my servants. I am only required to feed and clothe myself, an easy task in this land of opportunity.

A millionaire pays thousands of pounds for a gallery of paintings, and some poor boy or girl comes in, with open mind and poetic fancy, and carries away a treasure of beauty which the owner never saw. A collector bought at public auction in London, for one hundred and fifty-seven guineas, an autograph of Shakespeare; but for nothing a schoolboy can read and absorb the riches of "Hamlet."

Why should I waste my abilities pursuing this will-o'-the-wisp "Enough," which is ever a little more than one has, and which none of the panting millions ever yet overtook in his mad chase? Is there no desirable thing left in this world but gold, luxury, and ease?

"Want is a growing giant whom the coat of Have was never large enough to cover." "A man may as soon fill a chest with grace, or a vessel with virtue," says Phillips Brooks, "as a heart with wealth."

Shall we seek happiness through the sense of taste or of touch? Shall we idolize our stomachs and our backs? Have we no higher missions, no nobler destinies? Shall we "disgrace the fair day by a pusillanimous preference of our bread to our freedom"?

In the three great "Banquets" of Plato, Xenophon, and Plutarch the food is not even mentioned.

What does your money say to you: what message does it bring to you? Does it say to you, "Eat, drink, and be merry, for to-morrow we die"? Does it bring a message of comfort, of education, of culture, of travel, of books, of an opportunity to help your fellow-man, or is the message "More land, more thousands and millions"? What message does it bring you? Clothes for the naked, bread for the starving, schools for the ignorant, hospitals for the sick, asylums for the orphans, or of more for yourself and none for others? Is it a message of generosity or of meanness, breadth or narrowness? Does it speak to you of character? Does it mean a broader manhood, a larger aim, a nobler ambition, or does it cry "More, more, more"?

Are you an animal loaded with ingots, or a man filled with a purpose? He is rich whose mind is rich, whose thought enriches the intellect of the world. It is a sad sight to see a soul which thirsts not for truth or beauty or the good.

A sailor on a sinking vessel in the Caribbean Sea eagerly filled his pockets with Spanish dollars from a barrel on board while his companions, about to leave in the only boat, begged him to seek safety with them. But he could not leave the bright metal which he had so longed for and idolized, and was prevented from reaching shore by his very riches, when the vessel went down.

"Who is the richest of men," asked Socrates? "He who is content with the least, for contentment is nature's riches."

In More's "Utopia" gold was despised. Criminals were forced to wear heavy chains of it, and to have rings of it in their ears; it was put to the vilest uses to keep up the scorn of it. Bad characters were compelled to wear gold head-bands. Diamonds and pearls were used to decorate infants, so that the youth would discard and despise them.

"Ah, if the rich were as rich as the poor fancy riches!" exclaims Emerson.

Many a rich man has died in the poorhouse.

In excavating Pompeii a skeleton was found with the fingers clenched round a quantity of gold. A man of business in the town of Hull, England, when dying, pulled a bag of money from under his pillow, which he held between his clenched fingers with a grasp so firm as scarcely to relax under the agonies of death.

Oh! blind and wanting wit to choose,
Who house the chaff and burn the grain;
Who hug the wealth ye cannot use,
And lack the riches all may gain.
WILLIAM WATSON.

Poverty is the want of much, avarice the want of everything.

A poor man was met by a stranger while scoffing at the wealthy for not enjoying themselves. The stranger gave him a purse, in which he was always to find a ducat. As fast as he took one out another was to drop in, but he was not to begin to spend his fortune until he had thrown away the purse. He takes ducat after ducat out, but continually procrastinates and puts off the hour of enjoyment until he has got "a little more," and dies at last counting his millions.

A beggar was once met by Fortune, who promised to fill his wallet with gold, as much as he might please, on condition that whatever touched the ground should turn at once to dust. The beggar opens his wallet, asks for more and yet more, until the bag bursts. The gold falls to the ground, and all is lost.

When the steamer Central America was about to sink, the stewardess, having collected all the gold she could from the staterooms, and tied it in her apron, jumped for the last boat leaving the steamer. She missed her aim and fell into the water, the gold carrying her down head first.

In the year 1843 a rich miser lived in Padua, who was so mean and sordid that he would never give a cent to any person or object, and he was so afraid of the banks that he would not deposit with them, but would sit up nights with sword and pistol by him to guard his idol hoard. When his health gave way from anxiety and watching he built an underground treasure-chamber, so arranged that if any burglar ever entered, he would step upon a spring which would precipitate him into a subterranean river, where he could neither escape nor be heard. One night the miser went to his chest to see that all was right, when his foot touched the spring of the trap, and he was hurled into the deep, hidden stream.

"One would think," said Boswell, "that the proprietor of all this (Keddlestone, the seat of Lord Scarsfield) must be happy." "Nay, sir," said Johnson, "all this excludes but one evil, poverty."

John Duncan, the illegitimate child of a Scottish weaver, was ignorant, near-sighted, bent, a miserable apology for a human being, and at last a pauper. If he went upon the street he would sometimes be stoned by other boys. The farmer, for whom he watched cattle, was cruel to him, and after a rainy day would send him cold and wet to sleep on a miserable bed in a dark outhouse. Here he would empty the water from his shoes, and wring out his wet clothes and sleep as best he might. But the boy had a desire to learn to read, and when, a little later, he was put to weaving, he persuaded a schoolgirl, twelve years old, to teach him. He was sixteen when he learned the alphabet, after which his progress was quite rapid. He was very fond of plants, and worked overtime for several months to earn five shillings to buy a book on botany. He became a good botanist, and such was his interest in the study that at the age of eighty he walked twelve miles to obtain a new specimen. A man whom he met became interested at finding such a well-stored mind in such a miserable body, poorly clad, and published an account of his career. Many readers sent him money, but he saved it, and left it in his will to found eight scholarships and offer prizes for the encouragement of the study of natural science by the poor. His small but valuable library was left for a similar use.

Franklin said money never made a man happy yet; there is nothing in its nature to produce happiness. The more a man has, the more he wants. Instead of filling a vacuum, it makes one. A great bank account can never make a man rich. It is the mind that makes the body rich. No man is rich, however much money or land he may possess, who has a poor heart. If that is poor, he is poor indeed, though he own and rule kingdoms. He is rich or poor according to what he is, not according to what he has.

Who would not choose to be a millionaire of deeds with a Lincoln, a Grant, a Florence

Nightingale, a Childs; a millionaire of ideas with Emerson, with Lowell, with Shakespeare, with Wordsworth; a millionaire of statesmanship with a Gladstone, a Bright, a Sumner, a Washington?

Some men are rich in health, in constant cheerfulness, in a mercurial temperament which floats them over troubles and trials enough to sink a shipload of ordinary men. Others are rich in disposition, family, and friends. There are some men so amiable that everybody loves them; some so cheerful that they carry an atmosphere of jollity about them. Some are rich in integrity and character.

One of the first great lessons of life is to learn the true estimate of values. As the youth starts out in his career, all sorts of wares will be imposed upon him, and all kinds of temptations will be used to induce him to buy. His success will depend very largely upon his ability to estimate properly, not the apparent but the real value of everything presented to him. Vulgar Wealth will flaunt her banner before his eyes, and claim supremacy over everything else. A thousand different schemes will be thrust into his face with their claims for superiority. Every occupation and vocation will present its charms in turn, and offer its inducements. The youth who would succeed must not allow himself to be deceived by appearances, but must place the emphasis of life where it belongs.

No man, it is said, can read the works of John Ruskin without learning that his sources of pleasure are well-nigh infinite. There is not a flower, nor a cloud, nor a tree, nor a mountain, nor a star; not a bird that fans the air, nor a creature that walks the earth; not a glimpse of sea or sky or meadow-greenery; not a work of worthy art in the domains of painting, sculpture, poetry, and architecture; not a thought of God as the Great Spirit presiding over and informing all things, that is not to him a source of the sweetest pleasure. The whole world of matter and of spirit and the long record of human art are open to him as the never-failing fountains of his delight. In these pure realms he seeks his daily food and has his daily life.

There is now and then a man who sees beauty and true riches everywhere, and "worships the splendor of God which he sees bursting through each chink and cranny."

Phillips Brooks, Thoreau, Garrison, Emerson, Beecher, Agassiz, were rich without money. They saw the splendor in the flower, the glory in the grass, books in the running brooks, sermons in stones, and good in everything. They knew that the man who owns the landscape is seldom the one who pays the taxes on it. They sucked in power and wealth at first hands from the meadows, fields, and flowers, birds, brooks, mountains, and forest, as the bee sucks honey from the flowers. Every natural object seemed to bring them a special message from the great Author of the beautiful. To these rare souls every natural object was touched with power and beauty; and their thirsty souls drank it in as a traveler on a desert drinks in the god-sent water of the oasis. To extract power and real wealth from men and things seemed to be their mission, and to pour it out again in refreshing showers upon a thirsty humanity. They believed that man's most important food does not enter by the mouth. They knew that man could not live by estates, dollars, and bread alone, and that if he could he would only be an animal. They believed that the higher life demands a higher food. They believed in man's unlimited power of expansion, and that this growth demands a more highly organized food product than that which merely sustains animal life. They saw a finer nutriment in the landscape, in the meadows, than could be ground into flour, and which escaped the loaf. They felt a sentiment in natural objects which pointed upward, ever upward to the Author, and which was capable of feeding and expanding the higher life until it should grow into a finer sympathy and fellowship with the Author of the beautiful. They believed that the Creation thunders the ten commandments, and that all Nature is tugging at the terms of every contract to make it just. They could feel this finer sentiment, this soul lifter, this man inspirer, in the growing grain, in the waving corn, in the golden harvest. They saw it reflected in every brook, in every star, in every flower, in every dewdrop. They believed that Nature together with human nature were man's great schoolmasters, that if rightly used they would carve his rough life into beauty and touch his rude manner with grace.

"More servants wait on man than he'll take notice of." But if he would enjoy Nature he must come to it from a higher level than the yardstick. He must bring a spirit as grand and sublime as that by which the thing itself exists.

We all live on far lower levels than we need to do. We linger in the misty and oppressive valleys, when we might be climbing the sunlit hills. God puts into our hands the Book of Life, bright on every page with open secrets, and we suffer it to drop out of our hands unread. Emerson says, "We have come into a world which is a living poem. Everything is as I am." Nature provides for us a perpetual festival; she is bright to the bright, comforting to those who will accept comfort. We cannot conceive how a universe could possibly be created which could devise more efficient methods or greater opportunities for the delight, the happiness, and the real wealth of human beings than the one we live in.

The human body is packed full of marvelous devices, of wonderful contrivances, of infinite possibilities for the happiness and riches of the individual. No physiologist nor scientist has ever yet been able to point out a single improvement, even in the minutest detail, in the structure of the human body. No inventor has ever yet been able to suggest an improvement in this human mechanism. No chemist has ever been able to suggest a superior combination in any one of the elements which make up the human structure. One of the first things to do in life is to learn the natural wealth of our surroundings, instead of bemoaning our lot, for, no matter where we are placed, there is infinitely more about us than we can ever understand, than we can ever exhaust the meaning of.

"Thank Heaven there are still some Matthew Arnolds who prefer the heavenly sweetness of light to the Eden of riches." Arnold left only a few thousand dollars, but yet was he not one of the richest of men? What the world wants is young men who will amass golden thoughts, golden wisdom, golden deeds, not mere golden dollars; young men who prefer to have thought-capital, character-capital, to cash-capital. He who estimates his money the highest values himself the least. "I revere the person," says Emerson, "who is riches; so that I cannot think of him as alone, or poor, or exiled, or unhappy."

Raphael was rich without money. All doors opened to him, and he was more than welcome everywhere. His sweet spirit radiated sunshine wherever he went.

Henry Wilson was rich without money. So scrupulous had he been not to make his exalted position a means of worldly gain, that when this Natick cobbler, the sworn friend of the oppressed, whose one question as to measures or acts was ever "Is it right; will it do good?" came to be inaugurated as Vice-President of the country, he was obliged to borrow of his fellow-senator, Charles Sumner, one hundred dollars to meet the necessary expenses of the occasion.

Mozart, the great composer of the "Requiem," left barely enough money to bury him, but he has made the world richer.

A rich mind and noble spirit will cast a radiance of beauty over the humblest home, which the upholsterer and decorator can never approach. Who would not prefer to be a millionaire of character, of contentment, rather than possess nothing but the vulgar coins of a Croesus? Whoever uplifts civilization is rich though he die penniless, and future generations will erect his monument.

Are we tender, loving, self-denying, and honest, trying to fashion our frail life after that of the model man of Nazareth? Then, though our pockets are often empty, we have an inheritance which is as overwhelmingly precious as it is eternally incorruptible.

An Asiatic traveler tells us that one day he found the bodies of two men laid upon the desert sand beside the carcass of a camel. They had evidently died from thirst, and yet around the waist of each was a large store of jewels of different kinds, which they had doubtless been crossing the desert to sell in the markets of Persia.

The man who has no money is poor, but one who has nothing but money is poorer than he. He only is rich who can enjoy without owning; he who is covetous is poor though he have millions. There are riches of intellect, and no man with an intellectual taste can be called poor. He who has so little knowledge of human nature as to seek happiness by changing anything but his own disposition will waste his life in fruitless efforts, and multiply the griefs which he purposes to remove. He is rich as well as brave who can face poverty and misfortune with cheerfulness and courage.

We can so educate the will power that it will focus the thoughts upon the bright side of things, and upon objects which elevate the soul, thus forming a habit of happiness and goodness which will make us rich. The habit of making the best of everything and of always looking on the bright side of everything is a fortune in itself.

He is rich who values a good name above gold. Among the ancient Greeks and Romans honor was more sought after than wealth. Rome was imperial Rome no more when the imperial purple became an article of traffic.

This is the evil of trade, as well as of partisan politics. As Emerson remarks, it would put everything into market,—talent, beauty, virtue, and man himself.

Diogenes was captured by pirates and sold as a slave. His purchaser released him, and gave him charge of his household and of the education of his children. He despised wealth and affectation, and lived in a tub. "Do you want anything?" asked Alexander the Great, forcibly impressed by the abounding cheerfulness of the philosopher under such circumstances. "Yes," replied Diogenes, "I want you to stand out of my sunshine and not to take from me what you cannot give me." "Were I not Alexander," exclaimed the great conqueror, "I would be Diogenes."

Brave and honest men do not work for gold. They work for love, for honor, for character. When Socrates suffered death rather than abandon his views of right morality, when Las Casas endeavored to mitigate the tortures of the poor Indians, they had no thought of money or country. They worked for the elevation of all that thought, and for the relief of all that suffered.

"I don't want such things," said Epictetus to the rich Roman orator who was making light of his contempt for money-wealth; "and besides," said the stoic, "you are poorer than I am, after all. You have silver vessels, but earthenware reasons, principles, appetites. My mind to me a kingdom is, and it furnishes me with abundant and happy occupation in lieu of your restless idleness. All your possessions seem small to you; mine seem great to me. Your desire is insatiate, mine is satisfied."

"Do you know, sir," said a devotee of Mammon to John Bright, "that I am worth a million sterling?" "Yes," said the irritated but calm-spirited respondent, "I do; and I know that it is all you are worth."

A bankrupt merchant, returning home one night, said to his noble wife, "My dear, I am ruined; everything we have is in the hands of the sheriff." After a few moments of silence the wife looked into his face and asked, "Will the sheriff sell you?" "Oh, no." "Will the sheriff sell me?" "Oh, no." "Then do not say we have lost everything. All that is most valuable remains to us,—manhood, womanhood, childhood. We have lost but the results of our skill and industry. We can make another fortune if our hearts and hands are left us."

What power can poverty have over a home where loving hearts are beating with a consciousness of untold riches of head and heart?

Paul was never so great as when he occupied a prison cell; and Jesus Christ reached the height of his success when, smitten, spat upon, tormented, and crucified, He cried in agony, and yet with triumphant satisfaction, "It is finished."

"Character before wealth," was the motto of Amos Lawrence, who had inscribed on his pocket-book, "What shall it profit a man, if he shall gain the whole world and lose his own soul?"

If you make a fortune let every dollar of it be clean. You do not want to see in it drunkards reel, orphans weep, widows moan. Your riches must not make others poorer and more wretched.

Alexander the Great wandered to the gates of Paradise, and knocked for entrance. "Who knocks?" demanded the guardian angel. "Alexander." "Who is Alexander?" "Alexander,—the Alexander,—Alexander the Great,—the conqueror of the world." "We know him not," replied the angel; "this is the Lord's gate; only the righteous enter here."

Don't start out in life with a false standard; a truly great man makes official position and money and houses and estates look so tawdry, so mean and poor, that we feel like sinking out of sight with our cheap laurels and gold. Millions look trifling beside character.

A friend of Professor Agassiz, an eminent practical man, once expressed his wonder that a man of such abilities should remain contented with such a moderate income as he received. "I have enough," was Agassiz's reply. "I have no time to waste in making money. Life is not sufficiently long to enable a man to get rich and do his duty to his fellow-men at the same time."

How were the thousands of business men who lost every dollar they had in the Chicago fire enabled to go into business at once, some into wholesale business, without money? Their record was their bank account. The commercial agencies said they were square men; that they had always paid one hundred cents on a dollar; that they had paid promptly, and that they were industrious and dealt honorably with all men. This record was as good as a bank account. They drew on their character. Character was the coin which enabled penniless men to buy thousands of dollars' worth of goods. Their integrity did not burn up with their stores. The best part of them was beyond the reach of fire and could not be burned.

What are the toil-sweated productions of wealth piled up in vast profusion around a Girard, or a Rothschild, when weighed against the stores of wisdom, the treasures of knowledge, and the strength, beauty, and glory with which victorious virtue has enriched and adorned a great multitude of minds during the march of a hundred generations?

"Lord, how many things are in the world of which Diogenes hath no need!" exclaimed the stoic, as he wandered among the miscellaneous articles at a country fair.

"There are treasures laid up in the heart—treasures of charity, piety, temperance, and soberness. These treasures a man takes with him beyond death when he leaves this world." (Buddhist Scriptures.)

Is it any wonder that our children start out with wrong ideals of life, with wrong ideas of what constitutes success? The child is "urged to get on," to "rise in the world," to "make money." The youth is constantly told that nothing succeeds like success. False standards are everywhere set up for him, and then the boy is blamed if he makes a failure.

It is all very well to urge youth on to success, but the great mass of mankind can never reach or even approximate the goal constantly preached to them, nor can we all be rich. One of the great lessons to teach in this century of sharp competition and the survival of the fittest is how to be rich without money, and to learn how to do without success, according to the popular standard.

Gold cannot make the miser rich, nor can the want of it make the beggar poor.

In the poem, "The Changed Cross," a weary woman is represented as dreaming that she was led to a place where many crosses lay, crosses of divers shapes and sizes. The most beautiful one was set in jewels of gold. It was so tiny and exquisite that she changed her own plain cross for it, thinking she was fortunate in finding one so much lighter and lovelier. But soon her back began to ache under the glittering burden, and she changed it for another cross very beautiful and entwined with flowers. But she soon found that underneath the flowers were piercing thorns which tore her flesh. At last she came to a very plain cross without jewels, without carving, and with only the word, "Love," inscribed upon it. She took this one up and it proved the easiest and best of all. She was amazed, however, to find that it was her old cross which she had discarded. It is easy to see the jewels and the flowers in other people's crosses, but the thorns and heavy weight are known only to the bearers. How easy other people's burdens seem to us compared with our own. We do not appreciate the secret burdens which almost crush the heart, nor the years of weary waiting for delayed success—the aching hearts longing for sympathy, the hidden poverty, the suppressed emotion in other lives.

William Pitt, the great Commoner, considered money as dirt beneath his feet compared with the public interest and public esteem. His hands were clean.

The object for which we strive tells the story of our lives. Men and women should be judged by the happiness they create in those around them. Noble deeds always enrich, but millions of mere money may impoverish. Character is perpetual wealth, and by the side of him who possesses it the millionaire who has it not seems a pauper. Compared with it, what are houses and lands, stocks and bonds? "It is better that great souls should live in small habitations than that abject slaves should burrow in great houses." Plain living, rich thought, and grand effort are real riches.

Invest in yourself, and you will never be poor. Floods cannot carry your wealth away, fire cannot burn it, rust cannot consume it.

"If a man empties his purse into his head," says Franklin, "no man can take it from him. An investment in knowledge always pays the best interest."

"There is a cunning juggle in riches. I observe," says Emerson, "that they take somewhat for everything they give. I look bigger, but I am less, I have more clothes, but am not so warm; more armor, but less courage; more books, but less wit."

Howe'er it be, it seems to me,
'T is only noble to be good.
Kind hearts are more than coronets,
And simple faith than Norman blood.
TENNYSON.

CHAPTER XIV. OPPORTUNITIES WHERE YOU ARE.

To each man's life there comes a time supreme;
One day, one night, one morning, or one noon,
One freighted hour, one moment opportune,
One rift through which sublime fulfillments gleam,
One space when fate goes tiding with the stream,
One Once, in balance 'twixt Too Late, Too Soon,
And ready for the passing instant's boon
To tip in favor the uncertain beam.
Ah, happy he who, knowing how to wait,
Knows also how to watch and work and stand
On Life's broad deck alert, and at the prow
To seize the passing moment, big with fate,
From opportunity's extended hand,
When the great clock of destiny strikes Now!
MARY A. TOWNSEND.
Once to every man and nation comes the moment to decide,
In the strife of Truth with Falsehood, for the good or evil side.
LOWELL.
What is opportunity to a man who can't use it? An unfecundated egg, which the waves of time
wash away into nonentity.—GEORGE ELIOT.

A thousand years a poor man watched
Before the gate of Paradise:
But while one little nap he snatched,
It oped and shut. Ah! was he wise?
W. B. ALGER.
Our grand business is, not to see what lies dimly at a distance, but to do what lies clearly at
hand.—CARLYLE.

A man's best things are nearest him,
Lie close about his feet.
R. M. MILNES.
The secret of success in life is for a man to be ready for his opportunity when it comes.—
DISRAELI.

"There are no longer any good chances for young men," complained a law student to Daniel
Webster. "There is always room at the top," replied the great lawyer.

No chance, no opportunities, in a land where many poor boys become rich men, where newsboys go to Congress, and where those born in the lowest stations attain the highest positions? The world is all gates, all opportunities to him who will use them. But, like Bunyan's Pilgrim in the dungeon of Giant Despair's castle, who had the key of deliverance all the time with him but had forgotten it, we fail to rely wholly upon the ability to advance all that is good for us which has been given to the weakest as well as the strongest. We depend too much upon outside assistance.

"We look too high
For things close by."

A Baltimore lady lost a valuable diamond bracelet at a ball, and supposed that it was stolen from the pocket of her cloak. Years afterward she washed the steps of the Peabody Institute, pondering how to get money to buy food. She cut up an old, worn-out, ragged cloak to make a hood, when lo! in the lining of the cloak she discovered the diamond bracelet. During all her poverty she was worth $3500, but did not know it.

Many of us who think we are poor are rich in opportunities, if we could only see them, in possibilities all about us, in faculties worth more than diamond bracelets. In our large Eastern cities it has been found that at least ninety-four out of every hundred found their first fortune at home, or near at hand, and in meeting common every-day wants. It is a sorry day for a young man who cannot see any opportunities where he is, but thinks he can do better somewhere else. Some Brazilian shepherds organized a party to go to California to dig gold, and took along a handful of translucent pebbles to play checkers with on the voyage. After arriving in San Francisco, and after they had thrown most of the pebbles away, they discovered that they were diamonds. They hastened back to Brazil, only to find that the mines from which the pebbles had been gathered had been taken up by others and sold to the government.

The richest gold and silver mine in Nevada was sold for $42 by the owner to get money to pay his passage to other mines, where he thought he could get rich. Professor Agassiz told the Harvard students of a farmer who owned a farm of hundreds of acres of unprofitable woods and rocks, and concluded to sell out and get into a more profitable business. He decided to go into the coal-oil business; he studied coal measures and coal-oil deposits, and experimented for a long time. He sold his farm for $200, and engaged in his new business two hundred miles away. Only a short time after the man who bought his farm discovered upon it a great flood of coal-oil, which the farmer had previously ignorantly tried to drain off.

Hundreds of years ago there lived near the shore of the river Indus a Persian by the name of Ali Hafed. He lived in a cottage on the river bank, from which he could get a grand view of the beautiful country stretching away to the sea. He had a wife and children, an extensive farm, fields of grain, gardens of flowers, orchards of fruit, and miles of forest. He had a plenty of money and everything that heart could wish. He was contented and happy. One evening a priest of Buddha visited him, and, sitting before the fire, explained to him how the world was made, and how the first beams of sunlight condensed on the earth's surface into diamonds. The old priest told that a drop of sunlight the size of his thumb was worth more than large mines of copper, silver, or gold; that with one of them he could buy many farms like his; that with a handful he could buy a province, and with a mine of diamonds he could purchase a kingdom. Ali

Hafed listened, and was no longer a rich man. He had been touched with discontent, and with that all wealth vanishes. Early the next morning he woke the priest who had been the cause of his unhappiness, and anxiously asked him where he could find a mine of diamonds. "What do you want of diamonds?" asked the astonished priest. "I want to be rich and place my children on thrones." "All you have to do is to go and search until you find them," said the priest. "But where shall I go?" asked the poor farmer. "Go anywhere, north, south, east, or west." "How shall I know when I have found the place?" "When you find a river running over white sands between high mountain ranges, in those white sands you will find diamonds," answered the priest.

The discontented man sold the farm for what he could get, left his family with a neighbor, took the money he had at interest, and went to search for the coveted treasure. Over the mountains of Arabia, through Palestine and Egypt, he wandered for years, but found no diamonds. When his money was all gone and starvation stared him in the face, ashamed of his folly and of his rags, poor Ali Hafed threw himself into the tide and was drowned. The man who bought his farm was a contented man, who made the most of his surroundings, and did not believe in going away from home to hunt for diamonds or success. While his camel was drinking in the garden one day, he noticed a flash of light from the white sands of the brook. He picked up a pebble, and pleased with its brilliant hues took it into the house, put it on the shelf near the fireplace, and forgot all about it. The old priest of Buddha who had filled Ali Hafed with the fatal discontent called one day upon the new owner of the farm. He had no sooner entered the room than his eye caught that flash of light from the stone. "Here's a diamond! here's a diamond!" the old priest shouted in great excitement. "Has Ali Hafed returned?" said the priest. "No," said the farmer, "nor is that a diamond. That is but a stone." They went into the garden and stirred up the white sand with their fingers, and behold, other diamonds more beautiful than the first gleamed out of it. So the famous diamond beds of Golconda were discovered. Had Ali Hafed been content to remain at home, had he dug in his own garden, instead of going abroad in search for wealth, and reaping poverty, hardships, starvation, and death, he would have been one of the richest men in the world, for the entire farm abounded in the richest of gems.

You have your own special place and work. Find it, fill it. Scarcely a boy or girl will read these lines but has much better opportunity to win success than Garfield, Wilson, Franklin, Lincoln, Harriet Beecher Stowe, Frances Willard, and thousands of others. But to succeed you must be prepared to seize and improve the opportunity when it comes. Remember that four things come not back: the spoken word, the sped arrow, the past life, and the neglected opportunity.

It is one of the paradoxes of civilization that the more opportunities are utilized, the more new ones are thereby created. New openings are as easy to fill as ever to those who do their best; although it is not so easy as formerly to obtain distinction in the old lines, because the standard has advanced so much and competition has so greatly increased. "The world is no longer clay," said Emerson, "but rather iron in the hands of its workers, and men have got to hammer out a place for themselves by steady and rugged blows."

Thousands of men have made fortunes out of trifles which others pass by. As the bee gets honey from the same flower from which the spider gets poison, so some men will get a fortune out of the commonest and meanest things, as scraps of leather, cotton waste, slag, iron filings, from which others get only poverty and failure. There is scarcely a thing which contributes to the welfare and comfort of humanity, not an article of household furniture, a kitchen utensil, an article of clothing or of food, that is not capable of an improvement in which there may be a fortune.

Opportunities? They are all around us. Edison found them in a baggage car. Forces of nature plead to be used in the service of man, as lightning for ages tried to attract his attention to the great force of electricity, which would do his drudgery and leave him to develop the God-given powers within him. There is power lying latent everywhere waiting for the observant eye to discover it.

First find out what the world needs and then supply that want. An invention to make smoke go the wrong way in a chimney might be a very ingenious thing, but it would be of no use to humanity. The patent office at Washington is full of wonderful devices of ingenious mechanism, but not one in hundreds is of use to the inventor or to the world. And yet how many families have been impoverished, and have struggled for years amid want and woe, while the father has been working on useless inventions. A. T. Stewart, as a boy, lost eighty-seven cents when his capital was one dollar and a half in buying buttons and thread which shoppers did not call for. After that he made it a rule never to buy anything which the public did not want, and so prospered.

It is estimated that five out of every seven of the millionaire manufacturers began by making with their own hands the articles which made their fortunes. One of the greatest hindrances to advancement in life is the lack of observation and of the inclination to take pains. An observing man, the eyelets of whose shoes pulled out, but who could not afford to get another pair, said to himself, "I will make a metallic lacing hook, which can be riveted into the leather;" he was so poor that he had to borrow a sickle to cut the grass in front of his hired tenement. Now he is a very rich man.

An observing barber in Newark, N. J., thought he could make an improvement in shears for cutting hair, invented clippers, and became rich. A Maine man was called in from the hayfield to wash clothes for his invalid wife. He had never realized what it was to wash before. Finding the method slow and laborious, he invented the washing-machine, and made a fortune. A man who was suffering terribly with toothache said to himself, there must be some way of filling teeth which will prevent their aching. So he invented the principle of gold filling for teeth.

The great things of the world have not been done by men of large means. Ericsson began the construction of the screw propellers in a bathroom. The cotton-gin was first manufactured in a log cabin. John Harrison, the great inventor of the marine chronometer, began his career in the loft of an old barn. Parts of the first steamboat ever run in America were set up in the vestry of a church in Philadelphia by Fitch. McCormick began to make his famous reaper in a gristmill. The first model dry dock was made in an attic. Clark, the founder of Clark University of Worcester, Mass., began his great fortune by making toy wagons in a horse shed. Farquhar made umbrellas in his sitting-room, with his daughter's help, until he sold enough to hire a loft. Edison began his experiments in a baggage car on the Grand Trunk Railroad when a newsboy.

As soon as the weather would permit, the Jamestown colonists began to stroll about the country digging for gold. In a bank of sand some glittering particles were found, and the whole settlement was in a state of excitement. Fourteen weeks of the precious springtime, which ought to have been given to plowing and planting, were consumed in this stupid nonsense. Even the Indians ridiculed the madness of the men who, for imaginary grains of gold, were wasting their chances for a crop of corn.

Michael Angelo found a piece of discarded Carrara marble among waste rubbish beside a street in Florence, which some unskillful workman had cut, hacked, spoiled, and thrown away. No doubt many artists had noticed the fine quality of the marble, and regretted that it should have been spoiled. But Michael Angelo still saw an angel in the ruin, and with his chisel and mallet he called out from it one of the finest pieces of statuary in Italy, the young David.

The lonely island of Nantucket would not be considered a very favorable place to win success and fame. But Maria Mitchell, on seventy-five dollars a year, as librarian of the Nantucket Athenaeum, found time and opportunity to become a celebrated astronomer. Lucretia Mott, one of America's foremost philanthropists and reformers, who made herself felt over a whole continent, gained much of her reputation as a preacher on Nantucket Island.

"Why does not America have fine sculptors?" asked a romping girl, of Watertown, Mass., in 1842. Her father, a physician, answered that he supposed "an American could be a stone-cutter, but that is a very different thing from being a sculptor." "I think," said the plucky maiden, "that if no other American tries it I will." She began her studies in Boston, and walked seven miles to and fro daily between her home and the city. The medical schools in Boston would not admit her to study anatomy, so she had to go to St. Louis. Subsequently she went to Rome, and there, during a long residence, and afterward, modeled and carved very beautiful statuary which made the name of Harriet G. Hosmer famous. Begin where you are; work where you are; the hour which you are now wasting, dreaming of some far-off success, may be crowded with grand possibilities.

Patrick Henry was called a lazy boy, a good-for-nothing farmer, and he failed as a merchant. He was always dreaming of some far-off greatness, and never thought he could be a hero among the corn and tobacco and saddlebags of Virginia. He studied law six weeks, when he put out his shingle. People thought he would fail, but in his first case he showed that he had a wonderful power of oratory. It then first dawned upon him that he could be a hero in Virginia. From the time the Stamp Act was passed and Henry was elected to the Virginia House of Burgesses, and he had introduced his famous resolution against the unjust taxation of the American colonies, he rose steadily until he became one of the brilliant orators of America. In one of his first speeches upon this resolution he uttered these words, which were prophetic of his power and courage: "Caesar had his Brutus, Charles the First his Cromwell, and George the Third—may profit by their example. If this be treason, make the most of it."

The great natural philosopher, Faraday, who was the son of a blacksmith, wrote, when a young man, to Humphry Davy, asking for employment at the Royal Institution. Davy consulted a friend on the matter. "Here is a letter from a young man named Faraday, he has been attending my lectures, and wants me to give him employment at the Royal Institution—what can I do?" "Do? put him to washing bottles; if he is good for anything he will do it directly; if he refuses he is good for nothing." But the boy who could experiment in the attic of an apothecary shop with an old pan and glass vials during every moment he could snatch from his work saw an opportunity in washing bottles, which led to a professorship at the Royal Academy at Woolwich. Tyndall said of this boy with no chance, "He is the greatest experimental philosopher the world has ever seen." He became the wonder of his age in science.

There is a legend of an artist who long sought for a piece of sandal-wood, out of which to carve a Madonna. He was about to give up in despair, leaving the vision of his life unrealized, when in a dream he was bidden to carve his Madonna from a block of oak wood which was destined for the fire. He obeyed, and produced a masterpiece from a log of common firewood. Many of us lose great opportunities in life by waiting to find sandal-wood for our carvings, when they really lie hidden in the common logs that we burn. One man goes through life without seeing chances for doing anything great, while another close beside him snatches from the same circumstances and privileges opportunities for achieving grand results.

Anna Dickinson began life as a school-teacher. Adelaide Neilson was a child's nurse. Charlotte Cushman's parents were poor. The renowned Jeanne d'Arc fed swine. Christine Nilsson was a poor Swedish peasant, and ran barefoot in childhood. Edmonia Lewis, the colored sculptor, overcame the prejudice against her sex and color, and pursued her profession in Italy. Maria Mitchell, the astronomer, was the daughter of a poor man who taught school at two dollars per week. These are but a few of the many who have struggled with fate and risen to distinction through their own personal efforts.

Opportunities? They are everywhere. "America is another name for opportunities. Our whole history appears like a last effort of divine Providence in behalf of the human race." Never before were there such grand openings, such chances, such opportunities. Especially is this true for girls and young women. A new era is dawning for them. Hundreds of occupations and professions, which were closed to them only a few years ago, are now inviting them to enter.

When I hear of a young woman entering the medical profession, or beginning the study of law, or entering school with a view to teaching, I feel like congratulating her for thus asserting her individuality.

We cannot all of us perhaps make great discoveries like Newton, Faraday, Edison, and Thompson. We cannot all of us paint immortal pictures like an Angelo or a Raphael. But we can all of us make our lives sublime, by seizing common occasions and making them great. What chance had the young girl, Grace Darling, to distinguish herself, living on those barren lighthouse rocks alone with her aged parents? But while her brothers and sisters, who moved to the cities to win wealth and fame, are not known to the world, she became more famous than a princess. This poor girl did not need to go to London to see the nobility; they came to the lighthouse to see her. Right at home this young girl had won fame which the regal heirs might envy, and a name which will never perish from the earth. She did not wander away into dreamy distance for fame and fortune, but did her best where duty had placed her.

If you want to get rich, study yourself and your own wants. You will find that millions have the same wants. The safest business is always connected with man's prime necessities. He must have clothing and a dwelling; he must eat. He wants comforts, facilities of all kinds for pleasure, luxuries, education, and culture. Any man who can supply a great want of humanity, improve any methods which men use, supply any demand of comfort, or contribute in any way to their well-being, can make a fortune.

"We cannot doubt," said Edward Everett, "that truths now unknown are in reserve to reward the patience and the labors of future lovers of truth, which will go as far beyond the brilliant discoveries of the last generation as these do beyond all that was known to the ancient world."

The golden opportunity
Is never offered twice; seize then the hour
When fortune smiles and duty points the way;
Nor shrink aside to 'scape the spectre fear,
Nor pause, though pleasure beckon from her bower;
But bravely bear thee onward to the goal.
ANON.
For the distant still thou yearnest,
And behold the good so near;
If to use the good thou learnest,
Thou wilt surely find it here.
GOETHE.
Do not, then, stand idly waiting
For some greater work to do;
Fortune is a lazy goddess—
She will never come to you.
Go and toil in any vineyard,
Do not fear to do or dare;
If you want a field of labor,
You can find it anywhere.
ELLEN H. GATES.
Why thus longing, thus forever sighing,
For the far-off, unattained and dim,
While the beautiful, all around thee lying
Offers up its low, perpetual hymn?
HARRIET WINSLOW.
Work for the good that is nighest;
Dream not of greatness afar:
That glory is ever the highest
Which shines upon men as they are.
W. MORLEY PUNSHON.

CHAPTER XV. THE MIGHT OF LITTLE THINGS.

Little strokes fell great oaks.—FRANKLIN.

Think naught a trifle, though it small appear;
Small sands the mountain, moments make the year,
And trifles, life.
YOUNG.
"Scorn not the slightest word or deed,
Nor deem it void of power;
There's fruit in each wind-wafted seed,
That waits its natal hour."
It is but the littleness of man that seeth no greatness in trifles.—WENDELL PHILLIPS.

He that despiseth small things shall fall by little and little.—ECCLESIASTICUS.

Often from our weakness our strongest principles of conduct are born; and from the acorn, which a breeze has wafted, springs the oak which defies the storm.—BULWER.

The creation of a thousand forests is in one acorn.—EMERSON.

Men are led by trifles.—NAPOLEON I.

"A pebble on the streamlet scant
Has turned the course of many a river;
A dewdrop on the baby plant
Has warped the giant oak forever."
The mother of mischief is no bigger than a midge's wing.—SCOTCH PROVERB.

"The bad thing about a little sin is that it won't stay little."

"A little bit of patience often makes the sunshine come,
And a little bit of love makes a very happy home;
A little bit of hope makes a rainy day look gay,
And a little bit of charity makes glad a weary way."

"Arletta's pretty feet, glistening in the brook, made her the mother of William the Conqueror," says Palgrave's "History of Normandy and England." "Had she not thus fascinated Duke Robert the Liberal, of Normandy, Harold would not have fallen at Hastings, no Anglo-Norman dynasty could have arisen, no British Empire."

We may tell which way the wind blew before the Deluge by marking the ripple and cupping of the rain in the petrified sand now preserved forever. We tell the very path by which gigantic creatures, whom man never saw, walked to the river's edge to find their food.

The tears of Veturia and Volumnia saved Rome from the Volscians when nothing else could move the vengeful heart of Coriolanus.

It was little Greece that rolled back the overflowing tide of Asiatic luxury and despotism, giving instead to Europe and America models of the highest political freedom yet attained, and germs of limitless mental growth. A different result at Plataea had delayed the progress of the human race more than ten centuries.

Among the lofty Alps, it is said, the guides sometimes demand absolute silence, lest the vibration of the voice bring down an avalanche.

The power of observation in the American Indian would put many an educated man to shame. Returning home, an Indian discovered that his venison, which had been hanging up to dry, had been stolen. After careful observation he started to track the thief through the woods. Meeting a man on the route, he asked him if he had seen a little, old, white man, with a short gun, and with a small bob-tailed dog. The man told him he had met such a man, but was surprised to find that the Indian had not even seen the one he described. He asked the Indian how he could give such a minute description of the man whom he had never seen. "I knew the thief was a little man," said the Indian, "because he rolled up a stone to stand on in order to reach the venison; I knew he was an old man by his short steps; I knew he was a white man by his turning out his toes in walking, which an Indian never does; I knew he had a short gun by the mark it left on the tree where he had stood it up; I knew the dog was small by his tracks and short steps, and that he had a bob-tail by the mark it left in the dust where he sat."

Two drops of rain, falling side by side, were separated a few inches by a gentle breeze. Striking on opposite sides of the roof of a court-house in Wisconsin, one rolled southward through the Rock River and the Mississippi to the Gulf of Mexico; while the other entered successively the Fox River, Green Bay, Lake Michigan, the Straits of Mackinaw, Lake Huron, St. Clair River, Lake St. Clair, Detroit River, Lake Erie, Niagara River, Lake Ontario, the St. Lawrence River, and finally reached the Gulf of St. Lawrence. How slight the influence of the breeze, yet such was the formation of the continent that a trifling cause was multiplied almost beyond the power of figures to express its momentous effect upon the destinies of these companion raindrops. Who can calculate the future of the smallest trifle when a mud crack swells to an Amazon, and the stealing of a penny may end on the scaffold? Who does not know that the act of a moment may cause a life's regret? A trigger may be pulled in an instant, but the soul returns never.

A spark falling upon some combustibles led to the invention of gunpowder. Irritable tempers have marred the reputation of many a great man, as in the case of Edmund Burke and of Thomas Carlyle. A few bits of seaweed and driftwood, floating on the waves, enabled Columbus to stay a mutiny of his sailors which threatened to prevent the discovery of a new world. There are moments in history which balance years of ordinary life. Dana could interest a class for hours on a grain of sand; and from a single bone, such as no one had ever seen before, Agassiz could deduce the entire structure and habits of an animal so accurately that subsequent discoveries of complete skeletons have not changed one of his conclusions.

A cricket once saved a military expedition from destruction. The commanding officer and hundreds of his men were going to South America on a great ship, and, through the carelessness of the watch, they would have been dashed upon a ledge of rock had it not been for a cricket which a soldier had brought on board. When the little insect scented the land, it broke its long silence by a shrill note, and this warned them of their danger.

"Strange that a little thing like that should cause a man so much pain!" exclaimed a giant, as he rolled in his hand and examined with eager curiosity the acorn which his friend the dwarf had obligingly taken from the huge eye into which it had fallen just as the colossus was on the point of shooting a bird perched in the branches of an oak.

Sometimes a conversation, or a sentence in a letter, or a paragraph in an article, will help us to reproduce the whole character of the author; as a single bone, a fish scale, a fin, or a tooth, will enable the scientist and anatomist to reproduce the fish or the animal, although extinct for ages.

By gnawing through a dike, even a rat may drown a nation. A little boy in Holland saw water trickling from a small hole near the bottom of a dike. He realized that the leak would rapidly become larger if the water was not checked, so he held his hand over the hole for hours on a dark and dismal night until he could attract the attention of passers-by. His name is still held in grateful remembrance in Holland.

The beetling chalk cliffs of England were built by rhizopods, too small to be clearly seen without the aid of a magnifying-glass.

What was so unlikely as that throwing an empty wine-flask in the fire should furnish the first notion of a locomotive, or that the sickness of an Italian chemist's wife and her absurd craving for reptiles for food should begin the electric telegraph?

Madame Galvani noticed the contraction of the muscles of a skinned frog which was accidentally touched at the moment her husband took a spark from an electrical machine. She gave the hint which led to the discovery of galvanic electricity, now so useful in the arts and in transmitting vocal or written language.

M. Louis Pasteur was usher in the Lyceum. Thursdays he took the boys to walk. A student took his microscope to examine insects, and allowed Pasteur to look through it. This was the starting of the boy on the microscopic career which has made men wonder. He was almost wild with enthusiasm at the new world which the microscope revealed.

A stamp act to raise 60,000 pounds produced the American Revolution, a war that cost 100,000,000 pounds. What mighty contests rise from trivial things!

Congress met near a livery stable to discuss the Declaration of Independence. The members, in knee breeches and silk stockings, were so annoyed by flies, which they could not keep away with their handkerchiefs, that it has been said they cut short the debate, and hastened to affix their signatures to the greatest document in history.

"The fate of a nation," says Gladstone, "has often depended upon the good or bad digestion of a fine dinner."

A young man once went to India to seek his fortune, but, finding no opening, he went to his room, loaded his pistol, put the muzzle to his head, and pulled the trigger. But it did not go off. He went to the window to point it in another direction and try it again, resolved that if the weapon went off he would regard it as a Providence that he was spared. He pulled the trigger and it went off the first time. Trembling with excitement he resolved to hold his life sacred, to make the most of it, and never again to cheapen it. This young man became General Robert Clive, who, with but a handful of European soldiers, secured to the East India Company and afterwards to Great Britain a great and rich country with two hundred millions of people.

The cackling of a goose aroused the sentinels and saved Rome from the Gauls, and the pain from a thistle warned a Scottish army of the approach of the Danes. "Had Acre fallen," said Napoleon, "I should have changed the face of the world."

Henry Ward Beecher came within one vote of being elected superintendent of a railway. If he had had that vote America would probably have lost its greatest preacher. What a little thing fixes destiny!

In the earliest days of cotton spinning, the small fibres would stick to the bobbins, and make it necessary to stop and clear the machinery. Although this loss of time reduced the earnings of the operatives, the father of Robert Peel noticed that one of his spinners always drew full pay, as his machine never stopped. "How is this, Dick?" asked Mr. Peel one day; "the on-looker tells me your bobbins are always clean." "Ay, that they be," replied Dick Ferguson. "How do you manage it, Dick?" "Why, you see, Meester Peel," said the workman, "it is sort o' secret! If I tow'd ye, yo'd be as wise as I am." "That's so," said Mr. Peel, smiling; "but I'd give you something to know. Could you make all the looms work as smoothly as yours?" "Ivery one of 'em, meester," replied Dick. "Well, what shall I give you for your secret?" asked Mr. Peel, and Dick replied, "Gi' me a quart of ale every day as I'm in the mills, and I'll tell thee all about it." "Agreed," said Mr. Peel, and Dick whispered very cautiously in his ear, "Chalk your bobbins!" That was the whole secret, and Mr. Peel soon shot ahead of all his competitors, for he made machines that would chalk their own bobbins. Dick was handsomely rewarded with money instead of beer. His little idea has saved the world millions of dollars.

Trifles light as air often suggest to the thinking mind ideas which have revolutionized the world.

A poor English boy was compelled by his employer to deposit something on board a ship about to start for Algiers, in accordance with the merchant's custom of interesting employees by making them put something at risk in his business and so share in the gain or loss of each common venture. The boy had only a cat, which he had bought for a penny to catch mice in the garret where he slept. In tears, he carried her on board the vessel. On arriving at Algiers, the captain learned that the Dey was greatly annoyed by rats, and loaned him the cat. The rats disappeared so rapidly that the Dey wished to buy the cat, but the captain would not sell until a very high price was offered. With the purchase-money was sent a present of valuable pearls for the owner of Tabby. When the ship returned the sailors were greatly astonished to find that the boy owned most of the cargo, for it was part of the bargain that he was to bring back the value of his cat in goods. The London merchant took the boy into partnership; the latter became very wealthy, and in the course of business loaned money to the Dey who had bought the cat. As Lord Mayor of London, our cat merchant was knighted, and became the second man in the city,—Sir Richard Whittington.

When John Williams, the martyr missionary of Erromanga, went to the South Sea Islands, he took with him a single banana-tree from an English nobleman's conservatory; and now, from that single banana-tree, bananas are to be found throughout whole groups of islands. Before the negro slaves in the West Indies were emancipated a regiment of British soldiers was stationed near one of the plantations. A soldier offered to teach a slave to read on condition that he would teach a second, and that second a third, and so on. This the slave faithfully carried out, though severely flogged by the master of the plantation. Being sent to another plantation, he repeated the same thing there, and when at length liberty was proclaimed throughout the island, and the Bible Society offered a New Testament to every negro who could read, the number taught through this slave's instrumentality was found to be no less than six hundred.

A famous ruby was offered to the English government. The report of the crown jeweler was that it was the finest he had ever seen or heard of, but that one of the "facets" was slightly fractured. That invisible fracture reduced its value thousands of dollars, and it was rejected from the regalia of England.

It was a little thing for the janitor to leave a lamp swinging in the cathedral at Pisa, but in that steady swaying motion the boy Galileo saw the pendulum, and conceived the idea of thus measuring time.

"I was singing to the mouthpiece of a telephone," said Edison, "when the vibrations of my voice caused a fine steel point to pierce one of my fingers held just behind it. That set me to thinking. If I could record the motions of the point and send it over the same surface afterward, I saw no reason why the thing would not talk. I determined to make a machine that would work accurately, and gave my assistants the necessary instructions, telling them what I had discovered. That's the whole story. The phonograph is the result of the pricking of a finger."

It was a little thing for a cow to kick over a lantern left in a shanty, but it laid Chicago in ashes, and rendered homeless a hundred thousand people.

You turned a cold shoulder but once, you made but one stinging remark, yet it lost you a friend forever.

Some little weakness, some self-indulgence, a quick temper, want of decision, are little things, you say, when placed beside great abilities, but they have wrecked many a career. The

Parliament of Great Britain, the Congress of the United States, and representative governments all over the world have come from King John signing the Magna Charta.

Bentham says, "The turn of a sentence has decided many a friendship, and, for aught we know, the fate of many a kingdom."

The sight of a stranded cuttlefish led Cuvier to an investigation which made him one of the greatest natural historians in the world. The web of a spider suggested to Captain Brown the idea of a suspension bridge. A man, looking for a lost horse, picked up a stone in the Idaho mountains which led to the discovery of a rich gold mine.

An officer apologized to General O. M. Mitchel, the astronomer, for a brief delay, saying he was only a few moments late. "I have been in the habit of calculating the value of the thousandth part of a second," was Mitchel's reply.

A missing marriage certificate kept the hod-carrier of Hugh Miller from establishing his claim to the Earldom of Crawford. The masons would call out, "John, Yearl of Crawford, bring us anither hod o' lime."

Not long ago the great steamship Umbria was stopped in mid-Atlantic by a flaw in her engine shaft.

The absence of a comma in a bill which passed through Congress several years ago cost our government a million dollars. A single misspelled word prevented a deserving young man from obtaining a situation as instructor in a New England college. A cinder on the eyeball will conquer a Napoleon. Some little weakness, as lack of courtesy, want of decision, a bad temper, may nullify the labor of years.

"I cannot see that you have made any progress since my last visit," said a gentleman to Michael Angelo. "But," said the sculptor, "I have retouched this part, polished that, softened that feature, brought out that muscle, given some expression to this lip, more energy to that limb, etc." "But they are trifles!" exclaimed the visitor. "It may be so," replied the great artist, "but trifles make perfection, and perfection is no trifle."

That infinite patience which made Michael Angelo spend a week in bringing out a muscle in a statue with more vital fidelity to truth, or Gerhard Dow a day in giving the right effect to a dewdrop on a cabbage leaf, makes all the difference between success and failure.

By scattering it upon a sloping field of grain so as to form, in letters of great size, "Effects of Gypsum," Franklin brought this fertilizer into general use in America. By means of a kite he established principles in the science of electricity of such broad significance that they underlie nearly all the modern applications of that science, with probably boundless possibilities of development in the future.

More than four hundred and fifty years have passed since Laurens Coster amused his children by cutting their names in the bark of trees, in the land of windmills, and the monks have laid aside forever their old trade of copying books. From that day monarchies have crumbled, and Liberty, lifting up her head for the first time among the nations of the earth, has ever since kept pace with the march of her sister, Knowledge, up through the centuries. Yet how simple was the thought which has borne such a rich harvest of benefit to mankind.

As he carved the names of his prattling children it occurred to him that if the letters were made in separate blocks, and wet with ink, they would make clear printed impressions better and more rapidly than would the pen. So he made blocks, tied them together with strings, and printed a pamphlet with the aid of a hired man, John Gutenberg. People bought the pamphlets at a slight reduction from the price charged by the monks, supposing that the work was done in the old way. Coster died soon afterward, but young Gutenberg kept the secret, and experimented with metals until he had invented the metal type. In an obscure chamber in Strasburg he printed his first book.

At about this time a traveler called upon Charles VII. of France, who was so afraid somebody would poison him that he dared eat but little, and made his servants taste of every dish of food before he ate any. He looked with suspicion upon the stranger; but when the latter offered a beautiful copy of the Bible for only seven hundred and fifty crowns, the monarch bought it at once. Charles showed his Bible to the archbishop, telling him that it was the finest copy in the world, without a blot or mistake, and that it must have taken the copyist a lifetime to write it. "Why!" exclaimed the archbishop in surprise, "I bought one exactly like it a few days ago." It was soon learned that other rich people in Paris had bought similar copies. The king traced the book to John Faust, of Strasburg, who had furnished Gutenberg money to experiment with. The people said that Faust must have sold himself to the devil, and he only escaped burning at the stake by divulging the secret.

William Caxton, a London merchant who went to Holland to purchase cloth, bought a few books and some type, and established a printing-office in Westminster Chapel, where he issued, in 1474, "The Game of Chess," the first book printed in England.

The cry of the infant Moses attracted the attention of Pharaoh's daughter, and gave the Jews a lawgiver. A bird alighting on the bough of a tree at the mouth of the cave where Mahomet lay hid turned aside his pursuers, and gave a prophet to many nations. A flight of birds probably prevented Columbus from discovering this continent, for when he was growing anxious, Martin Alonzo Pinzon persuaded him to follow a flight of parrots toward the southwest; for to the Spanish seamen of that day it was good luck to follow in the wake of a flock of birds when on a voyage of discovery. But for his change of course Columbus would have reached the coast of Florida. "Never," wrote Humboldt, "had the flight of birds more important consequences."

The children of a spectacle-maker placed two or more pairs of the spectacles before each other in play, and told their father that distant objects looked larger. From this hint came the telescope.

"Of what use is it?" people asked with a sneer, when Franklin told of his discovery that lightning and electricity are identical. "What is the use of a child?" replied Franklin; "it may become a man."

"He who waits to do a great deal of good at once," said Dr. Johnson, "will never do any." Do good with what thou hast, or it will do thee no good.

Every day is a little life; and our whole life but a day repeated. Those that dare lose a day are dangerously prodigal, those that dare misspend it, desperate. What is the happiness of your life made up of? Little courtesies, little kindnesses, pleasant words, genial smiles, a friendly letter, good wishes, and good deeds. One in a million—once in a lifetime—may do a heroic action. The atomic theory is the true one. Many think common fractions vulgar, but they are the components of millions.

He is a great man who sees great things where others see little things, who sees the extraordinary in the ordinary. Ruskin sees a poem in the rose or the lily, while the hod-carrier would perhaps not go a rod out of his way to see a sunset which Ruskin would feed upon for a year.

Napoleon was a master of trifles. To details which his inferior officers thought too microscopic for their notice he gave the most exhaustive attention. Nothing was too small for his attention. He must know all about the provisions, the horse fodder, the biscuits, the camp kettles, the shoes. When the bugle sounded for the march to battle, every officer had his orders as to the exact route which he should follow, the exact day he was to arrive at a certain station, and the exact hour he was to leave, and they were all to reach the point of destination at a precise moment. It is said that nothing could be more perfectly planned than his memorable march which led to the victory of Austerlitz, and which sealed the fate of Europe for many years. He would often charge his absent officers to send him perfectly accurate returns, even to the smallest detail. "When they are sent to me, I give up every occupation in order to read them in detail, and to observe the difference between one monthly return and another. No young girl enjoys her novel as much as I do these returns." The captain who conveyed Napoleon to Elba was astonished with his familiarity with all the minute details connected with the ship. Napoleon left nothing to chance, nothing to contingency, so far as he could possibly avoid it. Everything was planned to a nicety before he attempted to execute it.

Wellington too was "great in little things." He knew no such things as trifles. While other generals trusted to subordinates, he gave his personal attention to the minutest detail. The history of many a failure could be written in three words, "Lack of detail." How many a lawyer has failed from the lack of details in deeds and important papers, the lack of little words which seemed like surplusage, and which involved his clients in litigation, and often great losses! How many wills are contested from the carelessness of lawyers in the omission or shading of words, or ambiguous use of language!

Physicians often fail to make a reputation through their habitual blundering, carelessness in writing prescriptions, failure to give minute instruction. The world is full of blunderers; business men fail from a disregard of trifles; they go to the bank to pay a note the day after it has gone to protest; they do not pay their bills promptly; do not answer their letters promptly or file them away accurately; their books do not quite balance; they do not know exactly how they stand, they have a contempt for details.

"My rule of conduct has been that whatever is worth doing at all is worth doing well," said

Nicolas Poussin, the great French painter. When asked the reason why he had become so eminent in a land of famous artists he replied, "Because I have neglected nothing."

Not even Helen of Troy, it is said, was beautiful enough to spare the tip of her nose; and if Cleopatra's had been an inch shorter Mark Antony would never have become infatuated with her wonderful charms, and the blemish would have changed the history of the world. Anne Boleyn's fascinating smile split the great Church of Rome in twain, and gave a nation an altered destiny. Napoleon, who feared not to attack the proudest monarchs in their capitols, shrank from the political influence of one independent woman in private life, Madame de Staël. Had not Scott sprained his foot his life would probably have taken a different direction.

Cromwell was about to sail for America when a law was passed prohibiting emigration. At that time he was a profligate, having squandered all his property. But when he found that he could not leave England he reformed his life. Had he not been detained who can tell what the history of Great Britain would have been?

When one of his friends asked Scopas the Thessalian for something that could be of little use to him, he answered, "It is in these useless and superfluous things that I am rich and happy."

It was the little foxes that spoiled the vines in Solomon's day. Mites play mischief now with our meal and cheese, moths with our woolens and furs, and mice in our pantries. More than half our diseases are produced by infinitesimal creatures called microbes.

Most people call fretting a minor fault, a foible, and not a vice. There is no vice except drunkenness which can so utterly destroy the peace, the happiness, of a home.

"We call the large majority of human lives obscure," says Bulwer, "presumptuous that we are! How know we what lives a single thought retained from the dust of nameless graves may have lighted to renown?"

The theft of a diamond necklace from a French queen convulsed Europe. From the careful and persistent accumulation of innumerable facts, each trivial in itself, but in the aggregate forming a mass of evidence, a Darwin extracts his law of evolution, and Linnaeus constructs the science of botany. A pan of water and two thermometers were the tools by which Dr. Black discovered latent heat, and a prism, a lens, and a sheet of pasteboard enabled Newton to unfold the composition of light and the origin of colors. An eminent foreign savant called on Dr. Wollaston, and asked to be shown over those laboratories of his in which science had been enriched by so many great discoveries, when the doctor took him into a little study, and, pointing to an old tea tray on the table, on which stood a few watch glasses, test papers, a small balance, and a blow-pipe, said, "There is my laboratory." A burnt stick and a barn door served Wilkie in lieu of pencil and paper. A single potato, carried to England by Sir Walter Raleigh in the sixteenth century, has multiplied into food for millions, driving famine from Ireland again and again.

It seemed a small thing to drive William Brewster, John Robinson, and the poor people of Austerfield and Scrooby into perpetual exile, but as Pilgrims they became the founders of a mighty people. A cloud may hide the sun which it cannot extinguish.

"Behold how great a matter a little fire kindleth." "A look of vexation or a word coldly spoken, or a little help thoughtlessly withheld, may produce long issues of regret."

It was but a little dispute, a little flash of temper, the trigger was pulled in an instant, but the soul returned never.

A few immortal sentences from Garrison and Phillips, a few poems from Lowell and Whittier, and the leaven is at work which will not cease its action until the whipping-post and bodily servitude are abolished forever.

"For want of a nail the shoe was lost,
For want of a shoe the horse was lost;
For want of a horse the rider was lost, and all,"
says Poor Richard, "for want of a horse-shoe nail."

A single remark dropped by an unknown person in the street led to the successful story of "The Bread-winners." A hymn chanted by the barefooted friars in the temple of Jupiter at Rome led to the famous "Decline and Fall of the Roman Empire."

"Do little things now," says a Persian proverb; "so shall big things come to thee by and by asking to be done." God will take care of the great things if we do not neglect the little ones.

"Words are things," says Byron, "and a small drop of ink, falling like dew upon a thought, produces that which makes thousands, perhaps millions think."

"I give these books for the founding of a college in this colony;" such were the words of ten ministers who in the year 1700 assembled at the village of Branford a few miles east of New Haven. Each of the worthy fathers deposited a few books upon the table around which they were sitting; such was the founding of Yale College.

"He that has a spirit of detail," says Webster, "will do better in life than many who figured beyond him in the university."

The pyramid of knowledge is made up of little grains of information, little observations picked up from everywhere.

For a thousand years Asia monopolized the secret of silk culture, and at Rome the product was sold for its weight in gold. During the sixth century, at the request of Justinian, two Persian monks brought a few eggs from China to Europe in a hollow cane. The eggs were hatched by means of heat, and Asia no longer held the monopoly of the silk business.

In comparison with Ferdinand, preparing to lead forth his magnificent army in Europe's supreme contest with the Moors, how insignificant seemed the visionary expedition of Columbus, about to start in three small shallops across the unknown ocean. But grand as was the triumph of Ferdinand, it now seems hardly worthy of mention in comparison with the wonderful achievement of the poor Genoese navigator.

Only one hundred and ninety-two Athenians perished in the battle of Marathon, but Europe was saved from a host which is said to have drunk rivers dry, and to have shaken the solid earth as they marched.

Great men are noted for their attention to trifles. Goethe once asked a monarch to excuse him, during an interview, while he went to an adjoining room to jot down a stray thought. Hogarth would make sketches of rare faces and characteristics upon his finger-nails upon the streets. Indeed, to a truly great mind there are no little things. "The eye of the understanding is like the eye of the sense; for as you may see objects through small crannies or holes, so you may see great axioms of nature through small and contemptible instances," said Bacon. Trifles light as air suggest to the keen observer the solution of mighty problems. Bits of glass arranged to amuse children led to the discovery of the kaleidoscope. Goodyear discovered how to vulcanize rubber by forgetting, until it became red hot, a skillet containing a compound which he had before considered worthless. Confined in the house by typhoid fever, Helmholtz, with a little money which he had saved by great economy, bought a microscope which led him into the field of science where he became so famous. A ship-worm boring a piece of wood suggested to Sir Isambard Brunei the idea of a tunnel under the Thames at London. Tracks of extinct animals in the old red sandstone led Hugh Miller on and on until he became the greatest geologist of his time. Sir Walter Scott once saw a shepherd boy plodding sturdily along, and asked him to ride. This boy was George Kemp, who became so enthusiastic in his study of sculpture that he walked fifty miles and back to see a beautiful statue. He did not forget the kindness of Sir Walter, and, when the latter died, threw his soul into the design of the magnificent monument erected in Edinburgh to the memory of the author of "Waverley."

A poor boy applied for a situation at a bank in Paris, but was refused. As he left the door, he picked up a pin. The bank president saw this, called the boy back, and gave him a situation from which he rose until he became the greatest banker of Paris,—Laffitte.

It was the turning point in Theodore Parker's life when he picked up a stone to throw at a turtle. Something within him said, "Don't do it," and he didn't. He went home and asked his mother what it was in him that said "Don't;" and she taught him the purpose of that inward monitor which he ever after chose as his guide. It is said that David Hume became a deist by being appointed in a debating society to take the side of infidelity. Voltaire could not erase from his mind the impression of a poem on infidelity committed at the age of five. The "Arabian Nights" aroused the genius of Coleridge. A Massachusetts soldier in the Civil War observed a bird hulling rice, and shot it; taking its bill for a model, he invented a hulling machine which has revolutionized the rice business. A war between France and England, costing more than a hundred thousand lives, grew out of a quarrel as to which of two vessels should first be served with water. The quarrel of two Indian boys over a grasshopper led to the "Grasshopper War." George IV. of England fell in a fit, and a village apothecary bled him, restoring him to consciousness. The king made him his physician, a position of great honor and profit.

Many a noble ship has stranded because of one defective timber, when all other parts were strong. Guard the weak point.

No object the eye ever beheld, no sound however slight caught by the ear, or anything once passing the turnstile of any of the senses, is ever let go. The eye is a perpetual camera imprinting upon the sensitive mental plates, and packing away in the brain for future use every face, every tree, every plant, flower, hill, stream, mountain, every scene upon the street, in fact, everything which comes within its range. There is a phonograph in our natures which catches, however thoughtless and transient, every syllable we utter, and registers forever the slightest enunciation, and renders it immortal. These notes may appear a thousand years hence, reproduced in our descendants, in all their beautiful or terrible detail.

All the ages that have been are rounded up into the small space we call "To-day." Every life spans all that precedes it. To-day is a book which contains everything that has transpired in the world up to the present moment. The millions of the past whose ashes have mingled with the dust for centuries still live in their destinies through the laws of heredity.

Nothing has ever been lost. All the infinitesimals of the past are amassed into the present.

The first acorn had wrapped up in it all the oak forests on the globe.

"Least of all seeds, greatest of all harvests," seems to be one of the great laws of nature. All life comes from microscopic beginnings. In nature there is nothing small. The microscope reveals as great a world below as the telescope above. All of nature's laws govern the smallest atoms, and a single drop of water is a miniature ocean.

The strength of a chain lies in its weakest link, however large and strong all the others may be. We are all inclined to be proud of our strong points, while we are sensitive and neglectful of our weaknesses. Yet it is our greatest weakness which measures our real strength. A soldier who escapes the bullets of a thousand battles may die from the scratch of a pin, and many a ship has survived the shocks of icebergs and the storms of ocean only to founder in a smooth sea from holes made by tiny insects. Drop by drop is instilled into the mind the poison which blasts many a precious life.

How often do we hear people say, "Oh, it's only ten minutes, or twenty minutes, till dinner time; there's no use doing anything," or use other expressions of a like effect? Why, it is just in these little spare bits of time, these odd moments, which most people throw away, that men who have risen have gained their education, written their books, and made themselves immortal.

Small things become great when a great soul sees them. The noble or heroic act of one man has sometimes elevated a nation. Many an honorable career has resulted from a kind word spoken in season or the warm grasp of a friendly hand.

It is the little rift within the lute,
That by and by will make the music mute,
And, ever widening, slowly silence all.
TENNYSON.
"It was only a glad 'good-morning,'

As she passed along the way,
But it spread the morning's glory
Over the livelong day."
"Only a thought in passing—a smile, or encouraging word,
Has lifted many a burden no other gift could have stirred.
Only!—But then the onlys
Make up the mighty all."

CHAPTER XVI. SELF-MASTERY.

Give me that man
That is not passion's slave, and I will wear him
In my heart's core, ay, in my heart of heart.
SHAKESPEARE.
Strength of character consists of two things,—power of will and power of self-restraint. It requires two things, therefore, for its existence,—strong feelings and strong command over them.—F. W. ROBERTSON.

"Self-reverence, self-knowledge, self-control,
These three alone lead life to sovereign power."
The bravest trophy ever man obtained
Is that which o'er himself himself hath gained.
EARL OF STIRLING.
Real glory springs from the conquest of ourselves; and without that the conqueror is naught but the veriest slave.—THOMSON.

Whatever day makes man a slave takes half his worth away.—ODYSSEY.

Chain up the unruly legion of thy breast. Lead thine own captivity captive, and be Caesar within thyself.—THOMAS BROWNE.

He who reigns within himself, and rules passions, desires, and fears, is more than a king.—MILTON.

He that is slow to anger is better than the mighty: and he that ruleth his spirit than he that taketh a city.—BIBLE.

Self-trust is of the essence of heroism.—EMERSON.

Man who man would be
Must rule the empire of himself.
P. B. SHELLEY.

"Ah! Diamond, you little know the mischief you have wrought," said Sir Isaac Newton, returning from supper to find that his dog had upset a lighted taper upon the laborious calculations of years, which lay in ashes before him. Then he went calmly to work to reproduce them. The man who thus excelled in self-mastery surpassed all his predecessors and contemporaries in mastering the laws of nature.

The sun was high in the heavens when a man called at the house of Pericles to abuse him. The man's anger knew no bounds. He vented his spite in violent language until he paused from sheer exhaustion, and saw that it was quite dark without. He turned to go home, when Pericles calmly called a servant, and said, "Bring a lamp and attend this man home." Is any argument needed to show the superiority of Pericles?

The gladiators who were trained to fight in the Coliseum were compelled to practice the most graceful postures of falling and the finest attitudes to assume in dying, in case they were vanquished. They were obliged to eat food which would make the blood thick in order that they should not die quickly when wounded, thus giving the spectators prolonged gratification by the spectacle of their agonies. Each had to take this oath: "We swear that we will suffer ourselves to be bound, scourged, burned, or killed by the sword, or whatever Eumolpus ordains, and thus, like freeborn gladiators, we religiously devote both our souls and our bodies to our master." They were trained to exercise sublime self-control even when dying a cruel death.

The American Minister at St. Petersburg was summoned one morning to save a young, dissolute, reckless American youth, Poe, from the penalties incurred in a drunken debauch. By the Minister's aid young Poe returned to the United States. Not long after this the author of the best story and poem competed for in the "Baltimore Visitor" was sent for, and behold, the youth who had taken both prizes was that same dissolute, reckless, penniless, orphan youth, who had been arrested in St. Petersburg,—pale, ragged, with no stockings, and with his threadbare but well brushed coat buttoned to the chin to conceal the lack of a shirt. Young Poe took fresh courage and resolution, and for a while showed that he was superior to the appetite which was striving to drag him down. But, alas, that fatal bottle! his mind was stored with riches, yet he died in moral poverty. This was a soldier's epitaph:—

"Here lies a soldier whom all must applaud,
Who fought many battles at home and abroad!
But the hottest engagement he ever was in,
Was the conquest of self, in the battle of sin."

In 1860, when a committee visited Abraham Lincoln at his home in Springfield, Ill., to notify him of his nomination as President, he ordered a pitcher of water and glasses, "that they might drink each other's health in the best beverage God ever gave to man." "Let us," he continued, "make it as unfashionable to withhold our names from the temperance pledge as for husbands to wear their wives' bonnets in church, and instances will be as rare in one case as the other."

Burns exercised no control over his appetites, but gave them the rein:—

"Thus thoughtless follies laid him low
And stained his name."

"The first and best of victories," says Plato, "is for a man to conquer himself; to be conquered by himself is, of all things, the most shameful and vile."

Self-control is at the root of all the virtues. Let a man yield to his impulses and passions, and from that moment he gives up his moral freedom.

"Teach self-denial and make its practice pleasurable," says Walter Scott, "and you create for the world a destiny more sublime than ever issued from the brain of the wildest dreamer."

Stonewall Jackson, early in life, determined to conquer every weakness he had, physical, mental, and moral. He held all of his powers with a firm hand. To his great self-discipline and self-mastery he owed his success. So determined was he to harden himself to the weather that he could not be induced to wear an overcoat in winter. "I will not give in to the cold," he said. For a year, on account of dyspepsia, he lived on buttermilk and stale bread, and wore a wet shirt next his body because his doctor advised it, although everybody else ridiculed the idea. This was while he was professor at the Virginia Military Institute. His doctor advised him to retire at nine o'clock; and, no matter where he was, or who was present, he always sought his bed on the minute. He adhered rigidly through life to this stern system of discipline. Such self-training, such self-conquest, gives one great power over others. It is equal to genius itself.

It is a good plan to form the habit of ranking our various qualities, marking our strongest point one hundred and all the others in proportion, in order to make the lowest mark more apparent, and enabling us to try to raise or strengthen it. A man's industry, for example, may be his strongest point, one hundred, his physical courage may be fifty; his moral courage, seventy-five; his temper, twenty-five; with but ten for self-control,—which, if he has strong appetites and passions, will be likely to be the rock on which he will split. He should strive in every way to raise it from one of the weakest qualities to one of the strongest. It would take but two or three minutes a day to rank ourselves in such a table by noting the exercise of each faculty for the day. If you have worked hard and faithfully, mark industry one hundred. If you have lost your temper, and, in consequence, lost your self-control, and made a fool of yourself, indicate it by a low mark. This will be an incentive to try to raise it the next day. If you have been irritable, indicate it by a corresponding mark, and redeem yourself on the morrow. If you have been cowardly where you should have been brave, hesitating where you should have shown decision, false where you should have been true, foolish where you should have been wise, tardy where you should have been prompt; if you have prevaricated where you should have told the exact truth; if you have taken the advantage where you should have been fair, have been unjust where you should have been just, impatient where you should have been patient, cross where you should have been cheerful, so indicate by your marks. You will find this a great aid to character building.

It is a subtle and profound remark of Hegel's that the riddle which the Sphinx, the Egyptian symbol of the mysteriousness of Nature, propounds to Oedipus is only another way of expressing the command of the Delphic oracle, "Know thyself." And when the answer is given the Sphinx casts herself down from her rock. When man knows himself, the mysteriousness of Nature and her terrors vanish.

The command by the ancient oracle at Delphos is of eternal significance. Add to it its natural complement—Help thyself—and the path to success is open to those who obey.

Guard your weak point. Moral contagion borrows fully half its strength from the weakness of its victims. Have you a hot, passionate temper? If so, a moment's outbreak, like a rat-hole in a dam, may flood all the work of years. One angry word sometimes raises a storm that time itself cannot allay. A single angry word has lost many a friend.

A Quaker was asked by a merchant whom he had conquered by his patience how he had been able to bear the other's abuse, and replied: "Friend, I will tell thee. I was naturally as hot and violent as thou art. I observed that men in a passion always speak loud, and I thought if I could control my voice I should repress my passion. I have therefore made it a rule never to let my voice rise above a certain key, and by a careful observance of this rule, I have, by the blessing of God, entirely mastered my natural tongue." Mr. Christmas of the Bank of England explains that the secret of his self-control under very trying circumstances was due to a rule learned from the great Pitt, never to lose his temper during banking hours from nine to three.

When Socrates found in himself any disposition to anger, he would check it by speaking low, in opposition to the motions of his displeasure. If you are conscious of being in a passion, keep your mouth shut, lest you increase it. Many a person has dropped dead in a rage. Fits of anger bring fits of disease. "Whom the gods would destroy they first make mad." "Keep cool," says Webster, "anger is not argument." "Be calm in arguing," says George Herbert, "for fierceness makes error a fault, and truth discourtesy."

To be angry with a weak man is to prove that you are not strong yourself. "Anger," says Pythagoras, "begins with folly and ends with repentance." You must measure the strength of a man by the power of the feelings he subdues, not by the power of those which subdue him.

De Leon, a distinguished Spanish poet, after lying years in dungeons of the Inquisition, dreary, and alone, without light, for translating part of the Scriptures into his native tongue, was released and restored to his professorship. A great crowd thronged to hear his first lecture, out of curiosity to learn what he might say about his imprisonment. But the great man merely resumed the lecture which had been so cruelly broken off five years before, just where he left it, with the words "Heri discebamus" (Yesterday we were teaching). What a lesson in this remarkable example of self-control for those who allow their tongues to jabber whatever happens to be uppermost in their minds!

Did you ever see a man receive a flagrant insult, and only grow a little pale, bite his quivering lip, and then reply quietly? Did you ever see a man in anguish stand as if carved out of solid rock, mastering himself? Have you not seen one bearing a hopeless daily trial remain silent and never tell the world what cankered his home peace? That is strength. "He who, with strong passions, remains chaste; he who, keenly sensitive, with manly power of indignation in him, can be provoked, and yet restrain himself and forgive,—these are strong men, the spiritual heroes."

"You will be remembered only as the man who broke my nose," said young Michael Angelo to the man Torrigiano, who struck him in anger. What sublime self-control for a quick-tempered man!

"You ask whether it would not be manly to resent a great injury," said Eardley Wilmot: "I answer that it would be manly to resent it, but it would be Godlike to forgive it."

That man has conquered his tongue who can allow the ribald jest or scurrilous word to die unspoken on his lips, and maintain an indignant silence amid reproaches and accusations and sneers and scoffs. "He is a fool who cannot be angry," says English, "but he is a wise man who will not."

Peter the Great made a law in 1722 that a nobleman who should beat his slave should be regarded as insane, and a guardian appointed to look after his property and person. This great monarch once struck his gardener, who took to his bed and died. Peter, hearing of this, exclaimed with tears in his eyes, "Alas! I have civilized my own subjects; I have conquered other nations; yet have I not been able to civilize or conquer myself." The same monarch, when drunk, rushed upon Admiral Le Fort with a sword. Le Fort, with great self-possession, bared his breast to receive the stroke. This sobered Peter, and afterwards he asked the pardon of Le Fort. Peter said, "I am trying to reform my country, and I am not yet able to reform myself." Self-conquest is man's last and greatest victory.

A medical authority of highest repute affirms that excessive labor, exposure to wet and cold, deprivation of sufficient quantities of necessary and wholesome food, habitual bad lodging, sloth and intemperance, are all deadly enemies to human life, but they are none of them so bad as violent and ungoverned passion,—that men and women have frequently lived to an advanced age in spite of these, but that instances are very rare where people of irascible tempers live to extreme old age.

It was the self-discipline of a man who had never looked upon war until he was forty that enabled Oliver Cromwell to create an army which never fought without annihilating, yet which retired into the ranks of industry as soon as the government was established, each soldier being distinguished from his neighbors only by his superior diligence, sobriety, and regularity in the pursuits of peace.

How sweet the serenity of habitual self-command! When does a man feel more a master of himself than when he has passed through a sudden and severe provocation in silence or in undisturbed good humor?

Whether teaching the rules of an exact morality, answering his corrupt judges, receiving sentence of death, or swallowing the poison, Socrates was still calm, quiet, undisturbed, intrepid.

It is a great thing to have brains, but it is vastly greater to be able to command them. The Duke of Wellington had great power over himself, although his natural temper was extremely irritable. He remained at the Duchess of Richmond's ball till about three o'clock on the morning of the 16th of June, 1815, "showing himself very cheerful," although he knew that a desperate battle was awaiting him. On the field of Waterloo he gave his orders at the most critical moments without the slightest excitement.

Napoleon, having made his arrangements for the terrible conflict of the next day (Jena and Auerstadt), retired to his tent about midnight, and calmly sat down to draw up a plan of study and discipline for Madame Campan's female school. "Keep cool, and you command everybody," says St. Just.

"He that would govern others first should be
The master of himself,"
says Massinger.

He who has mastered himself, who is his own Caesar, will be stronger than his passion, superior to circumstances, higher than his calling, greater than his speech. Self-control is the generalship which turns a mob of raw recruits into a disciplined army. The rough man has become the polished and dignified soldier, in other words, the man has got control of himself, and knows how to use himself. The human race is under constant drill. Our occupations, difficulties, obstacles, disappointments, if used aright, are the great schoolmasters which help us to possess ourselves. The man who is master of himself will not be a slave to drudgery, but will keep in advance of his work. He will not rob his family of that which is worth more than money or position; he will not be the slave of his occupation, not at the mercy of circumstances. His methods and system will enable him to accomplish wonders, and yet give him leisure for self-culture. The man who controls himself works to live rather than lives for work.

The man of great self-control, the man who thinks a great deal and says little, who is self-centred, well balanced, carries a thousand times more weight than the man of weak will, always wavering and undecided.

If a man lacks self-control he seems to lack everything. Without it he can have no patience, no power to govern himself, he can have no self-reliance, for he will always be at the mercy of his strongest passion. If he lacks self-control, the very backbone, pith, and nerve of character are lacking also.

The discipline which is the main end in education is simply control acquired over one's mental faculties; without this discipline no man is a strong and accurate thinker. "Prove to me," says Mrs. Oliphant, "that you can control yourself, and I'll say you're an educated man; and, without this, all other education is good for next to nothing."

The wife of Socrates, Xanthippe, was a woman of a most fantastical and furious spirit. At one time, having vented all the reproaches upon Socrates her fury could suggest, he went out and sat before the door. His calm and unconcerned behavior but irritated her so much the more; and, in the excess of her rage, she ran upstairs and emptied a vessel upon his head, at which he only laughed and said that "so much thunder must needs produce a shower." Alcibiades his friend, talking with him about his wife, told him he wondered how he could bear such an everlasting scold in the same house with him. He replied, "I have so accustomed myself to expect it, that it now offends me no more than the noise of carriages in the street."

How many men have in their chain of character one weak link. They may be weak in the link of truthfulness, politeness, trustworthiness, temper, chastity, temperance, courage, industry, or may have some other weakness which wrecks their success and thwarts a life's endeavor. He who would succeed must hold all his faculties under perfect control; they must be disciplined, drilled, until they obey the will.

Think of a young man just starting out in life to conquer the world being at the mercy of his own appetites and passions! He cannot stand up and look the world in the face when he is the slave of what should be his own servants. He cannot lead who is led. There is nothing which gives certainty and direction to the life of a man who is not his own master. If he has mastered all but one appetite, passion, or weakness, he is still a slave; it is the weakest point that measures the strength of character.

Seneca, one of the greatest of the ancient philosophers, said that "we should every night call ourselves to account. What infirmity have I mastered to-day? what passion opposed? what temptation resisted? what virtue acquired?" and then he follows with the profound truth that "our vices will abate of themselves if they be brought every day to the shrift." If you cannot at first control your anger, learn to control your tongue, which, like fire, is a good servant, but a hard master.

Five words cost Zacharias forty weeks' silence. There is many a man whose tongue might govern multitudes if he could only govern his tongue. Anger, like too much wine, hides us from ourselves, but exposes us to others.

General von Moltke, perhaps the greatest strategist of this century, had, as a foundation for his other talents, the power to "hold his tongue in seven languages." A young man went to Socrates to learn oratory. On being introduced, he talked so incessantly that Socrates asked for double fees. "Why charge me double?" asked the young fellow. "Because," said the orator, "I must teach you two sciences: the one how to hold your tongue, the other how to speak." The first is the more difficult.

Half the actual trouble of life would be saved if people would remember that silence is golden, when they are irritated, vexed, or annoyed.

To feel provoked or exasperated at a trifle, when the nerves are exhausted, is, perhaps, natural to us in our imperfect state. But why put into the shape of speech the annoyance which, once uttered, is remembered; which may burn like a blistering wound, or rankle like a poisoned arrow? If a child be crying or a friend capricious, or a servant unreasonable, be careful what you say. Do not speak while you feel the impulse of anger, for you will be almost certain to say too much, to say more than your cooler judgment will approve, and to speak in a way that you will regret. Be silent until the "sweet by and by," when you will be calm, rested, and self-controlled.

"Seest thou a man that is hasty in his words? There is more hope of a fool than of him."

"Silence," says Zimmerman, "is the safest response for all the contradiction that arises from impertinence, vulgarity, or envy."

In rhetoric, as Emerson truly says, this art of omission is the chief secret of power. "Everything tells in favor of the man who talks but little. The presumption is that he is a superior man; and if, in point of fact, he is not a sheer blockhead, the presumption then is that he is very superior indeed." Grant was master of the science of silence.

The self-controlled are self-possessed. "Sir, the house is on fire!" shrieked a frightened servant, running into Dr. Lawson's study. "Go and tell your mistress," said the preoccupied professor, without looking up from the book he was reading; "you know I have no charge of household matters." A woman whose house was on fire threw a looking-glass out of the window, and carried a pair of andirons several rods to a safe place beside a stone wall. "Presence of mind and courage in distress are more than armies to procure success."

Xenophon tells us that at one time the Persian princes had for their teachers the four best men in the kingdom. (1) The wisest man to teach wisdom. (2) The bravest to teach courage. (3) The most just to train the moral nature. (4) The most temperate to teach self-control. We have them all in the Bible, and in Christ our teacher, an example. "If it is a small sacrifice to discontinue the use of wine," said Samuel J. May, "do it for the sake of others; if it is a great sacrifice, do it for your own sake." How many of nature's noblemen, who might be kings if they could control themselves, drink away their honor, reputation, and money in glasses of "wet damnation," more costly than the vinegar in which Cleopatra dissolved her pearls.

Experience shows that, quicker than almost any other physical agency, alcohol breaks down a man's power of self-control. But the physical evils of intemperance, great as they are, are slight, compared with the moral injury it produces. It is not simply that vices and crimes almost inevitably follow the loss of rational self-direction, which is the invariable accompaniment of intoxication; manhood is lowered and finally lost by the sensual tyranny of appetite. The drunken man has given up the reins of his nature to a fool or a fiend, and he is driven fast to base or unutterably foolish ends.

With almost palsied hand, at a temperance meeting, John B. Gough signed the pledge. For six days and nights in a wretched garret, without a mouthful of food, with scarcely a moment's sleep, he fought the fearful battle with appetite. Weak, famished, almost dying, he crawled into the sunlight; but he had conquered the demon, which had almost killed him. Gough used to describe the struggles of a man who tried to leave off using tobacco. He threw away what he had, and said that was the end of it; but no, it was only the beginning of it. He would chew camomile, gentian, toothpicks, but it was of no use. He bought another plug of tobacco and put it in his pocket. He wanted a chew awfully, but he looked at it and said, "You are a weed, and I am a man. I'll master you if I die for it;" and he did, while carrying it in his pocket daily.

Natural appetites, if given rein, will not only grow monstrous and despotic, but artificial appetites will be created which, like a ghastly Frankenstein, develop a kind of independent life and force, and then turn on their creator to torment him without pity, and will mock his efforts to free himself from this slavery. The victim of strong drink is one of the most pitiable creatures on earth, he becomes half beast, or half demon. Oh, the silent, suffering tongues that whisper "Don't," but the will lies prostrate, and the debauch goes on. What a mute confession of degradation there is in the very appearance of a confirmed sot. Behold a man no longer in possession of himself; the flesh is master; the spiritual nature is sunk in the mire of sensuality, and the mental faculties are a mere mob of enfeebled powers under bondage to a bestial or mad tyrant. As Challis says:—

"Once the demon enters,
Stands within the door;

Peace and hope and gladness
Dwell there nevermore."

Many persons are intemperate in their feelings; they are emotionally prodigal. Passion is intemperance; so is caprice. There is an intemperance even in melancholy and mirth. The temperate man is not mastered by his moods; he will not be driven or enticed into excess; his steadfast will conquers despondency, and is not unbalanced by transient exhilarations, for ecstasy is as fatal as despair. Temper is subjected to reason and conscience. How many people excuse themselves for doing wrong or foolish acts by the plea that they have a quick temper. But he who is king of himself rules his temper, turning its very heat and passion into energy that works good instead of evil. Stephen Girard, when he heard of a clerk with a strong temper, was glad to employ him. He believed that such persons, taught self-control, were the best workers. Controlled temper is an element of strength; wisely regulated, it expends itself as energy in work, just as heat in an engine is transmuted into force that drives the wheels of industry. Cromwell, William the Silent, Wordsworth, Faraday, Washington, and Wellington were men of prodigious tempers, but they were also men whose self-control was nearly perfect.

George Washington's faculties were so well balanced and combined that his constitution was tempered evenly with all the elements of activity, and his mind resembled a well organized commonwealth. His passions, which had the intensest vigor, owed allegiance to reason; and with all the fiery quickness of his spirit, his impetuous and massive will was held in check by consummate judgment. He had in his composition a calm which was a balance-wheel, and which gave him in moments of highest excitement the power of self-control, and enabled him to excel in patience, even when he had most cause for disgust.

It was said by an enemy of William the Silent that an arrogant or indiscreet word never fell from his lips.

How brilliantly could Carlyle write of heroism, courage, self-control, and yet fly into a rage at a rooster crowing in a neighbor's yard.

A self-controlled mind is a free mind, and freedom is power.

"I call that mind free," says Channing, "which jealously guards its intellectual rights and powers, which calls no man master, which does not content itself with a passive or hereditary faith, which opens itself to light whencesoever it may come, which receives new truth as an angel from heaven, which, whilst consulting others, inquires still more of the oracle within itself, and uses instructions from abroad, not to supersede, but to quicken and exalt its own energies. I call that mind free which is not passively framed by outward circumstances, which is not swept away by the torrent of events, which is not the creature of accidental impulse, but which bends events to its own improvement, and acts from an inward spring, from immutable principles which it has deliberately espoused. I call that mind free which protects itself against the usurpations of society, which does not cower to human opinion, which feels itself accountable to a higher tribunal than man's, which respects a higher law than fashion, which respects itself too much to be the slave or tool of the many or the few. I call that mind free which through confidence in God and in the power of virtue has cast off all fear but that of wrong-doing, which no menace or peril can enthrall, which is calm in the midst of tumults, and possesses itself though all else be lost. I call that mind free which resists the bondage of habit, which does not mechanically repeat itself and copy the past, which does not live on its old virtues, which does not enslave itself to precise rules, but which forgets what is behind, listens for new and higher monitions of conscience, and rejoices to pour itself forth in fresh and higher exertions. I call that mind free which is jealous of its own freedom, which guards itself from being merged in others, which guards its empire over itself as nobler than the empire of the world."

Be free—not chiefly from the iron chain
But from the one which passion forges—be
The master of thyself. If lost, regain
The rule o'er chance, sense, circumstance. Be free.
EPHRAIM PEABODY.

"It is not enough to have great qualities," says La Rochefoucauld; "we should also have the management of them." No man can call himself educated until every voluntary muscle obeys his will.

Every human being is conscious of two natures. One is ever reaching up after the good, the true, and the noble,—is aspiring after all that uplifts, elevates, and purifies. It is the God-side of man, the image of the Creator, the immortal side, the spiritual side. It is the gravitation of the soul faculties toward their Maker. The other is the bestial side which gravitates downward. It does not aspire, it grovels; it wallows in the mire of sensualism. Like the beast, it knows but one law, and is led by only one motive, self-indulgence, self-gratification. When neither hungry nor thirsty, or when gorged and sated by over-indulgence, it lies quiet and peaceful as a lamb, and we sometimes think it subdued. But when its imperious passion accumulates, it clamors for satisfaction. You cannot reason with it, for it has no reason, only an imperious instinct for gratification. You cannot appeal to its self-respect, for it has none. It cares nothing for character, for manliness, for the spiritual.

These two natures are ever at war, one pulling heavenward, the other, earthward. Nor do they ever become reconciled. Either may conquer, but the vanquished never submits. The higher nature may be compelled to grovel, to wallow in the mire of sensual indulgence, but it always rebels and enters its protest. It can never forget that it bears the image of its Maker, even when dragged through the slough of sensualism. The still small voice which bids man look up is never quite hushed. If the victim of the lower nature could only forget that he was born to look upward, if he could only erase the image of his Maker, if he could only hush the voice which haunts him and condemns him when he is bound in slavery, if he could only enjoy his indulgences without the mockery of remorse, he thinks he would be content to remain a brute. But the ghost of his better self rises as he is about to partake of his delight, and robs him of the expected pleasure. He has sold his better self for pleasure which is poison, and he cannot lose the consciousness of the fearful sacrifice he has made. The banquet may be ready, but the hand on the wall is writing his doom.

Give me that soul, superior power,
That conquest over fate,

Which sways the weakness of the hour,
Rules little things as great:
That lulls the human waves of strife
With words and feelings kind,
And makes the trials of our life
The triumphs of our mind.
CHARLES SWAIN.
Reader, attend—whether thy soul
Soars fancy's flights above the pole,
Or darkly grubs this earthly hole,
In low pursuits:
Know prudent, cautious self-control
Is wisdom's root.
BURNS.
The king is the man who can.—CARLYLE.

I have only one counsel for you—Be master.—NAPOLEON.

Ah, silly man, who dream'st thy honor stands
In ruling others, not thyself. Thy slaves
Serve thee, and thou thy slave: in iron bands
Thy servile spirit, pressed with wild passions, raves.
Wouldst thou live honored?—clip ambition's wing:
To reason's yoke thy furious passions bring:
Thrice noble is the man who of himself is king.
PHINEAS FLETCHER.
"Not in the clamor of the crowded street,
Not in the shouts and plaudits of the throng,
But in ourselves are triumph and defeat."